Tweeting to Power

OXFORD STUDIES IN DIGITAL POLITICS
Series Editor: Andrew Chadwick, Royal Holloway, University of London

Tweeting to Power

THE SOCIAL MEDIA REVOLUTION
IN AMERICAN POLITICS

JASON GAINOUS

KEVIN M. WAGNER

OXFORD
UNIVERSITY PRESS

Oxford University Press is a department of the University of Oxford.
It furthers the University's objective of excellence in research, scholarship,
and education by publishing worldwide.

Oxford New York
Auckland Cape Town Dar es Salaam Hong Kong Karachi
Kuala Lumpur Madrid Melbourne Mexico City Nairobi
New Delhi Shanghai Taipei Toronto

With offices in
Argentina Austria Brazil Chile Czech Republic France Greece
Guatemala Hungary Italy Japan Poland Portugal Singapore
South Korea Switzerland Thailand Turkey Ukraine Vietnam

Oxford is a registered trade mark of Oxford University Press
in the UK and certain other countries.

Published in the United States of America by
Oxford University Press
198 Madison Avenue, New York, NY 10016

© Oxford University Press 2014

Library of Congress Cataloging-in-Publication Data
Gainous, Jason, 1971–
    Tweeting to power : the social media revolution in American politics / Jason Gainous, Kevin M. Wagner.
        p.   cm.
    Includes bibliographical references and index.
    ISBN 978–0–19–996509–0 (pbk. : alk. paper) — ISBN 978–0–19–996507–6 (hardcover : alk. paper)
1. Communication in politics—Technological innovations—United States. 2. Political participation—
Technological innovations—United States. 3. Internet—Political aspects—United States. 4. Social media—
Political aspects—United States. 5. Twitter. I. Title.
    JA85.2.U6G35 2014
    320.97301'4—dc23

                                                            2013018996

9780199965076
9780199965090 (pbk.)

I would like to dedicate this book to my loving parents: John and Kay Gainous, Pamela and Rick Steinberg, and Richard Carter. None of this is possible without their undying support throughout my life.—Jason Gainous

To my wife Jodie, the best writer I know. Your love and unwavering support make everything I do possible. To my children: Madeleine, Alexander, and Harrison. Nothing helps you consider the future and its endless possibilities like three imaginative and wonderful children. Never shy away from a challenge. Believe in yourselves, and know that I believe in you.—Kevin M. Wagner

Contents

List of Figures in Chapters

List of Tables in Chapters

Acknowledgments

We would like to thank the following people for their comments and assistance with this project: Kevin Fahey, Philip Habel, and Amanda LeDuke.

Jason Gainous and Kevin M. Wagner*

---

*Each author contributed equally to this book project. They are listed alphabetically.

Tweeting to Power

1

Social Media—The New Dinner Table?

Online social networking websites have exploded in popularity. The number of adult Internet users actively using online networking websites, such as the hugely popular social portal Facebook, more than quadrupled between 2005 and the end of 2009 (Lenhart 2009; Pew 2011a; Pew 2011b). Between December 2008 and December 2009, global consumers spent nearly six hours per month on social networking sites (SNSs), an 82% increase from the previous year and more than double the previous annual growth rate (Nielsen 2010). Twitter, which allows users to send out short messages to potentially large numbers of followers (sometimes called microblogging) has become one of the most popular sites on the Internet with an estimated 200 million users and growing (Alexa.com 2011; Quantcast 2010). An estimate of Twitter's growth was calculated at 1,300% in one year (Golbeck, Grimes, and Rogers 2010). The use of Twitter daily by users also quadrupled from late 2010 to 2012 (Pew 2012c). The growth in the use of SNSs generally, including Facebook and Twitter, is particularly significant among younger demographics. By 2012, around 92% of young adults (18–29) used SNSs (Pew 2012a). The frequency with which older generations used social media by 2012 is nothing to scoff at either. Nearly 73% of Internet users ranging from 30 through 49 years of age used social media, approximately 57% from the ages of 50 through 64 used social media, and even many of those Internet users over 65 used social media at 38%.

In the political sphere, the importance of this growth in the use of online social networking websites ("social media") is grounded in our understanding of American political thought. The foundational notion of American democracy is the idea that people exercise sovereignty through a republican form of governance, or as James Madison noted, a "scheme of representation" (Wagner 2010). Information communication systems are vital to that process, as they structure what people know and how they understand it (Bennett 2011). Social media alters the political calculus in the United States by shifting who controls information, who consumes information, and how that information is distributed. We posit that social media changes two vital elements of the political learning process. First, by enabling the consumer to pick his or her own network of communication, social media allows citizens to self-select their content in a way that avoids any disagreeable ideas or interpretations. Second, the networks themselves exist outside the traditional media machine, allowing political actors—including parties and candidates—to shape and dictate their content.

Understanding how these new networks affect political information and communication is increasingly relevant. The expansion and intensification of social media use for political gain is significant even by Internet growth standards (Pew 2012a). In just a few short years, the American political system is awash in social media from candidates, interest groups, parties and even the voters themselves. Members of Congress are using Twitter to send short statements to their supporters and followers at almost all times, including while the President is speaking to Congress at the State of the Union address. By 2011, one measure had 387 members of Congress using Twitter (TweetCongress.com 2011), and virtually every member had some kind of Internet and social media presence (Gainous and Wagner 2011). As the use of social media becomes ubiquitous, measures of the impact of the new medium and testable theories of its importance are becoming vital to understanding this new political environment.

While the term "social media" is typically used in reference to the networking websites Facebook or Twitter, it is actually a more general term. Social media[1] includes a broad and growing portion of the Internet that is designed as a platform which allows users, and groups of users, to create and exchange content, often in an interactive or collaborative fashion (see Kaplan and Haenlein 2010). The Internet has been moving in the direction of more user-generated content for some time, with the first iteration of the idea referred to as Web 2.0 (see Stanyer 2008). Users of Web 2.0 were given the ability to personalize news or entertainment web pages by indicating what they want to see, hear, or read (Gainous and Wagner 2011). This approach, based on a user-defined experience, is what underlies social media, and its popularity is fairly easy to understand. Instead of drawing users by trying to anticipate what content they might prefer, this system permits the user to define an entire experience based on exactly what they favor. Giving the consumer what they desire is good business. However, as we will explore throughout this book, the implications of consuming only the information you prefer to see has some clear consequences in the political sphere.

There is no defining protocol for social media, and many different approaches to it exist on the Internet. Some of the leading social media include Facebook, MySpace, LinkedIn, Twitter, YouTube, and Google+, just to name a few. While social media is becoming almost ubiquitous and integrated into many different activities online, the protocol of choice does change. In truth, the rise, evolution, and sometimes fall of social networking websites and protocols is happening at such a rapid pace, we are reluctant to name leading protocols as their popularity may be eclipsed by the next appealing idea. Just as few saw the meteoric rise of the networking website MySpace, just as few saw its rapid decline and replacement by Facebook (Hoge 2009). Newer, and perhaps more intuitive social networking protocols, are introduced regularly with mixed and somewhat unpredictable success.

Even if a particular social media protocol wanes in popularity, we anticipate that this user-dominated system will continue to expand and more people will flock to it. As noted above, the growth and participation of Americans in social media continues to grow at a significant pace. This is particularly true for the political aspects of the social media. By 2010, 22% of Internet users used social media websites for political activity (Smith 2011). This is likely to continue as social media becomes easier to access through mobile devices, allowing people to carry their networks with them. Already more than half of mobile phone users access the Internet from their device (Pew 2012b). The names and systems may change, but the importance of online social networking is likely to be a fixture going forward. We are not certain which social media protocol will draw the most users in the next few years, but we expect at least some of you are reading this book after being alerted to it by friends or acquaintances through a social media website.

In this research, we explore the implications of this new media and how it may alter the political landscape. Scholars have considered and measured how the Internet and technology are influencing political participation (Barber 2001; Bimber 1999; Bode 2012; Bonfadelli 2002; Boulianne 2009, 2011; Delli Carpini 2000; DiMaggio et al. 2004; Gainous and Wagner 2011, Gainous, Marlowe, and Wagner 2013; Gibson, Lusoli, and Ward 2005; Hendriks Vettehen, Hagemann, and Van Snippenburg 2004; Kittilson and Dalton 2011; Krueger 2002; Norris 2001; Polat 2005; Shah, Kwak, and Holbert 2001; Wagner and Gainous 2013; Ward, Gibson, and Lusoli 2003; Weber, Loumakis, and Bergman 2003; Xenos and Moy 2007). Some have also looked specifically at the relationship between social media use and political participation (Bode 2012; Conroy, Feezell, and Guerrero 2012; Gainous and Wagner 2011; Gainous, Marlowe, and Wagner 2013; Gil de Zúñiga, Jun, and Valenzuela 2012; Pasek, More, and Romer 2009; Valenzuela, Park, and Kee 2009) and at how politicians' use of social media influences the traditional media's news coverage (Wallsten 2011). We build on this impressive body of research to explore how and why social media may affect political discourse and participation and fill in the blanks with measures of the use and importance of social media in the political sphere. To do so, we rely on measures both of politicians' use of social media, Twitter in particular, and of public use of social media.

Beyond simple measures relating to the magnitude of usage, we use inferential statistics to examine the variables that are affecting, and are affected by, the use of social media. However, this is not simply a book of quantitative measures. Descriptions of social media are interesting, but alone are only fixed pictures of moments in time. Using the data, we develop our theoretic explanation to combine with our empirical examination of social media, in an attempt to create a larger comprehensive understanding of the implications for US politics. In this way, our research should have broader implications, as it is not tied to any social networking protocol but rather establishes a foundation for understanding how the very nature of digital communication through social networks will likely change the political processes in the United States.

While social media applications are the focus here, at its essence, this book is primarily concerned with measuring, understanding, and predicting a transformation in the political environment. It is about a fundamental shift in the way people interact with each other, obtain and process information, and ultimately use this information to choose who governs. Social media presents a foundational change in the preexisting media landscape and structures guiding political communication. It presents an alternative environment by which opinion leaders, politicians, and citizens can engage with each other that is multidimensional and largely unique in the history of our political system. Technology advances are not new, but we contend the character of the change here is. Rather than simply being just the latest progression in communication technology, social media presents an entirely new paradigm on how people engage with each other. Instead of waiting for traditional media to explain limited elements of the news, the networker is interacting with not just the news itself but with entire networks of friends and acquaintances without limits from borders or geography. It is a network that lacks an editor or gatekeeper, and one that is governed by a new set of rules and codes of behavior that are only now being developed.

In this chapter we lay the predicate for the measures and models in this book. We will offer a review of the literature and findings in the study of mass media, including the growing amount of research focused on the Internet and social media. This will be followed by a detailed explanation of our theory regarding how the nature and scope of political communication is changing and shifting the American political system. We will set forth our reasoning and supporting analysis for our theoretical assertion that social media allows consumers to create networks of preferred information which result in greater degrees of influence for political actors and interest groups. Finally, we will highlight upcoming chapters where we test our theories and model the effects of social media on the political landscape.

Rethinking Politics in the Age of Social Media

Social media has generated a broad set of implications, and we do not attempt to answer, let alone address, them all. In this book we examine, measure, and predict the likely changes in political communication and the implications for the greater political system. Our central questions are as follows: (1) How are political actors using social media to shape citizens' perceptions? (2) How does the new social media fit into traditional theories of citizen information processing? and (3) What are the implications of the answers to these questions for the relationship between those who govern and those being governed?

While there has been no moment when the media environment was static, the changes brought through the Internet, and the subsequent creation of social media, present a change of a different order than previous advancements. This is not to say that other advances were insignificant. Political scientists have long known that differences in the way information is propagated can generate changes in the political behavior of large populations (Converse 1962; Kernell 1994; Prior 2007). The most noticeable effect of this shift in information technology is in the amount and timeliness of the information available (Kinder 2003). There is a substantial difference between the media environment that existed in the 1930s, a time when newspaper circulation reached one out of three Americans, and the 1960s, when television became almost universal (Prior 2005). Television was particularly influential as it brought information directly into the home in a visual medium that was often easier to digest and more viscerally effective than previous channels, such as printed news (Graber 2010). Yet the improvements did not change who was speaking and who was listening.

The growth of social media is not simply an improvement in communication technology but rather a foundational change in how people communicate, not just between each other but with political actors and institutions. While all of the technological changes in how we communicate with each other are important milestones, social media is not only a huge leap in efficiency. It is also a substantively new way to interact. Each previous advance in communication technology influenced how we chose our leaders and even why we chose our leaders. It is no accident that the visual medium of television has led to an electoral advantage for taller candidates (Sommers 2002). Nonetheless, we suggest that social media, while a progression on this continuum, is not just another step but rather a leap into a fundamentally different environment because of the nature of the communication. Online social networking is a change of a different order and will create a new paradigm by redefining to whom each citizen is talking and how, when, and why that communication occurs.

Our assertion is based on significant differences that online social networking present from previous advances. Most significantly, social media is a two-way form of mass communication. Each previous advance was a form of one-way mass communication. Campaigns have been a singular message from a candidate, distributed through mass media to constituents and voters. Politicians spoke through the media, and the people were a largely passive audience. Social media allows the user to not only choose what network to be part of but also to be an active participant in the network. The user is a news creator, not simply a receptacle. This ground-shifting advance creates an entirely new way to view politics and the values attributed to advertising and campaigning. Different political behaviors are incentivized, including short video messages and virtual town halls, while some traditional behaviors, such as printing and mailing physical brochures, are no longer as useful or productive. The direct interaction generated by retail politics is far more costly and reaches far fewer people than digital strategies (Gainous and Wagner 2011). Social media creates interaction without regard to geography, and substantial increases in the efficiency of political communication create a new calculus in the political arena.

The true story of social media is bigger than choosing more effective political campaigning strategies. A larger shift is occurring. Social media presents a substantial change to our media system in both how information is reported and distributed, with significant implications for the industries that make up modern media. While the business implications are both interesting and worthy of discussion and research, it is beyond our scope. The political implications alone are substantial.

Contrasting Old and New Media

Social media presents significant departures from the traditional political media model that has existed and dominated political communication in the United States (see Bennett 2011; Graber 2010; Prior 2005). Each previous advance from the penny press to the radio to television was an advance in efficiency and distribution. However, the paradigm of one-way communication controlled by a small and readily identifiable group or groups of people was unchanged. Social media has created a different news paradigm alongside, and in some ways replacing, the traditional model. It operates in both directions allowing the parties to communicate with each other, rather than one side speaking and the other listening. Further, the conversation works in a remarkably open environment that allows information that is perceived as the most interesting or appealing to be distributed to the widest audience. The user chooses not only what to access but also what content is worth redistributing across the network.

The traditional media, such as newspapers and broadcasts, were ways for those with means to transmit ideas and information to the mass public. The conversation largely had one party talking and another party listening. Corporations, governments or other groups of influence controlled the information conveyed with laws or sometimes simply by owning the means of distribution (Bennett 2011). The power of the content provider has repeatedly been shown to be influential for both television (Prior 2007) and radio (Barker 2002). In the radio sphere, talk show hosts such as Rush Limbaugh have influence often by framing and priming issues for their audience in ways that lead to support for particular outcomes and conclusions (Barker 2002). In an environment where the information provider controls how and what is distributed, the framing, especially when articulated through preferred value positions, can be very persuasive. Talk radio in particular allows the show host great latitude to control his or her message and to use heuristics to frame it in a particular value structure (Barker 2002). As the owner of the means of communication has the ability to not only control what information is conveyed but also how that information is framed and contextualized, the traditional media concern has often been over the diversity, or the absence of diversity of media ownership. More directly, where there are only a few microphones, the owners of those microphones have an outsized role.

In contrast, the social media universe is user driven. This is not to say that the consumer of social media has replaced the owners of the media machines as the producer of content. But rather, the user has greater control of his or her content in an environment where the user has far more choices than exist for radio or television. Further, as an active participant in the news network, the user is more attentive and engaged because it is the user who chooses the content that is available to them to watch, read, and listen. This type of engagement increases the attention span of the user. People who choose their content, such as clicking on a link to a website in their social media stream, are going to spend more time reading and digesting the information (Klotz 2004). The end result is a new media that is more effective in conveying information and engaging its audience.

In addition, the information itself is not limited in time, scope, and content. A physical copy of a newspaper has a finite amount of space, and it cannot be updated after it is printed. The content is limited to what was known at the time of printing and the number of pages available. Even broadcasts, which are not frozen in time, are limited by the nature of the medium to address only one idea or event at a time. If the broadcast is not covering an issue important to the viewer, the viewer has no recourse and cannot alter the nature of the program, though he or she can certainly change the channel. Social media is by far the most versatile, comprehensive, and interactive form of communication. It differs from traditional media in not just speed and scope of distribution but in the character of the interaction between the news and the consumer of the news. Further, what makes this particularly significant is that the nature of the interaction widens and deepens as new protocols and applications are added and expanded. Social media grows more interactive and accessible with each day that passes.

Social media connects people to each other and binds them with no concern for distance, geography or traditional political cleavages. Unlike other mediums, the communications can be immediate. The feedback and the discovery of some information and its distribution can travel at speeds never before seen. During the 2012 Democratic National Convention, President Obama's nomination acceptance speech generated huge networks of social media discussions. While the speech was being delivered, over 50,000 Obama-related tweets per minute were happening. The three-day event generated nearly 10 million tweets that were directly relevant, and countless more that were related in some way but not easily sorted (Twitter 2012). The growth of broadband connections has multiplied the speed, and newer technology will likely make distribution limitless in breadth and scope. As the Internet grows and its penetration throughout the world increases, the changes will accelerate. The nature of the way society is linked with itself and with the state is shifting around us.

At its most basic level, social media captures all of the elements of the previous mediums. In operation, social media can distribute everything that television, magazines, radio, and newspapers do, and in a more timely manner with an easily accessible and interactive interface on demand (Tewksbury 2003). Beyond being simply a compilation of the previous mass media, the social media presents a mass, multidirectional conversation. One can respond to a video with a video. One can discover an issue, research that issue and respond to it, respond to the responses or even chat about it, and then distribute it to networks of other people from any of a multitude of mobile or fixed computing devices. The versatility of this interaction and engagement is unprecedented. Over three-quarters of Twitter users access the network through wireless devices such as laptop computers or even mobile phones (Williams and Gulati 2010). Content can be organized over several platforms, understood, and engaged using multiple applications, restricted only by the access and knowledge of the user.

Mixed Early Returns from Digital Democracy

While there has been a fair amount of excitement concerning the rise of the Internet campaign as political strategy, systematic measures of its importance are inconsistent in their findings. There is still little understanding of how important the rise of these communication protocols is on the overall system. Scholars fall largely into two camps when considering the implications of the Internet on politics. Some propose that the Internet will provide the means by which people and politicians can even the otherwise limited political field, creating more opportunities for ideas and candidates (Barber 2003; Corrado and Firestone 1996; Hagen and Mayer 2000). In this view, the Internet is a positive democratizing entity that helps remove the barriers that favor some groups and individuals in the electorate. This projection is regularly called the equalization theory (Barber 2001).

This view of the Internet is commonly found in the way media frame democratic movements in the world and in particular the Middle East, in nations such as Tunisia, Egypt, Libya, Oman, and the Palestinian territories (Howard 2011). Various opposition or democratization movements in Egypt, Tunisia, Kuwait, Iraq, Iran, Albania, and Afghanistan have successfully organized and avoided government crackdowns by migrating to the web (Howard 2011). The use of the web has created a communication protocol that is difficult to contain and limit using the more traditional heavy-handed approaches to opposition media (Giustozzi 2001). Since many repressive nations maintain themselves through state institutions that restrict political communication and organization, the Internet appears, at least facially, as a potential antidote. Many contemporary journalists are willing to give the Internet, and communication protocols such as Twitter, at least partial credit for uprisings in Egypt and Tunisia (Dyson 2011).

The alternative view, grounded more in the study of Western democracies, does not have such an optimistic view of the Internet. Some scholars see modern technology as standard politics by another means (Bimber and Davis 2003; Margolis and Resnick 2000; Ward, Gibson, and Lusolli 2003). As a result, any change will be marginal, preventing a shift in the basic power balance of the political systems. In this view, the use of the Internet will be "normalized" into the current electoral paradigm (Bimber and Davis 2003). In application, the supporters of normalization see the Internet as a new tool to be used as part of the conventional political structure. While normalization theorists do not discount the Internet as an important tool, these theorists see it as just the latest tool in the hands of traditional interests (Hindman 2008).

The seminal work in the area of Internet politics is Bimber and Davis's *Campaigning Online: The Internet in U.S. Elections* (2003). In that study, the authors use data from the 2000 election to illustrate that while candidates are moving to the Internet, the voters are likely to be reinforced in their positions rather than persuaded by the websites. Bimber and Davis show a remarkable foresight in both anticipating the questions that online technology brings, and the likely behavioral influences that will affect its impact. They approach the Internet from both the candidate's side and the voter's side, a structure we will also use and restate as supply and demand sides respectively. Further, Bimber and Davis grapple with the importance of self-selection of media content and how it will reinforce beliefs. We start with the same foundation, but as we illustrate throughout this book, social media leads to larger and more substantial changes than Bimber and Davis (2003) find and anticipate in their study. While some of the same influence are in play, the social media sphere is a very different environment than the one that existed for early Internet campaigns.

While we argue that the effects of social media will be substantial, we acknowledge that other scholars have found more limited results to date. Early findings do support a more limited impact for the Internet on politics, particularly in established democracies (see Chadwick 2006; Gainous and Wagner 2011). Some of these findings are driven by the limitations of measuring a medium that is evolving more rapidly than the pace of the scholarship. For example, how social media affected campaigning in 2000 or 2004 bears almost no resemblance to its implications in 2008. While this should lead to a stronger relationship over time, more recent measures have not been supportive of this projection (Bimber and Copeland 2013). Nonetheless, the political repercussions of online social media are still in flux as politicians have only relatively recently adopted the platform. The microblogging website Twitter was not widely used by political candidates prior to 2010, but it became broadly adopted, if not effectively used, during the 2010 election cycle (Garrison-Sprenger 2008; Headcount.com 2011; Senak 2010; Sifry 2009).

Some of the adoption in Congress was driven by its successful use by other representatives (Chi and Yang 2010). However, the importance and potential usefulness of Twitter as a tool was limited in this period. Studies have shown that most members of Congress use Twitter primarily to forward a link to press releases or summaries of a legislator's activities or duties (Ammann 2010; Glassman, Straus, and Shogan 2009; Golbeck, Grimes, and Rogers 2010). This actually mimics the initial use of Internet web pages by politicians, which were similarly used as an electronic billboard (Chadwick 2006; Cornfeld, Rainie, and Horrigan 2003). When used in this limited fashion, social media is fairly anticipated as having a minor role.

However, seeing this limited use and projecting a small campaign role for social media is a temporal error. As in the case of Internet web pages, the use of social media is changing and evolving as political actors begin to understand and maximize their potential for campaign and communication functions. In truth, they already have begun to do so, though the pace of academic research has not been able to keep up. Early research from the 1997 and 1998 campaigns in the United Kingdom concluded that, though the candidates made use of technology, they and the parties were limited in the use of online resources and used the Internet primarily as an electronic newspaper or online brochure with limited interactivity (Gibson and Ward 1998; Ward and Gibson 2003). As in the United States, the use of the Internet as a campaign tool increased in subsequent elections as a means of organization and communication (Wagner and Gainous 2009). The pace of this change is difficult to anticipate as it took more than fifty years for telephones to reach half the population, while computer penetration reached a majority in a fraction of that time (West 2005). Internet, and social media growth, is even faster (Gainous and Wagner 2011).

Campaigns and parties are often slow to adapt to new political environments, but they are often forced to adapt to win (Appleton and Ward 1997). The changes required by social media are occurring quickly, but are significant. By 2012, almost a third of likely voters were not watching live television on a weekly basis (Say Media 2012). Reaching voters now requires more than just covering the broadcast media with thirty-second advertisements. With the increasing use of digital devices to access social networks of information, the landscape is evolving each elections cycle even if the political actors themselves are behind the fast-moving curve. Anticipation has never been the strength of political organizations, which are traditionally resistant to change (Appleton and Ward 1997). But there is little doubt that they will do so.

As a result, the larger picture concerning Internet and social media usage is still being developed as the adoption and application of the technology accelerates. In the United States, only approximately one-quarter of candidates had campaign websites in 2001 (Ward and Gibson 2003). Today, virtually all do. The growth of social networking is similar, though at a strikingly faster pace with strong evidence that universal adoption is likely. A survey of the Congressional Management Foundation (Williams and Gulati 2010) found that approaching half of congressional staffers believe that Twitter is somewhat or very important for understanding constituent views and opinions. Just as web pages went from billboards to fundraising machines with interactive content, social media is and will continue to evolve into a significant form of interactive communication in the political system.

Yet the importance of social media in the present environment can be difficult to see or measure. Due in part to the rapid rates of adoption, even the most basic questions concerning the role that social media can play in the political system are still largely unclear Much of the use of social networks in politics is experimental based on optimistic hopes, rather than clear data and results. Each political player is maneuvering to see if a particular strategy can raise money, rally support, or even simply allow one to manipulate the public image and perception of a person or idea. Some presumption exists that social media or the Internet in general is a solution to many political problems ranging from publicity to fundraising to influencing the media (see Gainous and Wagner 2011; Mossberger, Tolbert, and Stansbury 2003; Wagner and Gainous 2009). Some of these assertions concerning the usefulness of social media are based on the logic that political players would not engage in online social media so strongly if the results were not significant. Certainly, political scientists have begun to take note of the role of social media and its impact on politics (Barber 2001; Corrado and Firestone 1996; Hagen and Mayer 2000; Rash 1997; Wallsten 2011).

Despite its relatively recent arrival, social media has been the subject of study by scholars who have sought to measure and anticipate how social networking online fits into the current political paradigm. Much of the scholarship has focused on why politicians use social media such as Twitter or Facebook (Chi and Yang 2010; Lassen, Brown, and Riding 2010; Williams and Gulati 2008). Other research has cataloged how it is used or the nature of the networks developed (Glassman, Straus, and Shogan 2009; Golbeck, Grimes, and Rogers 2010; Honeycutt and Herring 2009; Senak 2010; Romero et al. 2010; Ostermeier 2009). Scholars have looked at the effects of information technology on politics (Davis 2009; McKenna and Pole 2008; Wallsten 2008). Some scholars have attempted to measure the winners, or perhaps the most proficient users, of social media based on the number of followers or subscribers or even how often their posts are redistributed or "retweeted" (Romero, Meeder, and Kleinberg 2011; Senak 2010; Sifry 2009). Such research presents an interesting and significant view of how social media is being used and an increasing picture of its growth. In this book, we build on the findings of this earlier work and present a new way to understand social media as not an extension of the current paradigm, but rather as a new and potentially paradigm-shifting approach to understanding political interactions and communication.

Remaking the Gatekeeper: Networks of Ideas in the Digital Age

Previous research has already established that a changing media environment can cause changes in the electorate and ultimately changes in the composition of elected offices including Congress. In reviewing the effects of cable news, Markus Prior (2007) found a significant correlation between cable penetration and partisan polarization. Interestingly, he noted that the polarization in the electorate preceded the polarization in Congress. This chronology casts some doubt on the theories that it is elite leadership that polarized and the public which followed (Carmines and Stimson 1986, 1989). Prior's research confirms the importance of the type of information that is readily available, and the means by which people have to choose which information to view or read.

One of the larger implications of social media, as noted above, is the change in how information is distributed, and more directly, who operated and now operates the levers. Though the tradition of an independent media as a government watchdog is a long-held American tradition, at the time of the founding of the United States the media was not independent from the political system. Newspapers or, more precisely, pamphlets were distributed regularly with political goals in mind. Thomas Paine's *Common Sense* was supportive of independence from England. The *Federalist Papers* were authored and distributed with the intention of convincing delegates to adopt the Constitution. It was not until the rise in mass literacy and the subsequent invention of the penny press that journalism as a profession began in earnest (Graber 2010). A professional journalist acts as an intermediary or sometimes gatekeeper between the political actors and the people. Newspapers and television networks choose what to cover, what questions to ask, even what not to convey to the public, presumably using journalistic ethics. It is a system that has regularly been criticized as biased, though the evidence of such is mixed at best (Bennett 2011; Graber 2006; Turner 2007).

Social media has no obvious gatekeeper. Anyone can join and participate given sufficient knowledge and resources. While this is a limitation of sorts, it is a very low threshold established by the virtually uncountable number of posts on social media like Twitter and Facebook every day. Search tools catalog information so efficiently that any person with Internet access can find information on virtually any topic they can type into a search query and what people are saying and thinking about it. Social media is an incredible aggregator of sortable information that is virtually free for millions of people. Each individual in a social network chooses whether to read, redistribute or even add to each stream of information that comes to them. One may question whether the American public chooses wisely—videos of cats playing with yarn are particularly popular (YouTube.com 2011)—but it is the users' choices that allow social media to drive a topic, including many political topics. Videos of political mistakes can be become well-known in a day or sometimes a few hours with repeated distributions across social networks online. Some political videos have become so popular that the video distribution site YouTube has created a channel that consists of nothing but political clips, with the most popular clips ranked atop the page and displayed with a button allowing users to distribute the clip to their social network through their preferred social media protocol (YouTube.com 2011).

Yet while each user decides what information to read and distribute, this is not a random process, nor is each user equal in the process. Some users have vast networks that regularly read their posts. Others lack a large audience, or for some, any audience at all. The political implications of such an arrangement present an interesting model. Politicians are some of the most followed or subscribed to users in social media. They regularly distribute content to very large audiences who then redistribute it along different networks, making the potential reach of each post substantial. Further, the distribution is not random. It is made to individuals who choose to receive the posts, making them a particularly receptive audience. This presents a new type of media network. It is a network of largely like-minded individuals that is easily accessed once built and operates entirely outside the editing and gatekeeping function of the traditional media.

In short, social media is a unique opportunity for politicians to control their message. This new type of message control is evident in the more recent campaigns. Scholars have noted that the use of social media has altered traditional campaign tactics to avoid traditional media outlets as they often filter and interpret the campaign message. By 2010 candidates were using social media to bypass the media and control their own message and distribution. Using protocols like Facebook and Twitter allowed Senate candidates to simply avoid traditional media and still reach and target voters (Bode et al. 2011b). The usefulness of this approach has become so apparent that a new political industry has started to aid and instruct politicians on how to maximize their influence in the social media (Agranoff and Tabin 2011). As a result, both the most optimistic and the most pessimistic views of social media have elements of truth. The medium is open and democratizing, however; the political players appear to be the most able originators of content.

The resulting environment for political communication is unique and still developing. Policymakers, interest groups, activists, and politicians seek to make or create news on the supply side of the information flow using social media platforms, which are perfect tools to drive news stories and events while circumventing the traditional media such as television and newspapers. Even the traditional media conglomerates recognize the value of the social media platform and attempt to use it to drive users back to their content. On the demand side, consumers can be more selective about to what and to whom they pay attention, in part, by joining and participating in social networks. These networked citizens develop patterns of consumption that are predictable and allow for targeted marketing of news and points of view. Facebook and Twitter facilitate this process and the flow of information by making available large audiences and by providing a platform for the exchange of information between trusted friends/followers. As a result, opinion leaders can maximize their influence on public opinion in ways never before possible by distributing information widely, but in a targeted manner. Social media may be making politicians and candidates much more effective drivers of news and content.

Politics in the One-sided Information Universe

The implications of this new structure are better understood in the context of the epistemology of how people develop attitudes and opinions. This is especially true for voters whose decisions are not fixed by consistent ideological patterns. These voters are often referred to as floating voters (Zaller 2004; Key 1966). The study of uncommitted or floating voters has historically been important, as studies illustrate they often have a disproportionately large impact on electoral outcomes (Burden and Kimball 2002; Kelley 1983). The impact of these floating voters falls in two ways. The first is whether they will even vote; voters lacking consistent ideological constraints are irregular voters at best (Campbell 1960; Converse 1962; Kelley 1983; Key 1966). Second, when they do vote, what influences their choices?

The answer to both questions is the nature and the intensity of political information. The public forms opinions based on the information available to it. Political scientists often refer to public opinion in the aggregate, but it is essentially an individual-level process, even if eventually aggregated together (Cassino, Taber, and Lodge 2007; Dahl 1961, 1989; Page and Shapiro 1992). Sometimes the information is sought and obtained directly and other times it is the byproduct of everyday activities (Downs 1957; Popkin 1994. There are two well-held models of information processing. The receive, accept, and sample (RAS) model developed by Zaller and Feldman 1992) posits that an individual's political attitudes are developed by averaging across a range of considerations they hold, influenced in part by those ideas or beliefs that are the most recent to be considered (Zaller 1992). Alternatively, the online processing model (OPM) proposes that citizens essentially keep a running tally on issues or candidates. As they are exposed to information, a citizen will determine if that information improves or hurts their assessment and then retain the resulting calculation (Lodge, McGraw, and Stroh 1989; Lodge, Steenbergen, and Brau 1995; Lodge 1995). Interestingly, the citizen will often forget the reasons for their standing assessment of the issue or candidate, while still feeling very strongly and certain about their decision. From the outside this may make decisions appear irrational, when they are in fact rational, though the citizen has no ability to articulate the reasoning for the belief.

In either model, it is apparent that the nature of the informational environment is vital. Whether creating the sampling frame in the RAS model or the information that alters or shifts the running calculation in the OPM model, the information that is readily available in a person's network is the key. We build on both of these models later, arguing that the memory-based assessment (long-term memory) inherent in the RAS model (Zaller and Feldman 1992) guides the self-selection, where citizens tend to consume congenial news and screen out opposing viewpoints via social media and the OPM then explains how new information obtained from social media shapes opinion (see for discussion of self-selection, Arceneaux and Johnson 2013; Bennett and Manheim 2006; Bimber and Davis 2003; Garrett 2009a, 2009b; Goldman and Mutz 2011; Iyengar and Hahn 2009; Iyengar et al. 2008; Manjoo 2008; Mutz and Martin 2001; Prior 2007; Stroud 2008, 2011; Sunstein 2009; Taber 2003; Taber and Lodge 2006; Valentino et al. 2009).

Further, an understanding of how media highlight certain events and issues for viewers (Bennett 2011; Graber 2007) is crucial to the theoretical framework we create using these models. The modern mass media has adopted a strategy on most issues to present two different sides of each issue, usually from ideologically liberal and conservative positions. This is generally referred to as a two-sided information flow (Zaller 1992). While this may not constitute exactly a balanced approach, it shapes the considerations or information that individuals consider when reaching decisions, especially political decisions. As one might suspect, the nature of the information flow influences the levels of political polarization (Gainous and Wagner 2011; Zaller 1992). In the traditional mass media, two-sided flows encourage polarization because people on both sides have sufficient information to take an ideological position.

One-sided information flows have a depolarizing effect because they stimulate agreement by avoiding the presentation of alternative possible positions (Zaller 1992). This is particularly important as studies have shown that people will actively seek information with which they agree and avoid contrary positions (Lodge and Taber 2000). Interestingly, those with higher levels of information or more firmly held opinions were much more likely to engage in this behavior. Given the opportunity to control their media environment, citizens will maximize this effect (Lodge and Taber 2000). While clinically interesting to psychologists, this has had limited import in the larger political environment, as most of the mass media experience in the United States is based on two-sided information flows that are outside the control of the user. Technology has reversed this, first with talk radio (see Barker 2002), then cable television (see Arceneaux and Johnson 2013), next with the advent of the Internet (see Bimber and Davis 2003), and now with social media.

The Internet presents an environment with not just two-sided information flows, but potentially infinite flows. Rather than letting the user simply tune out the information with which they do not agree, as is often the case with television broadcasts, the Internet allows them to avoid any contrary information in its entirety. This process began with cable television, which created flows of one-sided information that users could self-select (Arceneaux and Johnson 2013; Prior 2007). Cable news was increasingly fine-tuned to particular points of view. Escalating measures of polarization in the electorate followed the growth and penetration of cable (Bennett 2011; Prior 2007). Scholars studying these changes noted the polarizing effect of these information flows (Arceneaux and Johnson 2013; Hamilton 2004).

At first blush, the openness of the Internet might lead one to believe that the diversity of viewpoints will lead to less ideological positions. The Internet is more open, accessible, and diverse, but it also allows users to avoid anything with which they may disagree (Bimber and Davis 2003). In fact, social media often leads to this result by placing one in a network of like-minded friends and family that often hold consistent political views. This allows users to avoid cognitive dissonance, or any discomfort they would feel when confronted or exposed to information that is contrary to their disposition (Chen and Risen 2010; Elliot and Devine 1994; Festinger 1957; Lashley 2009). The power of television, even with cable and hundreds of channels, is nothing compared to the Internet. On the Internet, this polarizing effect is maximized by providing networks containing flows of information that cater to multiple ideological positions. These networks are rewarded with increased importance by the absence of moderating influences. Social media has accelerated this by several magnitudes. The users of social media can opt to follow particular flows of information creating not just polarization but entire networks of reinforced beliefs (Sunstein 2002).

Understood in this context, social media has the significant potential to polarize people by offering readily available one-sided information combined with an interface that easily rewards a preference for such information. This structure by its nature will allow users to interrupt and avoid contrary information flows. People are allowed to choose their content, and they tend to choose information that is consistent with what they already believe (Chen and Risen 2010). Cable started the trend, but it is the Internet and social media that removed the content of news as a constant for the entire society. The end result is very different groups of people, living in entirely different informational networks, creating increasingly isolated cultural and ideological bubbles.

A political sphere dominated by isolated networks will produce some less-than-optimal results. The source of the people's attitudes is shaped by the messages that dominate their social media networks. Those messages will increasingly be the most often seen sources of the considerations that they have cognitively accessible. In addition, the existence of these networks has an additional effect. Deliberation among like-minded persons does not result in a middle position. More directly, if a group of conservatives deliberates, the result is not the median of their ideological views, it is often the extreme conservative position (Sunstein 2009). The mechanism of this movement is driven by the repeated reinforcement of the groups' central tendencies. When the argument is skewed in one direction, liberal or conservative, the average group member moves in that direction (Sunstein 2009).

Yet this state of increasingly ideological and polarized networks of people is only part of the story. In the absence of the traditional media's mediating role as a gatekeeper, the vacuum of news aggregator, framer, and agenda-setter has not been left vacant. Consumers of news will always need someone to distill it into digestible pieces. With the limited influence of the traditional media to shape the flow of information or present a two-sided information flow, the network will create its own flow of information dominated in part, not by the media, but by the political actors and other interest groups (Agranoff and Tabin 2011). The new social media has created a new paradigm with the public as

consumers of information (demand side) and the elite actors as prov
tion (supply side). The social media presents a perfect opportunity
the public wants information that does not challenge their predisposi
want to give it to them.

The Plan for the Book

In the following chapters, we will explore how social media shifts more power to political actors and interests relative to the traditional media arrangement and how "Tweeting to Power" has become the de facto standard. In this book we will illustrate the power
of this new media paradigm though the use of public opinion data to show three basic
things: (1) people receive the flow of information through social media through political actors and they prefer information that does not challenge their predispositions,
(2) social media use stimulates participation, and (3) social media use crystallizes attitudes creating more polarized and extreme positions. We will be analyzing multiple
datasets, quantitative and qualitative, comprised of data from both elite and nonelite
sources. The chapters of this book are organized nonsequentially covering two primary
subject areas: (1) The US Congress and Twitter, and (2) The American Public and
Social Media. For the first area, we gathered the population of tweets from the 2010 US
congressional candidates for six months leading up to the elections. We explore both
how candidates utilized Twitter to shape the information voters had to rely on come
election time and how effective this effort was at garnering votes. For the second area,
we analyze recent survey data from Pew (2010) that assesses social media use broadly
as well as the specific ways that people are using Facebook and Twitter to exchange political information.

The theory laid out in this chapter also conforms to the two basic areas described
above: Congress and the public. Without expending high media costs, those in power
or seeking power can use these new communication platforms to circumvent traditional
media. This provides political actors with more control over their message, and as a
result, an ability to shape the information that consumers have cognitively accessible
and the attitudes and understandings that result. This is a foundational shift, as social
media platforms provide a more direct opportunity for campaigns, candidates, and political leaders to guide the very way people obtain and process information. There is a
change in information consumption as well. Facebook and Twitter permit consumers
the ability to self-select information and choose to whom they pay attention. These consumers will likely select opinion leaders and politicians whom they trust. Thus, a direct
conduit, with limited intermediary influence, from those in power to their constituents
and potential supporters is constructed. The rest of the book documents this process
along with its attitudinal and behavioral consequences.

In Chapter 2, we set the predicate for our examination by presenting the foundation
for the narrative of the demand side (public opinion) here. In this chapter, we create a
framework for understanding the analysis that comes in the following chapters. This
includes the development of our theory as related to selective exposure and the com-
pulsion for people to avoid information contrary to their predispositions because it may
cause them discomfort (developed more fully in Chapter 8). We then offer a descriptive

ysis of the primary public opinion measures used in this book, based on 2010 data .om the Pew Research Center's Internet and American Life Project. Here we explore some of the questions about social media applications necessary to understand their relationship to politics such as: (1) How pervasive is social media use? (2) How much of this use involves political exchanges? and (3) Do people seek out shared viewpoints and networks of like-minded people? The results here suggest that social media use has become quite pervasive and a fair amount of political communication is taking place. On the final question, it is central to our theory here that people actually prefer information that does not challenge their predispositions. This provides an opportunity structure on which politicians can capitalize. The results clearly indicate that many people prefer one-sided information and believe the Internet makes it easier for people to connect with people who share their political views. Further, the evidence also suggests that many people believe the information provided by politicians they follow is interesting and relevant, indicating that they are receptive to this information flow. Finally, and critical to our overall theory, the results suggest that those who prefer one-sided information are more likely to use social media such as Facebook and Twitter to gather political information.

In Chapter 3, we remain focused on the demand side of social media, further exploring the 2010 Pew survey data. We examine the nature and characteristics of the individuals who are using these platforms to exchange politically relevant information to build a foundation for understanding group behavior as it relates to social media use. We consider the importance of these trends in use based on the theory of information flows and develop our theory as it relates to cognitive dissonance or discomfort that people may experience as a result of the psychological commonalities associated with group membership (race, gender, etc.). If candidates can use social media to circumvent the traditional gatekeepers and control the flow of information, then those who are more frequent users should be more susceptible to their influence. Individuals can select to follow the people who provide information that gives them the least amount of discomfort as a result of exposure to information contrary to their predispositions. This makes social media particularly effective in providing messages that are likely to be read and considered. Not only can candidates use social media to circumvent the media's gatekeeping function, they can also control the message and direct it to individuals who are particularly receptive to it. To explore and test this theory, we examine who is using social media across several platforms including Facebook and Twitter using an index of social media use and construct a series of multivariate models to explore who is using social media, ceteris paribus.

In Chapter 4, we begin the in-depth analysis of the supply side information flow by examining the ways in which US congressional candidates utilized Twitter to control their respective messages. This is a qualitative and quantitative content analysis. We gathered the universe of Twitter activity by all major candidates in the 2010 US congressional races for the six months leading up to the elections. These data allow us to describe in detail how social media is used in campaigns and to be the first to measure that impact. On the qualitative side, we analyze the actual content of tweets, creating a typology that characterizes the varied nature and purpose of these tweets. This typology includes policy-driven tweets, attack/negative tweets, campaign information tweets, and personal/candidate characteristic tweets. On the quantitative side, first we categorize and measure the tweets across the typology. Next, we analyze what types of candidates are most likely to fit within each of these categories. This analysis draws comparisons across party identification, incumbency, district competitiveness, levels of spending, and a host of other controls. We conclude by estimating multivariate models to make causal inferences centered on how candidates are trying to control the flow of information and shape voter perceptions in the process.

In Chapter 5, we offer an analysis of the total Twitter activity across party identification, race of candidate, chamber (House or Senate), and incumbency status. The results indicate that variation clearly exists in the frequency with which different types of candidates tweet. Republicans, minorities, challengers, and senators tend to tweet more. Additionally, we look for differences in the frequency of tweets across each of the typographies identified in Chapter 4. The results show similar patterns across the same groups. The differences across party and incumbency become important to the theory we build both here and later in the book. We argue that context provided an opportunity structure that permitted both Republicans and incumbents to capitalize on the use of Twitter to greater benefit than their respective counterparts. We discuss the implications of this asymmetrical adoption and use of social media in political campaigns.

In Chapter 6, we examine the role of online social networks in encouraging political participation both online and in more traditional political forums and activities. We present an alternative view of the American political future that is substantively different from theories of apathy and declining participation that have dominated the scholarship within political behavior. We accept the foundational premise that democracy is rooted in an understanding of social networks and communicated ideas. However, we propose that the Internet, through social networking, is a solution to decaying social capital and the decline of political participation. We contend that the ease with which information flows through digital networks on Facebook and Twitter facilitates the opportunity for people to join civic and political groups. We go beyond previous research, which has primarily been aimed at addressing whether social media can stimulate online political participation (Bode 2012; Gainous and Wagner 2011), and explore whether social media use facilitates activity in offline civic groups. We argue that this is essential to knowing whether it can actually stimulate social capital and generate political activity beyond cyberspace.

To measure this effect, we estimate multivariate models of the relationship between social media use for both joining groups and taking political action. Beyond creating a forum for civic engagement, we examine the magnitude of the effect of social media on political participation. We theorize that the influence of social media is multiplied, since online social networks lower the required effort and the potential cost of the exchange of politically relevant information. As a result, Facebook and Twitter stimulate political action. The lower cost of political mobilization extends to politicians, interest groups, and opinion leaders who can mobilize citizens using online networks at a fraction of the cost of traditional media, or even the mail.

In Chapter 7, we move beyond exploring the relationship between social media and civic attentiveness to examine how social media creates a direct and substantially different link between the opinion makers and the population. We explore and measure how political actors seek to direct and control the flow of information. If people self-select whom and what to follow via their social media because of relevant considerations stored by long-term memory (Zaller 1992), people are keeping a running tally of the new information they obtain (Lodge, McGraw, and Stroh 1989; Lodge, Steenbergen, and Brau 1995; Lodge 1995), and this information comes from external sources, then Twitter is a new medium that candidates can use to provide these considerations. In doing so, they can circumvent the traditional media, the normal gatekeepers.

The analysis in this chapter is based on counts of the number of times candidates use specific social media tools such as linking, highlighting topics, labeling topics, and redistributing other messages. Specifically we measure, both qualitatively and quantitatively, how candidates are using these different strategies on Twitter to direct and control their messages. These measures include counts of the number of external links, the inclusion of @Twitter names, and hashtags. By including external links, candidates can direct consumers to their preferred information flow. They can also include @Twitter names to guide their followers to other Twitter users who are likely to reinforce the preferred information flow. Finally, they can use hashtags to guide the information flow by including the # symbol to mark keywords or topics in a tweet, making them identifiable in a Twitter search. We explore how different subsets of candidates apply these strategies, and create multivariate models to isolate the effects. The results again add to the building narrative suggesting that Republicans and challengers were more effectively capitalizing on the opportunity offer by Twitter to control the flow of information.

In Chapter 8, we explore the implications of the new controls that political actors have to direct and influence the flow of information. If social media is providing a direct conduit from those in power to citizens, then those citizens who are actively using social media to gather political information are likely to have more crystallized attitudes than those still relying on traditional media for information. Simply, social media users will have less conflicting information accessible because they actively choose to consume information coming directly from those courting them. Further, by declining to engage in online social networks with competing political actors or alternate ideological frameworks, they remove any dissonance in their political thought. It is in this chapter where we detail this theory, addressing the memory-based models and OPM (Lodge 1995; Lodge, McGraw, and Stroh 1989; Lodge, Steenbergen, and Brau 1995; Zaller 1992; Zaller and Feldman 1992).

Our argument is that deeply held predispositions stored in long-term memory guide the selection of whom and what to follow on social media. Once this choice is made, the OPM suggests that people are not making decisions based in long-term memory but rather they are constantly updating, which explains how opinions are shaped. If the new information people are obtaining is biased based on the self-selection that has occurred, their attitudes are likely to become crystallized and more extreme. We use a scale to measure the combined use of SNSs, including Twitter, to gather political information and test how well it predicts measures of political attitude extremity. The results suggest, clearly, that attitude extremity is associated with heightened social media use.

In Chapter 9, we begin to draw broader conclusions about the importance of social media on political outcomes. This chapter brings together the theoretical and empirical foundations of the book. It is here where we answer the question of whether congressional candidates' social media activities and participation generate measurable positive results. We estimate a series of models of candidate vote share to test these premises and measure the effectiveness of campaign uses of social media. We estimate separate models for the full sample and then only for those candidates who had a Twitter account. This allows us to determine if those who are tweeting are faring better at the polls than those who are not, if how much they are tweeting matters, and if the way they are using Twitter matters. The results indicate that Republican and challenger Twitter efforts seemed to be more effective at increasing vote share in the 2010 congressional elections. We discuss the implications of these results in the context of public mood theory (Stimson 1999, 2004).

In Chapter 10 we conclude and assess the importance of the social media revolution as a general concern in light of all of our data. We revisit the question of why political scientists and people in general should care about the impact of social media on politics. In doing so, we connect each of our findings to our theory of information flow in a succinct way, illustrating the power of these Web 2.0 applications to change the very bedrock of politics—people. We end our analysis with projections and predictions concerning what the future of politics will be as social media applications continue to evolve and penetrate societies around the world.

2

Evolution or Revolution—Why Facebook and Twitter Matter?

While there has been a fair amount of discussion concerning the use of social media in political campaigns, the observations often focus on descriptions or simple measures of magnitude or growth. It is often a catalog of what is occurring, rather than why. Observing that politicians use Twitter is the simple task, and it has been done (TweetCongress. com 2011). This descriptive research describing the state of social media and its increasing use in the political sphere is essential, and in truth, precursory to further study. We do continue that here. Yet it is the beginning of the task, not the end. Understanding what motivates the rapid growth in the use of social media and what it means for the evolving political environment is the far more difficult, and ultimately interesting, inquiry. It is in understanding the why that we can create an explanatory framework beyond the immediate usage and consider the broader implications going forward.

The analysis in this chapter works toward this answer in two ways. First, we lay the descriptive foundation for understanding how the use of SNSs such as Facebook and Twitter affect both people's attitudes and politicians' strategies. How much of the public uses SNSs? Why do they use SNSs, and for what types of political activity are they using them? Second, how does the method that people use to organize and access social media affect the kind of information that is obtained and how that information is understood? This is followed by direct tests of hypotheses. We test the premise that people who use SNSs believe that the Internet makes it easier to connect with likeminded people on political issues. Additionally, we test whether people who prefer one-sided news are more likely to gather political information via SNSs. The results below lend support to both these premises.

As detailed in Chapter 1, it is our central assertion that SNSs such as Facebook and Twitter bring a new dimension to our understanding of political communication and behavior. Social media creates alternative channels of information distribution that alter the costs and incentives of political communication in foundational ways. This alternative environment presents opportunities for politicians and other political actors to control the nature and distribution of information. Presently, scholars contend that citizens' perceptions of the political world around them are shaped in large part by the information that the popular media has made available to them through its coverage of politics and government (Bennett 2011; Graber 2010). We suggest that social media offer the opportunity for a new information flow that is no longer being structured and limited by the popular media. Thinking of SNSs as having a demand side and a supply side provides a useful heuristic for understanding their political ramifications. As a relatively new means of communication and information dissemination, SNSs have consequences on the demand side for citizen's political attitudes and political behavior, and on the supply side, they have created a new vehicle for political candidates to shape the outcomes of elections by circumventing the traditional media and controlling the flow of information.

We begin to address the theoretical foundation for the demand side consequences in this chapter and will fully detail this theory as we move through the book (particularly in Chapter 8). We contend that people have a tendency to avoid information that challenges their own predispositions because they prefer not to be confronted with information or opinions that are in conflict with their beliefs and understandings. This argument originates from theories centered on cognitive dissonance (Chen and Risen 2010; Elliot and Devine 1994; Festinger 1957) and extends to more recent scholarship focused on people's inclination to seek out congenial news (Arceneaux and Johnson 2013; Bennett and Manheim 2006; Garrett 2009a, 2009b; Goldman and Mutz 2011; Iyengar and Hahn 2009; Iyengar et al. 2008; Manjoo 2008; Mutz and Martin 2001; Stroud 2008, 2011; Sunstein 2009; Valentino et al. 2009). This has attitudinal implications. Traditional forms of media can generate ambivalence in the news consumer through the presentation of multisided information flows that lead to the creation of conflicting considerations (Alvarez and Brehm 1995; Craig et al. 2005; Eagly and Chaiken 1993; Gainous 2008a, 2008b; Zaller 1992; Zaller and Feldman 1992). We briefly outline how we think such conflict can be averted for many by relying on social media as sources of information in the present chapter, and again, detail this theory in a later chapter.

In the previous media environment, media companies dictated content using a limited number of primarily two-sided news distribution channels that subscribed to preset journalistic standards that structured the content (Bennett 2011). As we noted in chapter 1, this was a fairly limited environment for the consumer and forced most users to digest a limited right/left dynamic. Journalism as a profession has a set of standards on how the news should be covered, including what is worthy of coverage. This journalism-driven approach to news was the case during the height of the print journalism era in the early to mid-twentieth century and during the television broadcast news era that followed (Prior 2007). Whether it was newspapers, radio, or television, the channels of communication were expensive to own and limited in number. For a viewer or a reader seeking to avoid contrary information, and the resulting ambivalence and/or cognitive dissonance or general discomfort, there was little they could do other than simply avoiding news. In the massive number of self-created channels in the social media, infinite single channels of information have recreated the information landscape.

It is in breaking from the two-sided tradition that the power of social media becomes apparent. SNSs significantly change the dynamic by making it easy to create information channels that are consistent with the users' beliefs and avoid any conflicting considerations (Gainous and Wagner 2011). In the 1930s, the average person had available to them the afternoon newspaper or the radio. Even by the 1960s with the broad penetration of network television, the broadcast news was only three networks applying the same goal of two-sided information flows and standardized journalistic content, though with some mixed degrees of success. It was not until cable television and the explosion of niche networks that the availability of single-sided information flows became readily available and accessible. The advent of the social media has virtually recreated the media environment with no channel or distribution limit. The almost limitless distribution channels themselves have no economic or structural need to appeal to large masses of people and are free to be increasingly narrow and focused to the users' particular views. In fact, the user can design their own network of information and distribute it to like-minded users through social media. The users' desire to avoid conflicting views or contrary information is easily accomplished with very little effort. In truth, the reverse is more probable. If one is gathering their information solely through SNSs, it is the broader two-sided information flow that is more difficult to obtain (Gainous and Wagner 2011).

The consequences of this type of media environment are still being understood, especially when considered in light of traditional models concerning how attitudes are formed and how people store and access political information (see Cassino, Taber, and Lodge 2007; Zaller 1992). While we will not test the attitudinal implications in this chapter (we will do so later in the book), we will explore whether the foundational propositions in our theory are accurate. In this chapter, we test both the propensity to prefer one-sided information and the relationship between that propensity and SNS use. Before doing so we first provide some descriptive background. The foundation for any analysis of the behavioral implications of using social media begins with the issue of magnitude. For our argument that this attitudinal phenomenon has a direct effect on political campaigns, the flow of information, and election outcomes, we have to establish that the use of SNSs is pervasive on both supply side (coming from candidates) and the demand side (potential voters). We will address the former later in the book, and explore the latter here.

This chapter study uses a large N survey conducted by the Pew Internet & American Life Project in 2010 to lay out this empirical foundation.[1] We begin with a general analysis of the public's reliance on the Internet to gather information. Next, we directly measure and explore the popularity of SNS use. Specifically, we consider SNS use for political purposes, followed by the reasons why people follow political candidates or political organizations, and finally the users' perceptions about the information they gather via SNSs. The evidence indicates that a large portion of the public is using SNSs to gather political information. They do so for a variety of reasons including getting information prior to other people, having a personal connection with the political candidates or groups that they follow, and believing the information from SNSs is more reliable than information gathered from traditional news organizations.

This last reason has a significant implication. If the average user believes in the reliability of social media in distributing news, those who influence and control the online information networks, such as politicians and political actors, are increasingly dominant players. The distrust of popular mass media is the opening for political actors to circumvent the traditional media. By 2012, the percentage of people who had little or no trust in the media reached 60% (Morales 2012). Social media consumers are generally attentive to preferred political leaders and their perceptions of them are positive. Thus citizens can self-select networks supporting these political leaders and those with whom they trust to friend and/or follow on SNSs. They do this because it permits them to be recipients of largely one-sided information helping them to avoid experiencing negative feelings that may result from exposure to views different from their own. The result is a network dominated by a single-sided flow of information that often originates with the political actors or their supporters. This will increase polarized beliefs along with magnifying the influence to the political actors themselves.

The analysis described up to this point is admittedly speculative based on our theory and the application, in a new context, of previous research on political learning. People seek information that is consistent with their own predispositions and SNSs help facilitate this pursuit. The final descriptive and inferential evidence presented in this chapter provides clear support for this central contention. First, we offer descriptive statistics indicating that a significant portion of the public believes that the Internet makes it easier for users to connect with people with whom they share political views. Second, we present evidence supporting the proposition that increasingly large numbers of Americans prefer news that is one-sided. While these descriptive statistics provide a baseline for understanding the impact of our theoretical assertion, the models that conclude this chapter are central for support of the theory developed throughout the book. First, we model peoples' belief that the Internet connects them with like-minded people as a function of how often they use SNSs/Twitter to gather political information. The results demonstrably illustrate that heightened SNS/Twitter use stimulates this belief. Next, we model the propensity to use SNSs/Twitter to gather political information as a function of a preference for news that shares ones' point of view. The findings are again consistent with our expectations. The results of both models suggest that a preference for one-sided information does, indeed, increase the use of SNSs/Twitter to gather political information.

Your News or My News: Information in the Internet Age

The growing reliance of the American public on the Internet for news provides some context for making sense out of our theoretical assertions. The potential for the effects of SNSs to have widespread influence on public opinion and politicians' campaigning strategies that attempt to circumvent the media and control the flow of information is largely dependent on the degree to which people use the Internet. If the consequence of this control over the flow of information is ultimately going to shape election outcomes, it must reach a certain threshold. Simply, the larger the population reliant on the Internet as their primary source of news, the greater the impact such reliance will have on the aggregate consciousness of the American public. More people will be afforded the opportunity to self-select their news information leading to a less ambivalent public because they are reinforcing their cognitive predispositions. This, in turn, could lead to a more polarized public (Gainous and Wagner 2011). It will shape the attitudes and support of the public for candidates who effectively use SNSs to manage the content and flow of information.

The results presented in Figure 2.1 in the left graph labeled 1st Mention indicate that about 69% of the American public claimed that television was their primary source of news, around 12% relied on newspapers, 6% listened to the radio, 1% read magazines,

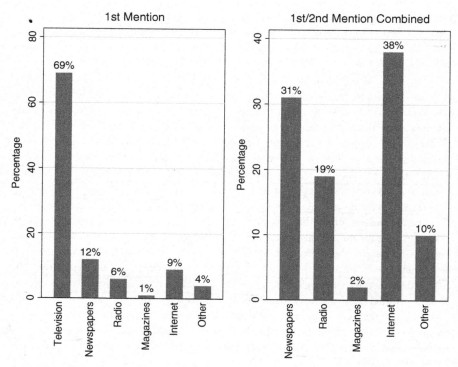

Figure 2.1 Distribution of Primary Source of News. Source: 2010 Pew Internet & American Life Project Post-Election Survey.

and most importantly for our purposes, roughly 9% of the American public relied on the Internet as their primary source of news in 2010.[2] Initially, this marginal distribution may seem low. Yet it is approaching the penetration of the formerly prominent print media in our data and will likely have surpassed it by the time you read this. Print media has already fallen to second position and continues to decline. Further, in the current media environment, primary information sources are a less reliable indicator. People are regularly exposed to multiple channels and sources daily or even hourly.

Considering how many sources are available, the rank ordering could change fairly regularly. In the survey, respondents were asked to give a second source of information and the right graph labeled 1st/2nd Mention Combined represents the distribution of those who mentioned these sources as either their first of second source. The results here show that about 38% of those in the sample mentioned the Internet as one of their primary sources of news. This estimate does not include those who would have listed it as third if given the opportunity to do so. As Americans are exposed to multiple sources (and many likely do not see the information learned on the Internet, often as a byproduct of other activities, as actual news consumption), the actual number of users relying at least in part on the Internet is likely higher.

Regardless, these conservative estimates represent significant growth across time. According to trend data from the Pew Project, the percentage of Americans who claim to rely on the Internet as a primary source of news has more than doubled since 2000 and has increased by nearly 33% since 2004. The public's reliance on the Internet for campaign news is on the rise and has increased to a significant level. Near half of the American public used the Internet in 2010 in at least some way to get news. Further, given that those who are older are generally less likely to use the Internet (Gainous and Wagner 2007, 2011; Mossberger, Tolbert, and Stansbury 2003; Rainie and Bell 2004), there is every reason to believe that use of the Internet for campaign news will become even more widespread as the more technologically savvy younger generations become larger parts of the electorate.

Is Everyone Really Doing It? How Pervasive Are Facebook and Twitter?

While having a general sense of how important the Internet is becoming in the political sphere is a good foundation, it is insufficient for our purposes. More pertinent to our theoretical framework is establishing just how significant the growth in the use of SNSs, such as Facebook and Twitter, has become. The larger the magnitude in this use, the likelihood that the social media can affect political outcomes becomes greater. In the bar graph on the left side of Figure 2.2, use of SNSs such as Facebook (and also MySpace and LinkedIn) is quite pervasive among those who use the Internet at least

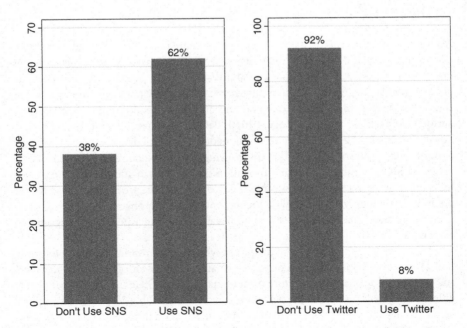

Figure 2.2 Mass SNS and Twitter Use. Source: 2010 Pew Internet & American Life Project Post-Election Survey. Results are based on those respondents who claim to use the Internet.

occasionally.[3] Roughly 62% claim to use an SNS. While any SNS such as MySpace, LinkedIn, Tumblr, and Instagram is included in the survey indicator, we believe that the majority of the affirmative responses stem from those who have a Facebook account. It is the most ubiquitous of the SNSs, and as of this writing still dwarfs the size and scope of the other far smaller websites.

As represented in the bar graph on the right side of Figure 2.2, Twitter use does not reach the heights of Facebook.[4] That said, we do not believe 8% is an inconsequential number of Twitter users (of Internet users). Eight percent of all Internet users is a staggeringly high number of users for any protocol. This is a suitably large enough number of the population to sway an election, even if one would presume that the influence of Twitter only affects its direct users and not the people with whom they interact. In fact, in many elections, especially ones conducted in competitive partisan districts, the winners and losers of the election are separated by less than 10% of the voting public (Konayne 2011). In addition, those who use Twitter happen to be among the most politically engaged. A t-test suggests that those who use Twitter are more likely to be attentive to news (p = 0.00).[5] Additionally, a second t-test illustrates that those who use Twitter are more likely to politically participate online (p = 0.00).[6] Finally, just as the proportion of the public who rely on the Internet as a source of news has trended upward and the number of Facebook users has done the same (see Pew post-election data trend, the number of Twitter users has nearly doubled since 2010, rising to 15% (see Pew Internet & American Life Project, 2012c). Twitter is rapidly becoming one of the most prominent avenues for the distribution of political information.

Gathering Political Information via SNSs

As noted above, the growth of Internet use in the United States is rapid and its penetration is increasing at a staggering rate, especially when compared to previous advances in communication technology (Gainous and Wagner 2011). Further, the adoption rate of social media is significant even by Internet standards. Twitter's growth in particular is massive, increasing 1,300% in one year and more than quadrupling over a two-year period (Golbeck, Grimes, and Rogers 2010; Pew 2012c). Yet the adoption rate alone does not speak to the importance of social media in political discourse. The next layer of our foundation is to establish that the growing masses migrating to social media are using the SNSs to gather political information. Before we can address our contention that people are using SNSs to seek out one-sided information, we must lay this broader predicate. Resultantly, we begin with the distribution of responses on a series of questions that gauge what types of political information exchanges people are engaging in via their SNS accounts.

At first blush the proportions of the public who engage in various political information gathering activities via SNSs may seem small, but when converted to raw numbers and juxtaposed against the total voter turnout in the United States in 2010, a completely different picture is revealed.[7] The percentages displayed in Table 2.1 are based on those who said they did use an SNS and that estimate is based on those who said they are Internet users, at least occasionally. This translates into 62% of the 70% of adults 18 years or older in the United States who claimed to use the Internet. There are approximately

Table 2.1 **Proportion Who Used SNSs for Various Political Purposes**

	Proportion	*Standard Error*
Get Campaign/Candidate Information	0.14	0.01
See Candidates Your Friends Voted for	0.16	0.01
Friend a Candidate/Campaign/Party/Group	0.10	0.01
Posted Political Content	0.12	0.01
Joined Political Group Supporting Cause	0.09	0.01
Started Political Group Supporting Cause	0.02	0.01
N = 1138		

237 million adults who are 18 or older in the United States according to the most recent U.S. Census (all calculations that follow are rounded to the nearest million). Therefore there are approximately 166 million Internet users and 103 million SNS users. Of those SNS users, roughly 52% claimed to have voted in the 2010 elections, making a total 54 million voting SNS users. Given that approximately 91 million Americans voted in the 2010 election, these calculations suggest that of that 91 million around 59% of them were SNS users.

While the numbers of total users are large and likely growing, the nature and scope of the use of SNSs for political purposes are more important subsets for our purposes. Initially, we calculate an estimate of how many of those voters were gathering political information via SNSs. According to Table 2.1, about 14% of those who use SNSs obtained campaign or candidate information from these sites. Other political behaviors varied. Sixteen percent or 17 million Americans claimed to have discovered the voting preferences of their friends and acquaintances on an SNS. Ten percent or 11 million Americans signed up on an SNS as a "friend" of a candidate, or a group involved in the campaign such as a political party or interest group. Twelve percent or 12 million posted content related to politics or the campaign. Nine percent or roughly 9 million joined a political group, or group supporting a cause on an SNS, and about 217,000 Americans claimed to have started a political group, or group supporting a political cause on an SNS. These numbers are sizable given that there were only approximately 91 million Americans who voted in the 2010 elections.

The percentages displayed in Table 2.2 regarding Twitter use for engaging in political exchanges are not as large as those for other SNSs, but they are still large enough to sway a competitive election.[8] Of those who claimed to use Twitter, 16% obtained campaign or candidate information on Twitter. Eleven percent followed a candidate or a group involved in the campaign such as a political party or interest group. 8% included links to political content in their tweets. Eleven percent used Twitter to follow the election results as they were happening. This translates to between one and two million Americans who engaged in such activity. While still relatively small in absolute numbers, the number of Twitter users nearly doubled by 2012, so these estimates would be larger in 2012 and subsequent years.

Table 2.2 **Proportion Who Used Twitter for Various Political Purposes**

	Proportion	*Standard Error*
Get Campaign/Candidate Information	0.16	0.03
Follow a Candidate/Campaign/Party/Group	0.11	0.03
Include Links to Political Content	0.08	0.03
Follow Election Results	0.11	0.03
N = 149		

Note: Data come from the 2010 Pew Internet & American Life Project Post-Election Survey. Results are based on those respondents who claim to use Twitter.

How Attentive Are Followers, Why Do They Follow, and Do They "Like" It?

Now that it has been established that many people do, indeed, gather political information through SNSs, the following descriptive data explore just how attentive they are to political candidates and organizations on SNSs, some of the reasons that people choose to follow them, and whether or not they find their postings interesting and relevant. Answers to these questions provide important context for understanding the effects of SNS use on political behavior. These indicators allow us to address the alternate reasons for why people are inclined to follow candidates and political organizations via SNSs. While we assert that the opportunity to easily avoid information inconsistent with ones' predispositions is one of the primary reasons why people may like to use SNSs to gather political information, we do not preclude the existence of other motivations or alternative hypotheses. Thus, these indicators provide a measured look at the possible alternatives.

As evident in the distributions displayed in Table 2.3, people will express reasons other than a preference for one-sided information to explain why they might follow candidates and political organizations on SNSs.[9] Yet these reasons are often consistent with a preference for one-sided information. A total of 64% of those sampled indicated that they used SNSs to find out news before other people (major and minor reason collapsed). Though this does not speak to a preference for one-sided information, it is not mutually exclusive. In fact, we can expect that someone who prefers news delivered when they want to read, or see it, would also prefer information that is tailored to their preferences. In addition, if they are getting information driven from a candidate, interest group, or even an ideologically definable network of friends, it is a safe assumption that the information is one-sided. Approximately 66% of the sample agreed that they follow political candidates or organizations on SNSs because they like to feel more connected. This, too, shares the same likely correlation with preferred one-sided information. People feel more connected if they are being given information from candidates and/or organizations that reinforce their predispositions.

Table 2.3 **Reasons Why People Follow Political Candidates or P**
Organizations

	Proportion	*Standard*
Find Out News before Other People		
Major Reason	0.22	0.06
Minor Reason	0.42	0.06
Not a Reason at all	0.36	0.07
To Feel More Personally Connected		
Major Reason	0.34	0.05
Minor Reason	0.32	0.08
Not a Reason at all	0.34	0.07
Information Is More Reliable		
Major Reason	0.23	0.04
Minor Reason	0.27	0.03
Not a Reason at all	0.50	0.04
N = 497		

Interestingly, around 50% of those sampled claimed that being able to get more reliable information is not one of the reasons that they follow candidates and organizations. This appears counterintuitive. If a user preferred one-sided information, it would follow that they would tend to believe it was reliable. Assuming that the answer itself is honest, it does present an interesting psychological implication. People may well prefer one-sided information even if they know it is not more reliable. Modern news distribution would then be driven far more by consistency of viewpoint rather than veracity. The viewer seeks reinforcement, even knowing that the reinforcement may not be from objective and reliable sources. Perhaps that explains the continued decline of the news organizations in the United States that strive most for the objective facts rather than the more palatable narrative view (e.g., Bennett 2011; Graber 2010, Prior 2007).

Alternatively, simply stating that reliability is not one of the reasons does not mean it is true. One could think the information is more reliable, but not claim that this is a reason why they follow candidates and/or organizations. Even if we thought this is unlikely, there are other reasons not to be overly concerned about this marginal distribution. There is likely a social desirability effect. People may feel uncomfortable claiming to a stranger that they think the organizations and candidates they follow give more reliable information, because they are not aware of the interviewer's positions. They also do not know if questions are going to follow that require them to specify which candidates and organizations they follow, generating a question order bias. They have already been asked a question that required them to indicate whether they would vote more Republicans or Democrats, so they could be assuming that the interviewer already knows which type of candidates and/or organizations they follow contributing to the social desirability effect. Even if we assume that the marginal distributions are completely accurate, we still need not be concerned. There is still roughly 50% of the public who follow candidates and/organizations on SNSs because they believe the information is more reliable. This is a sizable and clearly significant portion of the public.

The content of information generated from candidates and organizations presents interesting implications as well. Why people follow candidates and organizations and what they perceive of the information speaks to its influence. Do people find the information posted by candidates and groups attention-grabbing and pertinent? The results displayed in Figure 2.3 suggest that people who follow candidates' postings on SNSs clearly tend to find them both interesting and relevant.[10] Roughly 70% of those sampled who follow candidates on SNSs believe that the information that is posted to Twitter or SNSs such as MySpace or Facebook by the political candidates or groups that they follow meets this standard. This evidence is completely consistent with what we would expect if people were actually following candidates or groups because those candidates and groups were giving them information that reinforced their predispositions. People would certainly find information interesting and relevant to them if said information was consistent with their own views. News that meets their world view is likely to receive such a positive assessment and encourage the user to seek out more of it and to access it when it comes available.

If SNS use helps satisfy people's preference for one-sided information, the subsequent query is just how attentive these people are to the postings of candidates and

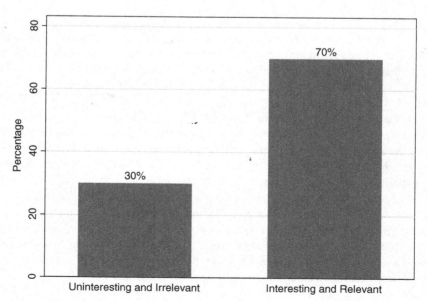

Figure 2.3 Perceptions of Political Candidates' Postings on SNSs. Source: 2010 Pew Internet & American Life Project Post-Election Survey. Results are based on those respondents who claim to use SNSs.

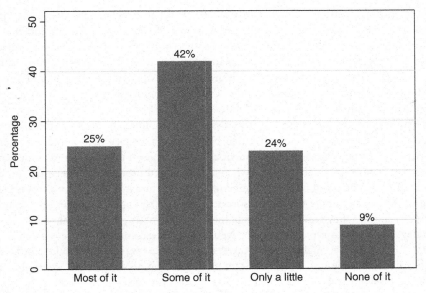

Figure 2.4 Attentiveness to Political Candidates' Postings on Twitter and SNSs.
Source: 2010 Pew Internet & American Life Project Post-Election Survey. Results are based on those respondents who claim to have signed up to follow a candidate or group on an SNS or Twitter.

groups. The marginal distribution displayed in Figure 2.4 shows that people who signed up to follow a candidate or political group on an SNS are fairly attentive to the information posted by that candidate or group.[11] In fact, 67% paid attention to at least some of the posts (42%) or all of the posts (25%). While 24% paid attention to only a little of the information posted, they are still following the post. Only nine percent claimed to not follow any of it. Taken altogether, these results illustrate that those who follow candidates/political organizations are attentive enough for there to be attitudinal and behavioral consequences if candidates can target these consumers by controlling the flow of information. Before we provide evidence of such later in the book, the next section will provide foundation, first, that people who use SNSs more often tend to think the Internet makes it easier to connect with people who share their point of view, and second, that people who prefer one-sided information are more likely to use SNSs.

Friendly Agreements: Connecting with the Like-Minded

Political psychology literature has long grappled with the preference of individuals for information that is consistent with their predispositions. The general proposition is that an uncomfortable state of "dissonance" is created when two or more beliefs or cognitions are inconsistent within a person's belief structure (Festinger 1957, 1964). People are motivated to resolve this conflict by changing their cognitions so that they become consonant or consistent (Chen and Risen 2010). When confronted with contrary information, this process can generally occur in one of two ways. When an individual digests information that is inconsistent with a previously held attitude, dissonance researchers predict that in the absence of an intervening cause, the initial attitude will shift to become more consistent with the information (Festinger 1957; Lodge and Taber 2000). Or alternatively, they will avoid or discard that information, maintaining a preference for the previous held belief structure.

The key proposition of the cognitive dissonance literature and theory is the premise that people strive for agreement in their beliefs. It is a balance that provides a structure for understanding their environment and the actions of people around them. This structure is resistant to change, and when a person is confronted with decisions or information that does not fit within their cognitive structure a level of discomfort is created. As a result, people will use dissonance-reducing strategies to regain the balance and equilibrium they previously held. In the context of news consumption, the obvious strategy is simply to avoid broadcasts, web pages, conversations, or other channels of communication that might increase the dissonance. This was thought to be a difficult proposition is modern societies' constant media environment. However, we propose it is an increasingly viable strategy in the social media universe.

While the theory of cognitive dissonance was created in the 1950s, its application is particularly significant in the digital age where the tools to respond to dissonance are readily available. One of the central tenets of our theory is the proposition that people tend to seek out information that reinforces their own point of view or predispositions in order to avoid experiencing unwanted cognitive conflict. This idea is based in a large literature focused on selective exposure, which will be described thoroughly in Chapter 8 (see Arceneaux and Johnson 2013 for a complete review). We suggest that SNSs such as Facebook and Twitter create a perfect vehicle to provide this opportunity for people. There are an increasingly large number of apparatuses within social media that are intended to provide the user with only the information they would want to see. Some of it is by direct design of the user. Facebook users can create their own universe of suitable information by "liking" reinforcing patterns of web portals and sources that the user defines as appropriate for their consumption. Twitter requires that the user define which sources of information they wish to follow and then organizes the information and provides an interface to access it. Some of this network formation and creation actually occurs without the direct action of the user, as the web protocols themselves attempt to anticipate the user's requirements and avoid any possible discomfort before it can even occur. From a practical and business perspective this makes perfect sense, as a user who is constantly forced to avoid uncomfortable information when using a social media protocol is likely to use such a protocol less or even stop using it all together.

Facebook uses the algorithm "EdgeRank" to select which friends' postings are more likely to appear in a user's News Feed[12] (described in detail in Chapter 8). Among other things, this algorithm uses the frequency with which one interacts with a friend, including reading their posts and clicking on the links they post, to determine whether this friend's postings make one's News Feed (Guildford 2011). Thus, the very nature of how Facebook presents information to someone is biased based on their self-selection. The nature of Twitter usage lends itself exactly to the process of information selection and avoidance. In using Twitter, people are actively deciding which networks of information they want to follow and which they prefer to avoid. Twitter should lead to greater selectivity in choosing whom to follow than Facebook because Twitter, by design, is specifically intended to connect users with certain people and organizations from whom they wish to receive information. This is an information-driven protocol rather than a simple connection between family and friends. Many users are likely to only follow or subscribe to those people, groups, and news organizations for which they have an affinity.

Since people tend to prefer information that reinforces their predispositions, those who use SNSs to gather political information frequently are more likely to believe the Internet helps them to connect with like-minded people when it comes to their political views. More directly, people are connecting with these like-minded people intentionally, as a result of web design, and even potentially subconsciously, to avoid being exposed to people, candidates, and organizations that post information that is inconsistent with their predispositions. As social media has both the tools and design to support this effort, users are more likely to believe that the Internet makes it easier to connect with like-minded people. We test this premise using a multivariate model that includes a number of important controls. However, support for this premise is apparent even before modeling the effects. The distribution on the scaled indicator is revealing. Of those who claim to use the Internet, a combined 57% believe that the Internet makes it a lot easier (46%) or at least a little easier (11%) to connect with like-minded people.[13]

While the distribution suggests that a majority of people do believe that the Internet makes it easier to connect with like-minded people, this does not directly test our hypothesis. To do so, we must first construct a measure that combines political use of SNSs such as Facebook and Twitter. We constructed a Guttman scale to measure the combined use of SNSs, including Twitter, to gather political information. We used the same dichotomous indicators displayed in Tables 2.1 and 2.2. We combined these indicators here as we expect the combined use of the SNSs, Facebook and Twitter, to influence how much people believe that the Internet improves their ability to connect with people who share their political positions. People who self-select whom they friend, follow, and pay attention to on multiple SNSs are more likely to believe the Internet connects them with the like-minded people than people who use only one SNS. Likewise, people who gather more political information on both single and multiple SNSs are more likely to believe the same.

We could have simply created an additive index, but we would have lost most of the cases because the number of Twitter users is much lower than the sample as a whole. Some of the other outcome variables are filtered as well, so we would have had an unacceptable loss of cases. We would have been unable to estimate the combined effect without bias. The Guttman scale approach we used simply assigns a 0 to respondents who didn't use any SNSs or Twitter to gather political information, a 1 to any respondent who claimed to do at least one thing to gather political information using any SNS including Twitter (e.g., get information about a campaign, friend or follow a candidate, etc.), a 2 to any respondent who did at least two of these things via any SNS including Twitter, and so on, up to 6.

We then created a dummy variable from the indicator of the belief that the Internet makes it easier to connect with like-minded people. We coded those who indicated that it makes a little or a lot easier as 1 and those who indicated it makes no difference as a 0.

This dummy is modeled as a function of the Guttman scale of political SNS/Twitter use and a series of controls including the frequency with which people use the Internet (Internet use), attentiveness to politics (attentiveness), partisanship strength, age, income, race (dummies for black, Asian, and Latino self-identification), and a dummy for female gender (female). The operationalization of all of these control variables is included in the Appendix.

As evidenced in Table 2.4, political SNS/Twitter use clearly has a strong positive relationship with the belief that the Internet makes it easier to connect with people who share similar political views. The odds ratio derived from the model indicates that for every one unit increase on political SNS/Twitter use, the odds of believing that the Internet makes it easier to connect with like-minded people increases by 1.75 times, ceteris paribus. The only other significant variables in the model are attentiveness and age. Nonetheless, it is important to include all these controls to assure that the effects of our primary variable of interest, political SNS/Twitter use, are not spurious. The bivariate model also predicts a significant effect ($p = 0.00$). As for the first of the significant controls, the model suggests that for every one unit increase in political attentiveness respondents were 1.37 times more likely to believe that the Internet makes it easier to connect with people who share their political views. Age also has a predictable effect

Table 2.4 **Political SNS/Twitter Use and the Belief that Internet Makes It Easy to Connect with Like-Minded People**

	Estimate	*Standard Error*	*p-value*	*OR*
Political SNS/Twitter Use	0.56	0.09	0.00	1.75
Internet Use	0.03	0.02	0.12	—
Attentiveness	0.31	0.08	0.00	1.37
Partisanship Strength	−0.05	0.12	0.65	—
Age	−0.43	0.09	0.00	0.65
Education	0.09	0.08	0.23	—
Income	−0.09	0.08	0.28	—
Black	0.06	0.20	0.78	—
Latino	0.19	0.21	0.37	—
Asian	0.20	0.40	0.62	—
Female	−0.07	0.11	0.50	—
Constant	0.41	0.37	0.27	—
Pseudo R^2	0.09			
N	1583			

Note: Data come from the 2010 Pew Internet & American Life Project Post-Election Survey. Table entries are logit estimates based on respondents who use the Internet at least occasionally, with associated standard errors in parentheses, and odds ratios (OR).

considering how social media use is more favored by younger people. A one quartile increase in age decreases the odds of one believing that that the Internet makes it easier to connect with people who share their political views.

While the results contained in Table 2.4 begin to lend support to the contention that people who use SNSs are avoiding information that is inconsistent with their own views, a more direct test is to simply ask people if they prefer news that is consistent with their own views and model SNS use as a function of that preference. Before doing so, we need to measure a baseline estimate of just how much people tend to prefer information that reinforces, or at least fails to challenge, their point of view. The results presented in Figure 2.5 indicate that a sizable segment of the American public does prefer information that shares their point of view.[14] Clearly, when respondents were asked whether they preferred news that shared their point of view, had no point of view, or challenged their point of view, the modal response was to prefer information that shared their point of view. Well over 40% of those in the sample chose this response.

A large segment of the public is willing to admit or even recognize that they prefer reinforcing information. This is a substantial population that would likely find the tools presented by SNSs to seek out reinforcing information attractive, given that they do lower the cost of gathering such information. Additionally, the estimate in these data may actually be lower than the true population parameter because there is a social desirability effect in this indicator. Many people who actually prefer to have news and information that shares their point of view will not say so when asked, as they want to present an image of objectivity. Some will not consciously realize that they do avoid contrary information. Yet the dissonance effect is an observable reaction in the general population (Risen and Chen 2010). So given this potential social desirability effect, this

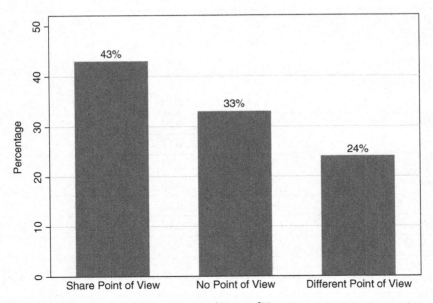

Figure 2.5 Preferences for News Sources' Point of View. Source: 2010 Pew Internet & American Life Project Post-Election Survey.

estimate, which exceeds 40%, is of a significant magnitude. This is especially persuasive considering the positive relationship between the propensity to gather political information on SNSs and the preference for news that shares one's point of view ($p = 0.01$).

Our final test of our theoretical assertion regarding people's preference for one-sided information and the opportunity that SNSs provide to satisfy this preference, is contained in Table 2.5. We model the Guttman scale of political SNS/Twitter use as function of the dummy variable of preference for news that shares one's point of view, the frequency with which people use the Internet (Internet use), attentiveness to politics (attentiveness), partisanship strength, age, income, race (dummies for black, Asian, and Latino self-identification), and a dummy for female gender (female). The tested premise here is straightforward. We assert that people who prefer one-sided news are more likely to use SNSs to gather political information because it facilitates this process for them. We include the controls to assure that the test accounts for as many alternative explanations as possible to avoid spuriousness. The results indicate that there is a strong positive relationship between the preference for one-sided information and the propensity with which people gather political information via their SNSs, including Facebook and Twitter. The odds ratio indicates that those who prefer one-sided news are 1.62 times more likely than those who prefer news that either has no point of view or different point of view than their own to be higher on the political SNS use scale. This is strong

Table 2.5 **Modeling Political SNS/Twitter Use as a Function of the Preference for One-Sided News**

	Estimate	Standard Error	p-value	OR
Preference One-Sided News	0.48	0.15	0.00	1.62
Internet Use	0.06	0.02	0.01	1.06
Attentiveness	0.99	0.10	0.00	2.69
Partisanship Strength	0.19	0.15	0.19	—
Age	−0.84	0.12	0.00	0.43
Education	−0.03	0.09	0.76	—
Income	−0.18	0.11	0.10	0.83
Black	−0.08	0.23	0.72	—
Latino	−0.10	0.25	0.71	—
Asian	−0.23	0.45	0.60	—
Female	0.27	0.14	0.05	1.31
Pseudo R^2	0.11			
N	1583			

Note: Data come from the 2010 Pew Internet & American Life Project Post-Election Survey. Table entries are ordered-logit estimates (threshold value are suppressed) based on respondents who use the Internet at least occasionally, with associated standard errors in parentheses, and odds ratios (OR).

evidence that those who prefer one-sided information use SNSs to gather political information more. It is not only statistically significant, it is a logically sound premise. SNS use should be preferred by people seeking to reinforce their beliefs, as it makes it easier for them to do so.

As noted above, it is important to include controls. There are several significant controls in the model, including Internet use, attentiveness, age, income, and gender. The odds ratio shows that for every one unit increase in the frequency with which people use the Internet, the odds of being higher on the political SNS/Twitter use scale increases by 1.06 times. This is a large effect, as should be expected. Yet the predicted odds are not as large as those predicted by preference for one-sided news. Political attentiveness is the only variable in the model that estimates higher odds of increasing on the dependent variable, political SNS/Twitter use, than preference for one-sided information (2.69). This is also consistent with our expectations. Those who are more attentive to politics should be more likely to gather political information than those who are not.

Two of the other significant variables in the model, age and income, estimate a negative relationship. As age and income increase by one quartile, the odds of being lower on the political SNS/Twitter use Guttman scale are 0.43 and 0.83, respectively. Finally, females are 1.31 times more likely to be higher on the scale. The demographic differences are significant findings and present interesting propositions for the impact of social media as a going concern. We will further explore these demographic differences in the next chapter. *Age / Income ⊖ relat.*

Summary

This chapter has provided a descriptive context for understanding the demand side of SNS use. There is a large segment of the public using the Internet as a source of news, and particularly, using SNSs, including both Facebook and Twitter, to gather political information. The numbers alone are large enough to make an impact on the aggregate public and, as a result, the strategies of interest groups, parties, and politicians. Further, and central to our theory, there was considerable evidence offered in this chapter to suggest that many actually prefer information that reinforces their own predispositions, and the Internet, including SNSs, helps them to find such information.

In the next chapter, we will expand our exploration of who is using SNSs. If candidates can use SNSs to circumvent the media and control the flow of information, then frequent users should be more susceptible to such influence. We will further detail the theory regarding people's preference for one-sided information and highlight those who are most likely to be targeted by politicians, or at least most affected by political campaigns, when they seek to control the flow of information through the social media.

3

Public Opinion 2.0—Read My Feed

In the previous chapter we established that people are using social media to gather political information and that information is often consistent with their predispositions and sourced from like-minded people, groups, and political actors. This chapter continues our exploration of the demand side of the use of social media. We make a more detailed examination of who is using social media the most and what characterizes those users. Additionally, we broaden our examination to see if the distribution has patterns across some identifiable groups. Chapter 2 provided the predicate evidence that people seek out information that reinforces their predispositions. We add an additional level onto this analysis by including group identification controls in our theory and subsequently our model of SNS/Twitter use. As we suggested earlier, there is some variance in the frequency with which people use SNSs across groups. This chapter will explore and explain those differences and propose some long-term implications for the political environment going forward.

Before we look at the distribution of SNS use across a range of individual level characteristics that shape public opinion, we detail how and why there are clear differences across groups in the acquisition and consumption of political information from the social media. There are nuances to understanding the demand side of our information consumption theory. In particular, we focus on the variable effect of the potential discomfort people may experience as a result of exposure to information that is contrary to their predispositions by offering a theoretical foundation for why we should see differences across groups concerning how and why they may collectively respond to such information. We also discuss the ways that groups may be targeted through SNSs by campaigns because of their collective and shared predispositions.

We begin by considering how different groups will access, consume, and understand political news. While there are always individual differences in how people respond to stimuli, there are measurable patterns in how different groups respond to media (Prior 2007). It is a long-held understanding in political science that members of certain groups such as racial, gender, and partisan ones have attitudes which are structured by membership in their respective group (Berelson, Lazarsfeld, and McPhee 1954; Mutz and Mondak 1997; Zinni, Rhodebeck, and Mattei 1997). That is not to say that each member of the group responds exactly the same, but rather at the aggregate level, there are definable group patterns that are both observable and predictable. This understanding of group behavior is so prevalent and popularized that even the broadcast media will regularly refer to collective group political behavior such as the women's vote, the Latino vote, or the African-American vote.

Building on the notion that there are definable predispositions in group behavior, the implications for social media and SNS use for groups are particularly instructive. Members of groups are likely to avoid certain types of information that is generally and collectively inconsistent with the positions of the group. This should orient them toward streams of information through SNSs from politicians, groups, and friends who share the group's viewpoint, or at least who understand it well enough to pander to it. This is far from an unknown behavior, even prior to the explosion of the Internet as a news source. Cable television has successfully pitched to group audiences fragmented along race, gender, wealth, and age, just to name a few (Prior 2007). This niche marketing is facially apparent. Networks such as "Oxygen" and "We" openly appeal to women, marketing both news and entertainment designed to appeal along gender lines (Patterson 2007). MTV attempts to market to a youth audience, and Univision to Latinos.

What makes the Internet and SNS use different is not the strategy itself, but the almost infinite capacity of the new medium to meet users' expectations for avoiding any contrary information. The process which began in earnest with cable television is enhanced because SNSs lower the cost of providing such information from the supply side and also lower the cost of gathering such information from the demand side. By subscribing to certain News Feeds and avoiding others, people easily create their own information bubble. While each individual News Feed is unique, we would expect groups with common identifiable predispositions to draw from similar sources and networks. Television could cater to large broad groups; SNSs can be created for very narrow ones. More directly, while there can be a few television channels for women, social media can create limitless News Feeds and information that are tailored to thousands of various subsets of women.

The implications are stark. If candidates can use SNSs including Twitter to circumvent the media and control the flow of information, then those who are more frequent users should be more susceptible to such influence. As we noted in Chapter 1, individual attitudes are made up of the averaging of considerations that people have cognitively accessible (Zaller 1992), and these considerations are constantly being updated (Bizer et al. 2006; Hastie and Park 1986; Lodge and Taber 2000). Increasingly these considerations are being generated and updated using information drawn through online social networking. This information is, by design and construction, consistent with previous predispositions. It reinforces the users in their predispositions and pushes them even further toward them. As we noted before, information exchanges among like-minded people tend to reach consensus at the extremes (Sunstein 2002). As a result, SNSs could be among the leading sources of group-level polarization in the media environment.

This process does not occur in a vacuum. The absence of media direction leaves political actors and their surrogates as prominent purveyors of political information. As they push information, analysis, and conclusions through the network, they accomplish two goals. The first is the obvious shaping of the information. The second is more subtle. As the information they previously provided has already been viewed and incorporated into a user's understanding, the new information is more readily digested and understood within the previously established context. The political actors have a remarkably powerful way to shape the cognitive understanding of the users, making them more likely to accept new information. Those who use SNSs, including Twitter, to follow candidates the most are likely to have more cognitively accessible information consistent with the direction and belief structure of the candidate or other political actor who has helped shaped and direct the News Feed. As a result, when the candidate or political actor places more information into the News Feed, it will be weighted more heavily in the consumers' own personal calculations when forming opinions.

While Chapter 2 included controls for group membership in the model of political SNS/Twitter use, it is useful to expand this avenue of inquiry and both look at general nonpolitical SNS use and break apart the index of political use herein to get a clearer understanding of how different groups are using different SNSs (Facebook and Twitter). This provides some context for interpreting the results of the chapters that will follow. Specifically, we look at differences in general SNS use, including Facebook, MySpace, LinkedIn, and Twitter, across party identification, race, age, education, income, and gender.[1] We follow this analysis with an exploration of differences in the use of SNSs for explicit political purposes across these same independent variables. Then we test whether these differences hold up in multivariate models. The bivariate results suggest, first, that when it comes to general SNS use, there are some important distinctions, especially in usage. Minorities, younger people, and women are more likely to be using SNSs. It then follows that members of these groups may be more susceptible to campaign targeting through all SNSs, and Twitter or Facebook in particular.

The findings clearly indicate that the use of social media websites such as Facebook to gather political information does significantly vary across party identification, age, education, and gender but not across race and income. Republicans, Caucasians, younger people, and men are more likely to use these sites to gather such information. So while minorities and women were more likely to use SNSs generally, they are both less likely to acquire information via such sites that would directly influence their own political dispositions. Interestingly, the results indicate that Republicans are far less likely than non-Republicans to be exposed to political information via Twitter. This is counterintuitive given the considerable effort by Republican politicians to reach out via Twitter (Almacy, Hauptman, and Newbert 2012). The only other significant bivariate finding regarding the use of Twitter to gather political information is that Caucasians are far more likely to do so than are minorities. Finally, we estimate multivariate models and the results show that there are still differences present across party identification, age, education, and gender (and minor race differences in political use of Twitter).

Before moving to a detailed description of the results, we consider why we might see differences/similarities across groups when it comes to how and why they may collectively experience cognitive dissonance or general discomfort. Finally, we provide a theoretical framework for understanding how and why certain groups may be targeted through SNSs by campaigns.

SNSs and Cognitive Dissonance/Discomfort across Groups

The power of social media to connect groups is only now being measured (Pew 2012a). SNSs allow users to form groups, and those groups can and do drive information to individual feeds. Some of the groups are openly partisan. Both the Republican and

Democratic parties have a social media presence on the two most prominent SNSs, Facebook and Twitter (Gainous and Wagner 2011). Both parties use their access to advocate for positions, persuade, inform, and, of course, raise money. These pages are supplemented by a multitude of groups, political actors, and news sites that supplement the partisan networks. Yet these overtly political presences on SNSs are only a small part of the larger narrative. For high information voters, the parties and politicians are likely important sources. For lower information voters, the individuals in the network are often followed on Twitter or "friended" on Facebook for nonpolitical reasons. These nonpartisan connections are more likely to define their News Feeds and indirectly create their political universe online. The partisan material can find its way into their network, but it is a product of the people they group with online. It is in studying that self-selection that we can find group-level patterns in social media for political content.

The previous chapter laid out why people actually prefer to avoid information that challenges their predispositions. As a baseline assumption for our models, we start with the null hypothesis, which is an electorate that had no patterns of predispositions. Yet we know that such an assumption is simply untrue. People bring a preset understanding of politics and political actors that is, in part, based on how they view themselves or more directly with whom they identify. Group identification remains an important lens on how people access and understand political information (Converse 1964; Nie, Verba, and Petrocik, 1976). For example, religion is a good predictor of party choice (Lijphart 1979). People are influenced by the groups with which they identify. Political scientists have long studied this group dynamic across race, ethnicity, gender, age, education, income, and many other factors (Dalton 1996).

We do not suggest that any particular group is more likely to experience dissonance or general discomfort. Rather, we assert that groups may collectively avoid similar sets of information types that would challenge their predispositions. In short, there should be predictable patterns of group behavior online. In the broadest terms, we would expect liberal groups to avoid Fox News or popular conservative radio talk host Rush Limbaugh. Conservative groups might avoid the Huffington Post or *New York Times'* editorials. Even narrower groups along regional, religious, or cultural differences should have cognitive schemas that are comparable (Conover and Feldman 1984). As a result, they should have predictable and measurable aggregate patterns of political engagement and avoidance over the Internet and social media in particular.

Starting with the well-researched premise that members of certain groups have attitudes that are structured by membership in their respective group (Berelson, Lazarsfeld, and McPhee 1954; Mutz and Mondak 1997; Zinni, Rhodebeck, and Mattei 1997), the implications are significant on the Internet. SNS users are likely to avoid certain types of information that are generally and collectively inconsistent with the positions of their group. This should open them up to the flow of information through SNSs from groups, political actors, and activists who share their viewpoint. Finally we contend this process is enhanced because SNSs, as they lower the cost of providing such information from the supply side, also lower the cost of gathering such information from the demand side.

SNS Campaign Targeting

As SNSs play such a powerful role in aggregating the individual predispositions of members of different groups, we would expect the social media to be an active arena for targeted political messaging and fundraising. Unsurprisingly, political actors are active online and the social media is awash with political activity. As expected, major political activities are ongoing, including fundraising, campaigning, and organizing online (Gainous and Wagner 2011). Supporting such behavior are early studies showing that online campaigning can and does affect electoral outcomes (Wagner and Gainous 2009). SNSs present a very cost-effective way to increase the speed, scale, and range of political actors as they seek to reach voters (Yang and Counts 2010). The usage statistics alone illustrate the importance that members of Congress place on social media. As of this writing, only 67 of the 535 members of Congress do not use Twitter (TweetCongress 2012). Being in the Senate, being a younger members of Congress, and party pressure are some of the key factors leading politicians to adopt Twitter (Lassen, Brown, and Riding 2010), but those distinctions are declining rapidly as the use of Twitter is becoming ubiquitous.

As a method of quickly and efficiently reaching voting groups with appeals that are tailored to them, SNSs, and Twitter in particular, are remarkably useful. Early research shows that constituent outreach is one of the driving motivations in using Twitter (Chi and Yang 2010). Campaigns can effectively target groups and tailor the message to them by appealing to perspectives that motivate and energize these groups. It is similar in many ways to the use of direct mail, but is strikingly more efficient, faster, interactive, and adjustable. It also allows for more frequent messaging and the use of followers to repeat or "retweet" the messages, links, and analysis at speeds that are unprecedented.

Successful politicians are among the quickest to adopt the use of Twitter in their campaigns and are among the most frequent users of the protocol. A large vote share in the previous election is one of the best predictors of high Twitter use in subsequent elections (Williams and Gulati 2010). Politicians see the efficacy of Twitter in targeting constituents. Early examinations of how Twitter is being used shows effective targeting of subgroups that can and do affect electoral outcomes (Bode, Dalrymple, and Shah 2011; Bode et al. 2011; Golbeck, Grimes, and Rogers 2010; Livene et al. 2011). Below, we explore the how this process works. We consider who is using these SNSs and ultimately how efficient group targeting may be among the largest benefits of social media adoption for politicians and other political actors.

Who Is Facebooking and Tweeting?

The results presented in Table 3.1 provide an initial look at differences in the use of SNSs, generally. These results are based on an index of the general use items presented in Figure 2.2 that simply asked respondents, first, if they used MySpace, Facebook, or LinkedIn, and second, if they used Twitter. We simply added the two indicators together to form a measure we call *SNS/Twitter Use*. The two items were correlated with each other ($p < 0.01$). Because these indices are ordinal, we rely on the Wilcoxon rank sum (Mann-Whitney) test to test for differences. Further, we created dummy variables

Table 3.1 **SNS and Twitter Use across Individual-level Characteristics**

	Mean	Standard Error	p-value
Party			
Republican	0.50	0.02	0.69
Democrat	0.53	0.02	0.50
Independent	0.50	0.02	0.69
Race			
White	0.48	0.01	0.00
Black	0.59	0.04	0.06
Latino	0.60	0.05	0.02
Age			
Lower Quartile	0.73	0.02	0.00
Interquartile Range	0.46	0.02	0.00
Upper Quartile	0.23	0.02	0.00
Education			
Tech/High School or Less	0.47	0.02	0.12
Some College	0.51	0.02	0.91
College/Post-College Graduate	0.53	0.02	0.17
Income			
Lower Quartile	0.55	0.03	0.15
Interquartile Range	0.49	0.02	0.13
Upper Quartile	0.51	0.02	0.76
Gender			
Male	0.44	0.02	0.00
Female	0.57	0.02	0.00

Note: Data come from 2010 Pew Internet & American Life Project Post-Election Survey. P-values are derived from a Wilcoxon rank sum (Mann-Whitney) test. They represent the probability that we cannot reject the null hypothesis that there is no difference between the respective category and the other categories combined.

for each category of the nominal and ordinal independent variables so that we could perform individual tests for differences between each response category and the combination of the other response categories.

The mean use across party identification, education, and income is not statistically distinguishable. The party identification result is interesting juxtaposed against a result from others' research (and confirmed in a subsequent chapter) suggesting that Republican candidates are more likely to Tweet (Bode et al. 2011; Peterson 2012; Peterson and Surzhko-Harned 2011). It would appear that their efforts are not increasing general use. While this may be the case, it does not mean that their social networking efforts are having the same impact as that of Democrats. Even effects at the margin can be important to certain subsets of voters. The relevance of targeting smaller groups of potential voters can be important depending on the election, the voting electorate, and the closeness of the race.

The results in Table 3.1 do indicate that minorities, younger people, and woman are more likely to be using SNSs. As a result, it may be easier for candidates to target these groups through Twitter or Facebook. Interestingly, and contrary to the access-based digital divide literature (Norris 2001; Gainous and Wagner 2007), it appears that Latinos and African-Americans are the most likely to be using SNSs. Latino mean use is only slightly higher than African-Americans, but both are significantly higher than whites. This high use in general is worth noting. Targeting the Latino vote is not a new phenomenon and is likely to grow as the Latino population in the United States rises (see Ramirez 2005). SNSs can potentially become a central vehicle for such targeting. This is especially true in light of the difficulties in reaching minority groups through conventional media.

As expected, younger people are more likely to use SNSs. The predicted pattern continues across the various age groups. Those in the lower quartile are more likely to use SNSs than those in the interquartile range. Those in the interquartile range are more likely to use SNSs than those in the upper quartile. Differences in political behavior across age are often attributable to life cycle or generational effects (Wilcox and Norrander 2002). There is little reason to believe that people simply decline to use social media as they get older. Hence it is unlikely that the differences across age are a life cycle effect. It is more logical and probable that it is a generational effect. The usage rates of older Americans will increase as the current older generation, which is resistant to online social media, is replaced with generations who have been using it most of their lives. As a result, we expect that the Internet's impact on politics will only increase in time as the difference between the generations on the use of social media dissipates. However, in the short term, the social media presents a strong opportunity to target younger voters who are often transient and hard to consistently locate in even current databases. While they also often lack a landline telephone, they do carry social media with them on their mobile devices, making targeting through SNS not only viable but likely preferred.

Finally, it appears that women are more likely than men to use SNSs. While the data does not provide us with conclusive answers as to why women are more likely to use social media (we will explore some hypotheses later), the fact that they do presents strong opportunities for political actors. The gender gap is one of the more important predictors of electoral success in the United States and its importance in elections is increasing (Kaufmann 2002). Women, like Latinos and African-Americans, have observable patterns of aggregate political behavior that make targeted campaign approaches viable, especially with a low-cost delivery mechanism such as an SNS.

The high usage rates of SNSs by women, Latinos, and African-Americans present opportunity for political actors and interest groups. These groups may be more susceptible to having their attitudes shaped through elite control of the flow of information simply because a refined and targeted appeal can be made directly to the large numbers of each group that use SNSs. However, the high usage rates by these groups alone does not make this so. While SNS use is a necessary condition for this causal relationship to exist, it is not sufficient. Results suggesting that these groups are likely to be gathering political information via these SNSs tend toward a sufficient condition.

The results presented in Table 3.2 offer an examination of how much people across the same groups examined above are using SNSs (including Twitter) to gather political information. We constructed two separate indices of the propensity people use both Facebook (and MySpace) and Twitter to gather political information. The first, *Political SNS Use*, is based on the six items contained in Table 2.1 ($\alpha = 0.65$), and the second, *Political Twitter Use*, is based on the four items contained in Table 2.2 ($\alpha = 0.62$). Interestingly, there is some divergence in the results relative to general SNS use. First, there appears to be some differences across party identification. Those who identify themselves as Republicans tended to be more likely than Democrats and Independents to gather political information via Facebook and MySpace. That said, they are less likely to gather political information via Twitter. As noted above, this is counterintuitive, considering that Republicans in Congress have made a concerted effort to utilize Twitter as a means of disseminating information (Chi and Yang 2010). While Republican voters may be less likely to gather political information than their partisan counterparts, this does not mean that Republican efforts have been fruitless. We will address the effectiveness of their efforts in Chapter 8.

It is well established that there are differences in the usage technology for politics based on access, training, and ability (Norris 2001; Gainous and Wagner 2011). As noted above, while the elements of the digital divide do appear in our findings, they are not always as we would expect. As for race, and the gathering of political information via SNSs, there were no significant differences in how much sites such as Facebook and MySpace were used. That said, whites were considerably more likely to gather political information via Twitter. This could certainly structure targeting strategies. Democratic politicians, who typically have a strong African-American base, may find it ineffective to attempt to reach this base through Twitter. Facebook would probably be more productive. However, it is important to consider that the visibility and popularity of Twitter has occurred more recently than with Facebook. The number of Twitter users, while increasing rapidly, is not yet equivalent to Facebook. As a result, it is certainly possible, maybe even probable, that some of these differences may dissipate in time, making both or either network a good avenue for targeted political information flows.

The results concerning age are particularly intriguing considering that age is often a factor in the adoption of technology (Norris 2001; Gainous and Wagner 2007). The results centered on gathering political information via Facebook and MySpace were consistent with those presented in Table 3.1. Younger people are more likely to utilize this avenue for obtaining information. However, there was a different result in regard to

Table 3.2 **Political Use of SNSs and Twitter across Individual Level Characteristics**

	Political SNS Use			Political Twitter Use		
	Mean	*S.E.*	*p-value*	*Mean*	*S.E.*	*p-value*
Party						
Republican	0.75	0.07	0.02	0.20	0.09	0.07
Democrat	0.58	0.05	0.68	0.49	0.12	0.61
Independent	0.56	0.06	0.06	0.59	0.15	0.26
Race						
White	0.65	0.04	0.44	0.60	0.12	0.07
Black	0.52	0.09	0.53	0.28	0.14	0.13
Latino	0.58	0.10	0.64	0.33	0.15	0.46
Age						
Lower Quartile	0.77	0.06	0.00	0.47	0.12	0.44
Interquartile Range	0.56	0.05	0.01	0.40	0.11	0.61
Upper Quartile	0.39	0.07	0.05	0.58	0.22	0.27
Education						
Tech/High School or Less	0.43	0.04	0.00	0.35	0.13	0.49
Some College	0.68	0.07	0.24	0.31	0.13	0.13
College/Post-College Grad	0.76	0.06	0.02	0.60	0.13	0.15
Income						
Lower Quartile	0.56	0.06	0.45	0.34	0.10	0.29
Interquartile Range	0.61	0.05	0.77	0.59	0.15	0.28
Upper Quartile	0.70	0.06	0.31	0.41	0.13	0.66
Gender						
Male	0.68	0.05	0.10	0.52	0.13	0.49
Female	0.58	0.04	0.10	0.41	0.08	0.49

Note: Data come from the 2010 Pew Internet & American Life Project Post-Election Survey. P-values are derived from a Wilcoxon rank sum (Mann-Whitney) test. They represent the probability that we cannot reject the null hypothesis that there is no difference between the respective category and the other categories combined.

Twitter. There was no significant difference across age with regard to political Twitter use. Interestingly, and while not statistically significant, the mean for the upper quartile of age was considerably higher than the lower quartiles. Older people do tend to vote more often than younger people (Rosenstone and Hansen 1993; Verba and Nie 1972), so perhaps certain subsets of older voters can be effectively targeted through Twitter.

Other noteworthy results included the differences across education. Those who are more educated tended to gather more political information via Facebook and MySpace than the less educated, but there were no significant education differences when it came to gathering political information via Twitter. These results are particularly distinctive as they represent a sharp contrast to the more typical technological divide between people of differing incomes and education (Norris 2001). Finally, it does appear that men were more likely than women to gather political information on Facebook and MySpace (though only significant at the 0.10 level). This runs counter to the results regarding general SNS use. While women were more likely to be on social media, men are, at least for now, more likely to use the network for political information.

Before we are ready to generalize from any of these findings, it is important to see how well they hold up in multivariate models holding constant each variable, respectively. The results of these models are in Table 3.3, and regarding party identification,

Table 3.3 **Models of Political SNS and Twitter Activity**

	SNS/Twitt. Use	OR	Pol. SNS Use	OR	Pol. Twitt. Use	OR
Republican	0.05	—	0.37**	1.44	−1.20**	0.30
	(0.11)		(0.16)		(0.57)	
White	−0.10	—	0.05	—	0.83*	2.30
	(0.13)		(0.19)		(0.48)	
Age	−1.05***	0.35	−0.38***	0.68	0.30	—
	(0.08)		(0.11)		(0.36)	
Education	0.16**	1.17	0.26***	1.30	0.25	—
	(0.07)		(0.08)		(0.35)	
Income	0.01	—	−0.10	—	0.03	—
	(0.09)		(0.09)		(0.30)	
Female	0.55***	1.73	−0.25*	0.78	−0.49	—
	(0.10)		(0.14)		(0.42)	
Pseudo R^2	0.06		0.02		0.06	
(a) N	(b) 1558		(c) 1095		(d) 134	

Note: Data come from the 2010 Pew Internet & American Life Project Post-Election Survey. Table entries are ordered-logit estimates (threshold values are suppressed), associated standard errors in parentheses, and odds ratios (OR). *** $p < 0.01$, ** $p < 0.05$, * $p < 0.1$.

do hold up. Even controlling for race, age, education, and income, it appears that Republicans were more likely than non-Republicans to use Facebook and MySpace to gather political information. Conversely, they were less likely to do so via Twitter. For the former, they were 1.44 times more likely to have higher political SNS use than non-Republicans, and for the latter, they are 0.30 times less likely to be higher on the political Twitter use index. The race effect persists in the political Twitter use model. Whites were 2.3 times more likely to be higher on this index than minorities, ceteris paribus. Consistent with the earlier findings, younger people were 0.35 times more likely to have more SNS use and 0.68 times more likely to use SNSs to gather political information. Next, those who are more educated were 1.17 times more likely to have more SNS use and 1.30 times more likely to gather political information via SNSs. Finally, women were 1.73 times more likely to use SNSs generally but 0.78 times less likely to use them to gather political information.

Summary

This chapter has built a theory explaining how and why certain groups may be more readily available to be targeted by political campaigns through the use of SNSs, including both Twitter and Facebook. Our basic argument is that people who belong to certain groups are likely to avoid certain types of information that is generally and collectively inconsistent with the positions of members of those groups. As a result, this opens them up for the flow of information through SNSs from politicians who share their viewpoint. SNSs lower the cost of providing such information from the supply side and also lower the cost of gathering such information from the demand side. We then examined which groups are more likely to both use SNSs generally and specifically to gather political information via SNSs. The resulted suggested there were some clear differences across partisanship, race, age, education, and gender.

In the next chapter, we move on to discussing the primary supply side of social networking information flow. Specifically, we will provide a descriptive framework of how candidates for the 2010 U.S. Congress utilized Twitter in their election bids. We will build the theory for a typology we constructed to categorize the ways in which these candidates relied on Twitter and will provide an empirical description of this typology using both quantitative and qualitative measures.

4

Congress 2.0—Internet-Style Politics

In previous chapters, we theorized why increased use of social media would lead to polarized positions and increased influence from political actors and groups. The focus up to this point has been largely on the consumer of information. In this chapter, we create a broader foundation for our approach from the supply side of the equation. In Chapter 3, we explored how people and groups of people are adapting and using social media to communicate and participate in politics. Politicians have become increasingly aware of the power of the Internet to organize for political purposes (Trippi 2005). Where the people go, the politicians follow. To understand how politicians are influencing and controlling the flow of information through the social media, we empirically describe and measure the ways members of the United States Congress (MCs) and challengers used Twitter in the 2010 election to reach out to their constituents and potential voters. We gathered the universe of tweets from MCs and the leading challengers for their seats. This data is comprised of 64,557 tweets. Of the 884 total candidates, 483 had Twitter accounts (55%). In the six-month time period leading up to the election for which we collected data, these MCs and challengers tweeted from as low as zero times (candidates who created a Twitter account and then never used it) to as high as 1,340 times by Tim Griffin, a successful Republican House challenger from Arkansas.

In this chapter we will explore and develop the theory that political leaders can use SNSs, Twitter in this case, to wrestle away control of the flow of information from the traditional gatekeepers in the modern media. There are two important changes that the social media networks alter about the flow of information. The first is a removal of the gatekeeping function normally practiced by the traditional media. The second is allowing the political actors to not only contribute to the flow of information but also to shape and direct it. After setting forth our assumptions and theory concerning the new media environment, we will use both quantitative and qualitative evidence to describe how politicians take advantage of the new information networks to accomplish their goals.

Prior to beginning the descriptive analysis, we will present the theoretical foundations in the research and findings from studies of campaigning to support the typology we created for characterizing the content of individual tweets. Our premise is that candidates tend to be single-minded seekers of reelection (Mayhew 1974, 2004) and are likely to rely on Twitter to serve this purpose. This makes the campaigning literature a reasonable theoretical avenue for developing expectations. Based on the patterns and activities found in research on modern campaigning, we have isolated four primary areas in which we would expect to find Twitter usage. These would be basic communication and organization, negative attacks, highlighting personal characteristics, and promoting policy.

Each typology is supported by research into modern campaign practices. We expect to observe tweets centered on campaign announcements, including fundraising activities, get out the vote efforts, requests for volunteers, and the calling of meetings (Bergan et al. 2005; Epstein and Zemsky 1995; Green, Gerber, Nickerson 2003; Heberlig, Hetherington, and Larson 2006; Hillygus and Jackman 2003; Shaw 1999). We expect that Twitter will be used for attacks on opposition and negative campaigning (see Lau, Sigelman, and Rovner 2007 for a complete review). It will serve to allow candidates to highlight their desirable personal characteristics (Funk 1999; Jacobs and Shapiro 1994; Kenney and Rice 1988; Kinder 1986; Markus and Converse 1979; Markus 1982; Miller and Miller 1976; Miller and Shanks 1996; Page and Jones 1979; Rahn et al. 1990). Finally, we expect to find tweets based on policy ideas (Kahn and Kenney 2001).

With this four category typology in mind, we are able to create workable categories to sort and explore the content of the tweets. However, before moving on to this description, we detail the theory centered on how politicians can use SNSs to circumvent the traditional media gatekeepers.

Circumventing the Gatekeeper

One of the great challenges for any politician is to effectively work the mass media to reach their constituents with the images and messaging that they prefer. A multitude of strategies exist for this purpose, including consistent talking points, made-for-media events, and even picking and choosing particular media outlets in order to obtain the most sympathetic coverage possible. The care and feeding of the media is a particularly important political skill (Bennett 2011). Yet even able politicians are at the mercy of the media's coverage, which can, and often does, reverse itself into hostile coverage with a fair degree of sensationalism at unexpected times and in unforeseen ways. An avenue to bypass the media is inherently appealing, as trusting a message through a third party has inbuilt limitations. News and political coverage are subject to many influences. In the modern media, news coverage is an ongoing struggle between competing interests, including political actors, media companies, advertisers, journalists, and consumers.

As a result, news, by its very nature, reflects multiple types of bias. Someone has to decide which people will be heard, which facts will be offered, and the manner in which they are organized and presented. Historically, that process occurs under the broad label of journalism. Though often intended to be an objective process based on journalistic standards, foundationally these are choices made by a few for the many. The process has multiple layers. Journalists and writers make choices. The editors will make their own choices as well. Yet these production-level decisions are only the beginning. Executives at news organizations often have input from the management and economic perspective. Additionally, in the modern media conglomerates, one also has to consider the role of lawyers and marketing experts in this process. News that results in expensive lawsuits or does not draw readers or viewers is not a long-term, or for that matter, even short-term, product for media corporations (Bennett 2011). Those are just some of the considerations that shape the regular news output.

Even before the explosion of the Internet and the mass adoption of social media, the ability of the traditional media companies to mediate between the people and the politicians was in decline. The ability of gatekeepers to limit what was available to consumers was already threatened by the expansion of cable networks and the increasing amount of sensational news coverage that had already crossed over into the entertainment media (Prior 2007). During the presidency of John F. Kennedy, national newspapers were reluctant to cover the personal foibles of the president. By Bill Clinton's terms in office, such coverage was constant and popular viewing. While a traditional journalist might have exercised a professional standard in not articulating personal indiscretions in the Kennedy era, such a choice was not available in the 1990s. If one journalist or reporter refused to cover the story, the growing and expanding cable and Internet media outlets would do so. That was the lesson taught by the explosive interest in Matt Drudge, who rose to prominence covering President Clinton's scandal with Monica Lewinsky through his then largely unknown website, *The Drudge Report*.

SNSs present an even larger threat to the gatekeeper. More than just creating additional outlets and more media, SNSs are user constructed and defined. This is a change not just in scale, but in structure. Rather than just increasing the number of available outlets, as the growth of cable television has done, SNSs have recreated the information market so that it is the user that creates their own outlet and solicits the content. It is an increase in magnitude, as there are now potentially infinite numbers of distribution channels. However, it is in the structure that this system is revolutionary. By allowing the user to create and control their network, there is no apparent or systematic form of gatekeeping. Each user is the gatekeeper and decides which information or flow of information that he or she wants to see or read. On its face, this is the most democratic and open informational system ever designed.

However, in practice it is not a totally free information system. There are two restrictions that predominate. First, information is not created in a vacuum. Someone must still gather, organize, and distribute it. The sources of information, even on the Internet, are often digital versions of traditional media outlets (Graber 2010). For example, The New York Times is both a traditional newspaper and an online distributor of news and interactive analysis. In choosing sources, the user has great freedom, but there are not an unlimited number of places that one can go for news. The gathering of information is still costly and requires an investment of time and resources. While the traditional media, such as newspapers, are a significant source of online content, they are one avenue among a number of possible options on the Internet. Along with the digital versions of traditional media, there are a myriad of blogs, web-based news services, and personal reporting. Internet-based sources ranging from blogs such as Matt Drudge's *The Drudge Report*, or online newspapers such as *The Huffington Post* are growing in number. It is a vast environment, but not an unlimited one.

Additionally, we know that people prefer information that meets their predispositions and expectations. As detailed above, cognitive dissonance, or the desire to avoid the discomfort caused by being confronted with information that is inconsistent with one's beliefs or understandings, drives people to familiar and accepted narratives of the news. This can be accomplished in two ways using social media. A person can create a network by sifting through the content and choosing information flows with which they find comfort and agreement. Alternatively, they can depend on agreeable outside sources to do the sifting and presenting, and simply join that already-developed network. It is in this second approach that we propose most Americans fall, providing an alternative to the traditional gatekeeping role of the media.

Since the nature of social media gives any interested party the ability to shape a network and drive content, it is a fertile ground for interested parties to market viewpoints, ideas, and content. Political actors are particularly well positioned to uses SNSs to become the de facto gatekeepers and control the narrative. The political actors can anticipate the needs of various subsets of voters and then enter their networks by designing content to appeal to these users. They can drive content through the network as well as help reshape and define it. The end result is that the user feels empowered to control his or her content but takes the short cut of adopting and adapting the networks that are designed to appeal to their predispositions. The political actor then uses the network to provide appealing content to the user and seize control of the narrative.

Twitter and Campaigning

With our four-category typology in mind, we are able to create workable categories to sort and explore the content of the tweets from candidates for Congress. While congressional elections are not the only elections that have a social media component, they are a window into likely strategies and behaviors. Before moving on to a description of the behavior of congressional candidates on Twitter, we need to detail how politicians are using SNSs in modern campaigns and what this new medium means for the political environment. While there are different ways that one can categorize the content of political Tweets, our organization is based on the foundational assertion that politicians are focused on winning office and their behaviors are determined in large part by that goal (Mayhew 1974).

Mayhew's formulation of congresspersons being motivated to act for reelection is not the only way to view their behavior. Others have argued that members of Congress are motivated by power-seeking (Dodd 1981), or that parties often shape behavior (Aldrich 1995), or even policy (Arnold 1990). We agree that members of Congress are motivated by things other than reelection, and the complexity of their actions, especially in committees, is strong evidence of alternative motivations (Fenno 1973). In fact, Mayhew does not make the claim that MCs have no motivation other than reelection (1974). However, he creates a viable theoretic foundation for congressional actions that helps explain structure and predict behavior. The power of the proposition is that his assumption is fairly adept at predicting many of the actions and activities of MCs.

For our purposes, Mayhew's theoretical construct is helpful in understanding the nature and scope of communication that happens during an election campaign. Though we adjust the framework for the Internet age, consistent with Mayhew's initial formulation, we predict that candidates seeking to win office would devote time and resources to online versions of advertising, credit claiming, and position taking. We should find tweets advertising the candidate's events, highlighting their desirable personal characteristics, and emphasizing their successes. Such advertising already occurs outside of Twitter (Bergan et al. 2005; Funk 1999; Heberlig, Hetherington, and Larson 2006; Jacobs and Shapiro 1994; Rahn et al. 1990). Additionally, we would expect that assigning credit and blame, as well as framing candidates' positions on important issues through negative advertising, would be a viable Twitter strategy as well (Lau, Sigelman, and Rovner 2007). Extending beyond Mayhew's initial argument, we would also expect policy positions to appear in the Twitter usage as long as it is not counter to their electoral prospects (Arnold 1990; Kahn and Kenney 2001).

While these strategies are well-known, Twitter makes these activities more efficient, inexpensive, and immediate. A campaign can dispatch a tweet in seconds to advertise a success, claim credit for a new policy, or even respond to the actions of their opponent. Not only can the dispatch occur rapidly, it can be carefully targeted to supporters for the largest impact. Previously such activity would have to occur through mail or telephone if targeted, or mass media such as broadcast television if not. Either is a relatively slow response. Further, direct outreach in traditional ways is time consuming, resource intensive, and expensive. Beyond the efficiency benefits, Twitter's structure suits campaigns. Each tweet is limited to 140 characters. While that may be too short to have an exhaustive policy conversation, it is remarkably useful for campaigns which are often intentionally short on details.

The initial evidence of this was at the presidential level, but it is likely to become common at the congressional level as the rates of adoption and usage of Twitter become more regular. The power of short political messages shared on Twitter was evident in the 2012 presidential election in the United States. Foreign policy can be, and often is, very nuanced and complex. How the United States engages with the world is a discussion that would facially appear ill suited for microblogging SNSs such as Twitter. Yet in the third presidential debate between Mitt Romney and Barack Obama, Twitter exploded with millions of short messages around themes within the debate (Cohn 2012). Barack Obama's assertion that Mitt Romney's concern over the number of ships in the Navy was akin to worrying about the number of horses or bayonets was the most tweeted about subject in the debate. The Twitter label, or hashtag, #horsesandbayonets, was being used at the rate of 105,767 tweets per minute out of approximately 6.5 million total tweets concerning the debate (Cohn 2012). This topic continued to trend highly on Twitter into the next day. Similarly, in the earlier second debate, Mitt Romney's use of the term "binders full of women" also launched millions of Twitter responses (Farley 2012). Consistent with our expectations, the campaigns themselves were fully engaged in these discussions and attempted to control the thematic messaging to their supporters. Inarguably, Twitter message control is now a foundational part of the process.

In the modern electoral environment, Twitter and similar kinds of microblogging are perfectly suited to the types of messaging in which candidates want to engage. Campaigns rarely seek to explain the minutia of complex legislation but instead seek to highlight victories and create short and succinct themes. Twitter not only supports such an approach, its absolute limit of 140 characters mandates it and both rewards and excuses parsimony in explanations. No one expects a tweet to be comprehensive. While people regularly assert that they want to see a candidates' policy plans, they are often more satisfied with simple policy statements or planned legislative direction as opposed to detailed plans (Kahn and Kenney 2001). In campaigns, voters want to know that there is a comprehensive strategy to address the larger problems or issues. More directly, they want to know that the candidate has a plan that is consistent with their values. As the campaign must work to capture the attention of voters who are otherwise disinterested or distracted, this is accomplished through an expression of direction rather than detail (Kahn and Kenney 2001). For a distracted constituent, a rendition of the details will often be received with less interest than the value-driven statement of direction. A tweet not only meets this need, it almost appears designed for that purpose.

Should some people seek details, a link to lengthy and even dense policy plans can be included with the Tweet. This gives the otherwise brief statement a perceived solid foundation, even if the actual plan is never accessed. In this way Twitter can convey both the theme and structure in a brief statement while appearing to suggest depth and detail. For candidates, Twitter presents one of the most inexpensive, unmediated, and closely focused forms of communication in campaign history. While not designed with campaigns in mind, Twitter is remarkably adaptable to the needs of the modern campaign. While many seeking to reach audiences inexpensively can make use of Twitter, few other activities have benefited as much as political outreach. With this understanding in mind, we will explore the specifics of this political activity on Twitter below.

Gathering and Coding the Data

To obtain a comprehensive picture of Twitter usage during the campaign, we gathered the universe of Twitter activity of all MCs and major party challengers for six months leading up to the November 2010 congressional elections.[1] We created a dummy Twitter account, signed up to follow all incumbent MCs and major party challengers, and then downloaded each of their Twitter posting histories from June 2010 through the election in November 2010. To sort this extensive volume of tweets, we created a list of keywords that represented the concepts we discussed above and encapsulated the four-category typology (campaign announcements, attack/negative campaigning tweets, tweets designed to highlight desirable personal characteristics about the candidates, and policy tweets).

We explored the qualitative data and the four-category typology and keywords structure. This exploration revealed a number of additional keywords that fit into each of the categories. After this qualitative examination, we performed a keyword search based on each of the identified words/phrases, verified that each time a keyword was identified the usage fit within the expected category, and then created counts of each keyword for each candidate, making the candidate the unit of analysis.[2] The categories are not mutually exclusive. One tweet could be counted more than once if it used multiple keywords. We decided that this is the optimal route as one tweet could simultaneously be used by a candidate to accomplish multiple strategic goals. Finally, we constructed additive indices of each of the four types of Twitter activity based on the summation of the keyword counts for each respective type.

We used the following keywords, including all roots and derivatives of each, for the four basic types of tweets that we categorized: (1) Campaign Announcements: *meeting*—campaign events not described as rally or event, *rally*—campaign events not described as meeting or event, *campaign*—used as both noun and verb, *volunteer*—used as both noun and verb, *help*—help/assist with campaign functions, *debate*—either to figuratively debate opponent on issues or the literal debates themselves, *run*—run for office, *event*—political, organizational, business events that are not categorized as meetings or rallies, *GOTV*—get out the vote, *fundraising, interview*—with all media, *contribution*—campaign/financial; (2) Attack/Negative Campaigning: *Boehner/Palin/ McConnell*—if used by a Democrat, *Pelosi/Obama/Reid*—if used by a Republican, *Tea Party/liberal, opponents' name, politicians*—when used derogatorily, *establishment*—to refer to Washington insiders, or state insiders; (3) Personal Characteristics: *principle*— principles such as "common sense," "conservative/liberal," or as a standalone, *victory* —as a forecast for election chances, or to refer to the advancement of goals, *progressive/ conservative, leader*—described self as a leader or working with other leaders, *hardwork- ing, fight*—fight for policies, principles, or for constituencies, *pray*—religious term, *faith*—religious term, *values*—personal values, "local" values, religious values, cultural values, *bipartisan*; and (4) Policy: *deficit, earmark/pork, abortion, taxes, healthcare, global warming, terrorism, education*).

Selecting Some Exemplary Tweets

The descriptive quantitative results indicated that around half of the congressional candidates, incumbents and challengers, had a Twitter account. Of those, around 45% used their Twitter account infrequently. In fact, around 3% of those with a Twitter account never tweeted. That said, the average number of tweets over the six-month period leading up to the 2010 election was approximately 134. One candidate tweeted 1,340 times, although the distribution is tilted toward the left side of the mean (see Figure 4.1). The standard deviation is quite high, suggesting that there was quite a bit of variance concerning how much Twitter activity each candidate had.

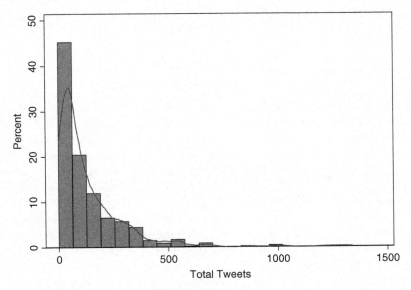

Figure 4.1 Distribution of Total Twitter Use by MCs and Challengers. Source: www.twitter.com.

The Twitter activity was varied and wide ranging, but it did fit our theoretical expectations. In this chapter we will lend qualitative evidence of the validity of the quantitative indices for each of the four types of candidate tweets that will follow. Below we explore some of the tweets that we categorized using our keywords and typology. This qualitative data is intended to provide context and nuance to the interpretation of the quantitative analysis that follows in this and subsequent chapters. The qualitative analysis is organized by section and subsection. Each section represents one of the four major categories in our typology. Under each section we offer examples of tweets that were categorized by each of the keywords we used.

While including tweets from the various types of accounts in the data (Democrats and Republicans, incumbents and challengers, House members and Senate members, etc.) is useful to the understanding of the nature of these data, including one qualitative example for each type and each keyword would become overwhelming. Thus in this chapter, and in the spirit of covering the various types of candidates from which each tweet may come, we rotate the type of candidate throughout our included examples across the keywords.

We start by offering an example of the first keyword under the first of the four type category (*Campaign Announcements*) from a Democrat House incumbent, and for the next keyword under *Campaign Announcements* we present a tweet from a Republican House incumbent. Then we present a tweet from a Democrat Senate incumbent, followed by a Republican Senate incumbent. Finally, we do the same thing for challengers continuing to move through the keywords under each of the four types of Tweets (*Campaign Announcements, Negative/Attack, Personal Characteristics*, and *Policy*). This will lead us back to the beginning of the cycle after eight examples of tweets. Given that there are 36 total keywords, we will offer at least four examples from candidates who fit into each of the eight types of candidates. After giving the descriptive statistics on the counts of each of the keywords falling under the four-category typology, respectively, we describe how each of these tweets reflects the respective category of the four-category typology, and finally, we provide the qualitative examples for each of the keywords.

Describing the Tweets

Generally, the quantitative descriptive results presented in Table 4.1 indicate that keywords used to represent the different types of tweets appeared quite frequently throughout the qualitative data. Some candidates used them repeatedly. Using the opponents' name (measuring attack/negative tweets) was the most frequent occurrence (mean = 18.59), but the highest percentage of candidates with Twitter accounts used the words "campaign" and "help" at least once (77%). The most infrequent keyword occurrence was "global warming" used to represent tweets about environmental policy. The data also show that there is substantial variability across all of these keywords. The standard deviations are quite high, suggesting that the frequency with which candidates used the words significantly varies. This is likely a result of the variance of Twitter activity in general. Broadly speaking, the keywords that seemed to be generally picking up most of the candidates fell under the campaign announcements category. On average, 48% of the candidates were picked up by one of the keywords (with a range from 25

Table 4.1 **Average Number of Tweets across Keywords**

	Mean	*Standard Deviation*	*Maximum*	*% of Candidates*
Meeting	2.81	4.41	32	60
Rally	2.45	6.11	69	46
Campaign	6.63	13.51	212	77
Volunteer	2.88	5.65	57	51
Help	6.86	12.94	135	77
Debate	4.73	10.92	97	53
Run	0.76	1.65	18	34
Event	2.62	4.26	35	60
GOTV	0.98	3.20	32	25
Fundraising	1.03	2.33	26	47
Interview	1.93	4.59	62	47
Contribution	0.71	2.57	38	26
Boehner/McConnell/Palin	0.39	1.21	12	17
Obama/Pelosi/Reid	8.12	14.96	129	76
TeaParty/Liberal	0.43	1.33	11	18
Opponent's Name	17.43	42.31	377	54
Politicians	0.24	0.69	5	15
Establishment	0.06	0.37	6	4
Principle	0.16	0.60	5	10
Victory	1.56	4.13	42	40
Progressive/Conservative	1.17	3.25	31	29
Leader	1.58	3.32	26	46
Hardworking	4.26	6.49	46	72
Fight	1.81	3.88	43	51
Pray	0.38	0.93	6	22
Faith	0.19	0.79	9	10
Values	0.26	0.95	12	14
Bipartisan	0.22	1.26	25	11
Deficit	0.61	1.55	16	28
Earmark/Pork	0.41	2.07	34	13
Abortion	0.09	0.37	3	6
Taxes	4.48	8.19	78	73

continued

Table 4.1 **(continued)**

	Mean	*Standard Deviation*	*Maximum*	*% of Candidates*
Healthcare	2.39	4.76	43	55
Global Warming	0.04	0.25	3	3
Terrorism	0.16	0.55	6	11
Education	0.75	2.18	24	29
Total # Tweets	134.49	163.40	1340	97

Note: Data come from www.twitter.com. Minimum is 0 for all cases. % of Candidates is the percentage of candidates with Twitter accounts who used the respective keyword at least once. The top five most used keywords are in bold print. The percentage for those who used the names Boehner/ McConnell/Palin was calculated only for Democrats with a Twitter account and only for Republicans with a Twitter account for those who said Obama/Pelosi/Reid.

to 77%). Next, 33% of candidates were picked up by the negative campaigning keywords (ranging from 4 to 76%). Additionally, 31% of the candidates were picked up by the keywords measuring tweets designed to reflect positive personal characteristics about themselves (ranging from 10 to 72%). Finally, roughly 27% were picked up by keywords that addressed policy (ranging from 3 to 73%).

Before moving on to the individual qualitative descriptions of each of the keywords, we briefly explore the relative distributions of these keywords when fitted into the typologies described above (campaign announcements, attack/negative campaigning, personal characteristics, and policy). First, this four-category typology effectively captured the structure, function, and characterizing of the tweets. On average approximately 54% of the total tweets were captured by our typology. That means that after eliminating those tweets which were identified by our keywords, but where the use of the word for our purpose was not a fit, over half of all tweets sent out by the population of incumbents and major party challengers were picked up by our typology. We do not claim that additional keywords would not categorize even more tweets, but we are comfortable asserting that the keywords we used are solid indicators of the general concepts we are trying to measure (the four types of tweeting). The qualitative evidence presented above in combination with the high percentage of total tweets captured by our typology leads us to this conclusion. If we were to add an additional type called "random information seemingly unrelated to the campaign" we believe that would account for most if not all of the remaining tweets.

Table 4.2 provides the relative distribution across the four types. We simply constructed an index for each type by summing the total number of counted words in each respective category for each candidate creating four indices. Then we summed the total number of counted tweets irrespective of category for each candidate. Then we divided the former by the latter giving us a relative percentage for each candidate. The results presented are the means of those relative percentages. On average 44% of the tweets by candidates that fit into our typology were some kind of campaign announcement, approximately 18% were attack/negative tweets, roughly 19% were tweets attempting to highlight the personal

Table 4.2 **Average Percentage of Classified Tweets across Each Type**

	Proportion	*Standard Deviation*
Campaign Announcements	0.44	0.23
Negative/Attack	0.18	0.15
Personal Characteristics	0.19	0.18
Policy	0.17	0.11

Note: Data come from www.twitter.com.

characteristics of the candidates, and about 17% were policy-centered tweets. As noted above, the categories are not mutually exclusive. Nonetheless, campaign announcements are the dominant use with mixed usage among the other tweet types.

A Qualitative Look at Congressional Tweets

Now we move on to the qualitative analysis of the four-category typology. The pattern that emerges from this analysis suggests that those candidates who seemed to be tweeting most often by using the keywords we identified as indicators of campaign announcements, attack/negative campaigning, personal characteristics about the candidates, and policy centered tweets tended to be candidates who ran unsuccessful bids for office. This will become important as we move into the later chapters of the book and begin to compare how the type of Twitter activity described in the present chapter fares against Twitter practices that focus more on trying to control the flow of information. We will present evidence later in the book consistent with our theory described up to this point that the latter is more electorally effective.

Campaign Announcements

MEETING

The word "meeting" was used as a keyword to identify tweets where candidates were making announcements about when they were going to meet with voters, supporters, or groups that would be important to the campaign. As evidenced in Table 4.1, the mean number of times some derivative of the word "meet" came up and passed the coding check to assure its usage was consistent with the campaigning announcement framework was 2.81, with a standard deviation of 4.41 and maximum of 32 by Dan Kapanke, an unsuccessful Republican challenger for a House seat in Wisconsin. Also, 60% of the candidates who had Twitter accounts used this keyword at least once. This is a quite common occurrence.

Example: Tammy Baldwin, Democrat, House incumbent
Tweet Heading down to the UW lake shore dorms to meet new students! Come stop by my field office open house today from 4 to 6 at 435 state #p2 #fb

This is an example of the type of tweet that got coded to represent a campaign announcement as a result of the word "meet" appearing in the tweet. Clearly, this is an example of a tweet from Representative Baldwin that was designed to advertise to her Twitter followers that she was going to be making an appearance on campus. This could really serve multiple purposes. It can generate attendees and instill confidence in followers because she was making sure they knew she was out on the campaign trail. The hashtags #p2 and #fb that appear at the end of the tweet are examples of the Twitter tool described in footnote 2 of this chapter and that will be expanded on in Chapter 9. These particular hashtags are used so that she was able link her followers to other tweets that used these hashtag; #p2, which is a resource for progressives using social media who prioritize diversity and empowerment and an umbrella tag for information for progressives on Twitter, and #fb, a hashtag used that will automatically add the tweet to Facebook if the user has installed the Selective Twitter Update application on Facebook. This allows her to simultaneously reach dual social media audiences.

RALLY

"Rally" was another word that was used to identify tweets that were making a campaign event announcement. The mean number of times candidates included the word "rally" was 2.45 with a standard deviation of 6.11 (see Table 4.1). Illiaro Pantano, a Latino Republican and an unsuccessful challenger for a House seat in North Carolina, used the word "rally" 69 times to make some kind of a campaign announcement. Roughly 46% of the candidates who had a Twitter account used this word at least once.

Example: Lynn Jenkins, Republican, House incumbent
Tweet It should be a beautiful day to for the GOP Clean Sweep Bus Tour. Our first rally begins in a few minutes here in Topeka! http://ht.ly/30Nel

This tweet is another good example of a message designed to attract people by making a simple campaign announcement. The link included at the end of the tweet led to Representative Jenkins' campaign homepage that provided more details about the campaign stop.

CAMPAIGN

The word "campaign" was also used to capture tweets that were making a campaign announcement. The idea is that candidates will use the word to announce events, to give updates on the campaign, and potentially to try to attract volunteers. It came up 6.63 times, on average, in candidates' tweets with a standard deviation of 13.51 (Table 4.1). The candidate with most number of tweets containing this word was again an unsuccessful Republican challenger, Joel Pollak, in the state of Illinois. He used this word extremely frequently at a count of 212 times. Other candidates seemed to use this word frequently as well. It was used by 77% of the candidates.

Example: Patty Murray, Democrat, Senate incumbent
Tweet Michelle & Jill spoke about the power of the grassroots. Join our campaign today: http://bit.ly/dAF6KA #wasen

This tweet is a typical example of the type of campaign announcement that is intended to draw positive attention to the campaign from the followers. Senator Patty Murray campaigned with First Lady Michelle Obama and Jill Biden. Clearly using these names is intended to garner positive attention. Given that most of Murray's followers are likely Democrats, this tweet probably accomplished that goal. Additional Murray's tweet offered a link to her campaign web page and a hashtag that taps into those tweeting about Washington Senate-related issues.

VOLUNTEER

The word "volunteer" was used simply to capture tweets that were aimed at seeking volunteers, offering information about volunteers, or making direct communications to volunteers. These are clear campaign announcements. As evidenced in Table 4.1, the word "volunteer" came up in tweets an average of 2.88 times with a standard deviation of 5.65. Current Senator Roy Blunt, a winning Republican challenger in the state of Missouri in 2010, used the word "volunteer" or some derivative of the word 57 times, the highest use in the data. Over half of the candidates used this word at least once (at 51%).

Example: Tom Coburn, Republican, Senate incumbent
Tweet Come to "Bartlesville Volunteer call night" Monday, October 25 from 4:00 pm to 8:30 pm. The Coburn for Senate Team . . . http://fb.me/LBbzUjFl

This tweet is a call for volunteers, a component that is clearly essential to any successful campaign. Senator Coburn is also using Facebook. The link connects his Twitter followers with the Facebook event page. Facebook event pages advertise the event to the friends of the person who created the event once they send out invitations. Additionally, the default setting for events in Facebook allows those who agree to attend to invite friends from their list. So, to say the least, the number of attendees can multiply quickly. This is a good example of how Twitter can be used to connect people to a larger SNS group by directing them to Facebook. It is a savvy use of SNSs.

HELP

The word or some derivative of the word "help" was included in our search to capture campaign announcements that were intended as calls for support. It came up on average 6.86 times with a standard deviation of 12.94. Sean Bielat, an unsuccessful Republican challenger for a Massachusetts seat in the House, used the word 135 times. The mean is higher than the use of the word "campaign," the maximum is lower, and the standard deviation is lower suggesting that this is a word that was used even more frequently across candidates. That said, the proportion of candidates who used the word at least once was the same as "campaign" at 77%.

Example: Steve Pougnet, Democrat, House challenger
Tweet watch our new ad, and help us keep it on the air by contributing online at www.electpougnet.com/donate http://fb.me/LxTaIux0

The high use of the word "help" in tweets probably reflects the need for campaigns to get support both financially and with labor. Of course, in the end, they cannot win without both. The links in this tweet go to the campaign webpage where contributions can be made and to a YouTube video of Pougnet's campaign commercial. This is another good use of multiple outlets through Twitter. It is important to begin to see here that the use of Twitter is much more than simply 140 characters. It opens the door to shaping the information to which followers are exposed.

DEBATE

The word "debate" was used as a search term to identify tweets that made campaign announcements about upcoming debates, announcements about the willingness to debate, and announcements about the success of debates that had happened. This word came 4.73 times on average with a standard deviation of 10.92. Bill Flores, a winning Republican house challenger for Texas, used this word the most frequently at 97 times. This word came up relatively frequently. Around 53% of the candidates used this word at least once in their tweets.

Example: Rich Iott, Republican, House challenger
Tweet Getting ready for tomorrow's debate sponsored by Fox Toledo and the Toledo Free Press.

    This tweet is a straightforward example of an announcement of an upcoming debate. The candidate is able to advertise the debate to his followers. Then the tweet may be retweeted, a reposting of someone else's tweet, so it reaches a wider audience.

RUN

The word "run" and its derivatives was used to capture tweets that were intended to announce that a candidate was running or to mention why a candidate was running. This word was not used frequently. It averaged 0.76 with a relatively low standard deviation of 1.65. That said, approximately 34% of the candidates who tweeted used this word at least once. Sean Bielat was again the most frequent user of this word. He used it 135 times.

Example: Jack Conway, Democrat, Senate challenger
Tweet I am running for the US Senate because of my daughter and her future. Help us win for all of our families! http://ow.ly/31U5h #KYDems

    This example is a straightforward candidacy announcement. It simultaneously lets people know the reason he wants people to believe he is running. The link directs followers to his web page and the hashtag connects his tweet to searches tweeters may do under the hashtag that includes discussions about Kentucky Democrats.

EVENT

The word "event" was included as a search term to pick up any tweets that were making announcements about a campaign event or to draw people's attention to the successes of an event. This word came up 2.62 times, on average, with a fairly tight distribution around the mean. The standard deviation was 4.26. Around 60% of the candidates who had

Twitter accounts used this word at least once. Joe DioGuardi, an unsuccessful Republican Senate challenger from New York, used this word the most frequently at 35 times.

Example: Joe DioGuardi, Republican, Senate challenger
Tweet New Right Now! Events: Campaign HQ Grand Opening & Special Event w/ Dick Morris! - staff #NYSen #tcot http://bit.ly/bCfgyI

This tweet is a clear example of how Twitter can be used to announce an event. It also simultaneously uses the tweet to include a link that connects followers to the Facebook advertisement for the Dick Morris event. This announces the event, reaches multiple audiences, and connects the candidate with a popular person in the Republican ranks. The hashtags will force the tweet to come up on any Twitter searches where others have used this hashtag that addresses New York Senate issues and issues being discussed by the group within the Top Conservatives hashtag. This is a popular hashtag that comes up frequently in candidate's tweets. It allows them to connect to a large national discussion among conservatives.

GOTV

The search term "GOTV" was intended to pick up any get out the vote plea for supporters to help push up participation. The full phrase "get out the vote," as opposed to the acronym, was also included in the search. This, too, was not an extremely popular phase but it did come up, on average, nearly one time across the sample at 0.98 with a standard deviation of 3.20. The standard deviation is three times the mean, suggesting that the distribution is spread around the mean. Rick Larsen, a winning Democratic House incumbent from Washington, used the phrase most frequently at 32 times and 25% of the candidates who had a Twitter account used it at least once.

Example: Carolyn Maloney, Democrat, House incumbent
Tweet StonewallDemsNY GOTV Rally: LG nominee Bob Duffy @TomDiNapoli @ChrisQuinn John Liu Jerry Nadler @CarolynBMaloney et al Wed 10/27 8pm LGBT Cntr 208 W 13th St

This example directly encourages followers to attend a get out the vote event. It is important to note that this is a retweet. Thus, Maloney reposted the tweet from another Twitter account. It comes from a group supporting gay rights in New York. She also links to others' Twitter accounts who will be attending the GOTV event. This is accomplishing multiple goals in one simple tweet: (1) it ties her to the gay rights Twitter group, which may get her additional followers, (2) provides the connection between her and these Twitter accounts for her followers, which we can assume is a good thing, (3) she may get additional followers from the others who are linked, (4) shows her support for gay rights, and (5) advertises the event. This is an example of a savvy Twitter campaign user.

FUNDRAISING

The word "fundraising" was used to capture any tweet that called for contributions, announced fundraising events, or provided information about the current fundraising status of the campaign. Fundraising or some derivative of the word was used 1.03 times on average with a relatively tight distribution around the mean. The standard deviation was 2.33. Approximately 47% of the candidates who had Twitter accounts used the word at least once and Francis Becker, an unsuccessful Republican House challenger form New York, used the word most frequently at 26 times.

Example: Brad Zaun, Republican, House incumbent

Tweet Come to "House Party Fundraiser!" Wednesday, September 29 from 5:00 pm to 7:00 pm. Dr. Pat Bertroche hosting this . . . http://fb.me/IMkaFlaH

This example is, simply, a campaign announcement about a fundraiser. The information about the event is provided and there is also a link to a Facebook event page. It is concise and maximizes opportunity by connecting to the Facebook event page.

INTERVIEW

The word "interview" is intended to pick up tweets that were intended to advertise an upcoming interview, provide information about the content of an interview, or highlight the success of an interview. This word came up, on average, 1.93 times with a standard deviation of 4.59. Approximately 47% of those candidates with Twitter accounts used this word or some derivative of the word at least once. Again Joe DioGuardi topped the list with the most use of this word at 62 times.

Example: Patrick Leahy, Democrat, Senate incumbent

Tweet Watch WPTZ tonight at 5:30pm for Senator Leahy's interview about the campaign. The Vermont Public Television is . . . http://fb.me/ztMJUN8I

This example provides all of the necessary information for followers to both know about the event and to potentially retweet it so that the audience can build. Additionally, it is linked to a Facebook event page.

CONTRIBUTION

The word "contribution" was used to capture tweets where the candidate was seeking financial contributions to the campaign, talking about the status of contributions, or thanking supporters for contributions. This word came up 0.71 times on average and had relatively large standard deviation at 2.57 suggesting the distribution was wide. In fact, the maximum number of uses of the word was 38, significantly higher than the mean. Tim Griffin, the same successful Republican House challenger from Arkansas mentioned at the beginning of the chapter who had the most overall tweets at 1,340 also had the most use of the word contribution. Roughly 26% of all candidates with a Twitter account used this word at least once.

Example: Johnny Isakson, Republican, Senate incumbent

Tweet 18 days until Election Day! Way #18 you can help us re-elect Johnny: Make a financial contribution at http://bit.ly/cntRwG!

The example here is a clear campaign announcement seeking financial contributions and the link went directly to his campaign web page, where contributions could be made.

Attack/Negative Campaigning

BOEHNER/MCCONNELL/PALIN (IF USED BY A DEMOCRAT)

This list of names was selected to represent an attack or negative tweet because, typically, if a candidate is using the name of a popular leader from the other party, they are doing so to mudsling or attack in some way. We only counted instances of these names for those candidates who were Democrats since John Boehner is the Republican speaker of the House, Mitch McConnell is the Republican Senate minority leader, and Sarah Palin is a popular, and divisive, former Republican vice-presidential candidate. Surprisingly, the mean use of at least one of these names was only 0.39 for Democrats with a standard deviation of 12 and only 17% of those candidates with Twitter accounts used one of these names at least once. Bryan Lentz, an unsuccessful challenger from Pennsylvania used these names the most times, topping out at 12 times.

Example: Jay Clough, Democrat, House challenger
Tweet @dccc Denounce Leader Boehner's Plan to raise the retirement age to pay for the GOP's destructive agenda http://dems.me/9aQGjX #p2 #Dems
　　This is a retweet from the Democratic Congressional Campaign Committee. It links to a petition on their website "to denounce Boehner's outrageous plan." This is a good example of an attack tweet. The language used in the Tweet ("denounce") and in the linked petition is clearly loaded. The hashtags link to the same progressive group Tammy Baldwin linked to and to anyone tagging a general Democrat discussion thread.

OBAMA/PELOSI/REID (IF USED BY A REPUBLICAN)

The use of these names worked the same way as the previous search terms but we used these to represent negative/attack tweets coming from Republicans. Clearly the use of President Obama's name by Republicans is going to be negative in most instances and the same can be said of House Minority Leader Nancy Pelosi and Senate Majority Leader Harry Reid. The mean use of one of these names was much higher for Republicans than was the use of the names in the Democratic example provided above, coming in at 8.12 with a standard deviation of 14.96. That said, we will not read too much into this, considering that one of the names in this set of search terms was a sitting president. This certainly boosted the average. This average was also boosted by John Faulk, an unsuccessful House challenger from Texas, who used these names a total of 129 times. While the mean may not be that telling, the percentage of those with Twitter accounts who tweeted one of these names is quite high at 77%.

Example: Jeff Miller, Republican, House challenger
Tweet Teacher who watched Obama sign stimulus is laid off http://fb.me/Je7UT1uj
　　The example provided here not only slings mud by trying to capitalize on any anti-Obama sentiment but it also provides a link to a story about a teacher being laid off that adds to the attack. Additionally, the story is linked through Facebook, which widens the reach of this tweet by hopefully connecting followers with the Facebook audience.

TEA PARTY/LIBERAL

The words "Tea Party" and "liberal" were used in the same spirit as the names described in the two previous sets of search terms. Democrats who use "Tea Party" are typically not doing so in a favorable light and the same can be said for when Republicans use the word "liberal." Our count here only included the use of these words in that context. We did not count how often Republicans used "Tea Party" or how often Democrats used the word "liberal" because this would not capture a negative/attack tweet, although it may be interesting for measuring and testing other concepts. The mean use of these terms, respectively, was 0.43 with a standard deviation of 1.21, so it was not common. In fact, only 18% of those candidates with Twitter accounts used one of these terms at least once. Jesse Kelly, an unsuccessful Republican House challenger from Arizona used "liberal" 11 times.

Example: Joseph Sestak, Jr, Democrat, Senate challenger
Tweet ICYMI: Joe #Sestak crashes the tea party: http://bit.ly/94DMlu #toomey #p2

   ICYMI is an Internet slang acronym for "In Case You Missed It." Notice that the tweet contains a hashtag for the candidate, a hashtag linking to the progressive group #p2, a link to a story that talks about how Sestak is giving the Republican Tea Party-supported candidate a serious challenge, and most interestingly, a hashtag for the opposing candidate. This means that people who follow and do searches for the opposing candidate, Patrick Toomey, may get a tweet and link to a story that does not benefit that candidate. This is a clever strategy.

OPPONENT'S NAME

It is typical that when a candidate uses his or her opponent's name, it is not being used positively. This is especially true in a tweet that only allows for 140 characters. Thus, this turns out to be a good indicator of attack/negative tweeting. In fact, the mean number of times the opponent's name came up in tweets was high at 17.43, with a standard deviation of 42.31. This is the highest average in our search terms. That said, not all candidates included the opponent's name. Approximately 54% of those with Twitter accounts used their opponent's name. Sean Bielat, was again the most frequent user in this category. He stated his opponent's name a staggering 377 times.

Example: Mark Kirk, Republican, Senate challenger
Tweet RT @kevingoody: For real RT @Kirk4senate: RT @bradleydj: I'm a Democrat . . . but Mark Kirk would make a better Senator than Alexi Giannoulias

   The example here is quite interesting. Kirk managed to include a retweet from a voter of the opposite party who stated that he preferred him to the incumbent sharing his party identification. Not only was this a retweet, but Kirk was actually retweeting a retweet. This provides a great example of how a tweet can move through various people and groups. A single tweet can have reach well beyond the people who follow the original tweeter.

POLITICIANS

The word "politicians" was used to pick up tweets where candidates were trying to separate themselves from the negative connotations that people often associate with politicians. This clearly often requires a subtle interpretation. It did not occur very often, with the mean not even reaching 1 at 0.24, with a standard deviation of 0.69. Only 15 of those candidates with a Twitter account used this word at least once. Two unsuccessful Republican challengers for seats in the House used this word five times. The first, was again Sean Bielat, and the second was Donna Campbell from Texas.

Example: Luis Gutierrez, Democrat, House incumbent
Tweet "It seems inconsistent to me that politicians who are pro-life and pro-family are also pro-deportation for newborns" http://bit.ly/ceh6ve

Gutierrez is not directly slinging mud on all politicians, but he is trying to distance himself from politicians with certain positions. In doing so, he essentially slings mud on politicians from the opposing party who tend to support such immigration laws. He offers a link to a news story consistent with the content of his tweet.

ESTABLISHMENT

The word "establishment" was included to identify tweets that were references to Washington insiders, state insiders, or the existing power structure in general. Our thinking here was that this type of anti-establishment rhetoric is often used among challengers to separate themselves from the insiders who challengers have identified as perpetuating the problem. This word did not come up often. The mean was only 0.06 with a relatively large standard deviation at 0.37 and only 4% of those with a Twitter account used this word at least once. Christine O'Donnell, an unsuccessful Republican Senate challenger from Delaware, used this word the most at only six times.

Example: Mike Coffman, Republican, House incumbent
Tweet Noonan in the @WSJ: #TeaParty allowed GOP establishment to get out from under Bush. http://bit.ly/do2xX1 Agree?

The @ tag links to *The Wall Street Journal*, a popular newspaper with conservatives, the hashtag obviously connects people to Tea Party discussion, and the link is to a news story in *The Wall Street Journal* about how the Tea Party is saving the Republican Party from the traditional establishment, including former President George W. Bush.

Personal Characteristics

PRINCIPLE

The word "principle" was only counted in our search when it represented tweets seeking to convey principles such as common sense, conservative/liberal, or if it was simply on its own (i.e., "I am principled" or "I have strong principles"). The idea here is that the candidate is using the word to try to present an image that is favorable to voters. As described earlier in this chapter, elections have increasingly become candidate centered. Candidates now have a new tool to try and cultivate their image successfully. This word came up on average 0.16 times with a standard deviation of 0.60 and around 10% of those candidates with Twitter accounts used it at least once. This word was used as many as five times by three different candidates: (1) Jim DeMint, a successful Republican incumbent Senator from South Carolina, (2) Christine O'Donnell, and (3) Justin Amash, a successful Republican incumbent House member from South Carolina.

Example: Russell Feingold, Democrat, Senate incumbent
Tweet STAFF Manitowoc Herald Times Reporter: Arguably the most principled member of the Senate http://bit.ly/bzCxBX

This tweet does a great job of portraying the candidate, Feingold, as principled because he does not have to say it himself. Rather he just quotes from news story written by a staff reporter from a newspaper in his state. Additionally, the link went to the story referenced in the tweet so people could read it themselves and the information could be reinforced.

VICTORY

The word "victory" was included in our search to identify tweets where that candidate offered a forecast of his or her election chances, or to refer to the advancement of goals. The thinking here is that such communication would make the candidate appear confident which is certainly a personal characteristic that voters find appealing. This word came up 1.56 times on average, with a standard deviation of 4.13. Approximately 40% of those with Twitter accounts used this word at least once. Richard Burr, a Republican Senate incumbent who was reelected in the state of North Carolina used this word 42 times.

Example: Richard Burr, Republican, Senate incumbent
Tweet One week to Victory! Read our latest blog post on Road to Victory tour, early voting, GOTV now: http://bit.ly/ciVVVc #ncsen #ncgop

This tweet from Burr is a perfect example of a tweet that used the word "victory" to present a confident image. Additionally, the tweet is using this confidence to try and encourage people to get out and vote early so they can be a part of the victory. The link connected followers to the blog referenced in the tweet and the hashtags connected them to discussions on the North Carolina Senate and the North Carolina Republican Party.

PROGRESSIVE/CONSERVATIVE

The keywords "progressive" and "conservative" were used to pick up tweets where candidates were referring to their own ideological dispositions. Typically, candidates will do this to appeal to their own base (e.g., "I am a true conservative," or "I want to bring progressive values to Washington"). So we recorded the use of the word "conservative" when used by a Republican and the word "progressive" when used by a Democrat. These words, respectively, came up 1.17 times on average with a standard deviation of 3.25. About 29% of the candidates with Twitter accounts used this word at least once, and Sean Bielat was again the most frequent user at 31 times.

Example: David Gill, Democrat, House challenger
Tweet I was featured in a new Huffington Post article called "A Progressive Candidate Ignored by the Democratic Party" http://tinyurl.com/285zts8

The candidate, Gill, was clearly pleased with how the article from *The Huffington Post* characterized him both in the title and the actual article. The link connects to the story referenced in the tweet. Both the title and the story clearly paint the idea of being progressive as a good thing, at least for appealing to Gill's Democratic base.

LEADER

The word "leader" was counted when a candidate used it to describe herself or himself as a leader or working with other leaders. Thus, this word really captures two different things. When a candidate calls herself a leader or quotes someone calling her a leader, she is attempting to instill confidence among her followers in her ability, simply, to lead. When she mentions working with other leaders it instills confidence by letting her followers know that she is supported by other leaders and it also presents an image of someone who works with others, something which will be perceived positively if those she works with are also viewed positively. So they are likely to mention working with others who are popular among their base voters. This word came up 1.58 times on average with a standard deviation of 3.32. About 46% of those candidates with a Twitter account used this word at least once. Peter Roskam, a successful Republican Hose incumbent from Illinois, used this word the most frequently at 26 times.

Example: Scott DesJarlais, Republican, House challenger
Tweet #TN04 Tossup ranking is no surprise 2 us. #TN is conservative state that wants to be represented by strong conservative leaders. #GOP #TCOT
This tweet is referring to election predictions suggesting that DesJarlais would win. This in itself paints the candidate in a positive light but the tweet goes further by reinforcing the positive image by essentially calling the candidate a strong conservative leader. The hashtags seek to extend the reach of this tweet by connecting it to tweeters who follow discussions about the Fourth Congressional District of Tennessee, the state of Tennessee, the Republican Party, and top conservatives.

HARDWORKING

The reasoning behind why we included the word "hardworking" in our search is straightforward. Candidates want to be perceived as people who will put in the work for the benefit of their constituents. Using this word in their tweets helps cultivate this image. This word came up fairly frequently with a mean of 4.26 and a relatively low standard deviation of 6.49. Around 72% of those who had Twitter accounts used this word at least once. Sheila Jackson Lee, a successful Democrat House incumbent from Texas, used this word the most frequently at 46 times.

Example: Elaine Marshall, Democrat, Senate challenger
Tweet "I've worked hard as a public servant to cut down red tape."- Why we love @Elaine4NC #UNCyoungdems #ncsen
This tweet simultaneously presents the image of a hard worker and provides an appealing message, helping to cut back on bureaucratic red tape. It is also a good practice to include one's own Twitter name (referred to as @Twitter name for the rest of the book)

as does Marshall here. This way, it makes it easy to build new followers if this tweet is retweeted. The hashtags are for North Carolina Democrats and the North Carolina Senate.

FIGHT

The word "fight" was used to identify tweets expressing that the candidate would fight for policies, principles, or for their constituency. The mean use of this was 1.81 times, with a standard deviation of 3.88. Approximately 51% of those candidates with a Twitter account used this word at least once. Jack Conway, an unsuccessful Democrat Senate challenger from Kentucky, used this word 43 times.

Example: Roy Blunt, Republican, Senate challenger
Tweet Video: Powerful stories from Missourians who have lost their jobs. I want to fight for them in the U.S. Senate. http://youtu.be/eh67J8Z8_Yw

This tweet clearly presents the candidate, Blunt, as willing to fight for his prospective constituency. This is a good example of a tweet that tries to also utilize other Internet media such as YouTube. The link connects to a YouTube video that presents stories about Missourians who lost their jobs.

PRAY

The reason we included the word "pray" in our search for tweets representing personal characteristics of the candidate is self-explanatory. Those who use the word present themselves as people of faith, which will be appealing to many voters. That said, this could also turn off many voters, so they may be careful about how and when they use it. This may explain why the mean use is fairly low at 0.38 with a standard deviation of 0.93. Roughly 22% of those candidates with Twitter accounts used this word at least once. Three unsuccessful Republican challengers for seats in the House used this word six times. The first was Sean Bielat again, the second was Donna Campbell, and the third was Dan Kapanke from Wisconsin.

Example: Jim Himes, Democrat, House incumbent
Tweet Worshiped 3.5 spirit-filled hours with the good people of Prayer Tabernacle in Bridgeport. Wow! Really recommend a soul-nourishing visit.

This tweet provides a good example of the nuance with which we interpreted the tweets overall. A derivative of the word "pray" got coded here as candidate use. Himes does not actually say he prayed and the word is a noun here instead of a verb. That said, it clearly gets at the underlying concept we are trying to measure. That is, it is an example of a candidate presenting his personal characteristics in a way that could be an attempt to appeal to certain voters. Here, Himes presents himself as pro-religion. We have to assume that he believes this message will bode well with his constituency.

FAITH

The inclusion of the word "faith" in our search is also self-explanatory. Just as the use of the word "pray" was included to identify those tweets where candidates presented themselves as people with faith to appeal to certain voters, the word "faith" is included for the same reason. The use of this word was also relatively infrequent with a mean of 0.19 and a standard deviation of 0.79. About 10% of those candidates with Twitter accounts used this word at least once. Chuck Smith, an unsuccessful Republican House challenger from Virginia, used this word most frequently at nine times.

Example: John Boehner, Republican, House incumbent
Tweet "Faith & Freedom Coalition Praises House GOP Agenda" http://is.gd/fpdKb via @ralphreed

This tweet clearly paints Republicans, and John Boehner himself, the House Speaker since 2011, as pro-faith, which we again can assume that he believes to be positive for his candidacy. The link reinforces as such. It goes to a story about how the Faith and Freedom Coalition supports House Republicans. The "via" term is used to denote that story came from Ralph Reed's Twitter feed. Reed is a popular Christian activist best known for being the first executive director of the Christian Coalition and currently leading the Faith and Freedom Coalition.

VALUES

We also included the generic term "values" to tap tweets about personal characteristics of the candidates. We counted the use of this word when it reflected personal, "local," religious, or cultural values. This word was used on average 0.26 times with a standard deviation of 0.95. Around 14% of those candidates with Twitter accounts used this word at least once. Joyce Elliott, an unsuccessful Democrat House challenger from Arkansas, used this word the most frequently at 12 times.

Example: Daniel Inouye, Democrat, Senate incumbent
Tweet "Vote Democrat not because of the party label, but because we fight for our values." D. Dela Cruz

This is a good example of a tweet being used to represent the candidate with values that appeal to the voter. It is generic so people can ascribe their own values to the comment. It also is a quote from a state senator from Inouye's home state, Hawaii. Inouye must believe his attachment to this leader is a good thing.

BIPARTISAN

The word "bipartisan" was included because candidates may seek to present themselves as one who will cooperate and rise above partisan bickering. This image may be particularly efficacious for candidates who reside in competitive districts. This word came up, on average, 0.22 times with a standard deviation of 1.26. Approximately 11% of those candidates with Twitter accounts used this word at least once. Raj Goyle, an unsuccessful Democrat House challenger from Kansas, used this word most frequently at 25 times.

Example: David Vitter, Republican, Senate incumbent
Tweet Received bipartisan endorsement of leaders in Jefferson, Terrebonne, Lafourche, Plaquemines, and St. Bernard Parishes. http://bit.ly/cRNeM5

This tweet clearly attempts to present this candidate as someone who will cooperate across partisan lines. The information obtained by clicking the link reinforces this
image. It is goes to a press release that highlights the endorsement referenced in the
tweet.

Policy

DEFICIT

These next set of keywords seek to identify tweets that addressed popular policy issues.
These are all straightforward and require little explanation. The first policy-related term
we use is "deficit." This word came up 0.61 times on average with a standard deviation
of 1.55. About 28% of those candidates with a Twitter account used this word at least
once. John Faulk, an unsuccessful Republican House challenger from Texas, used this
word most frequently at 16 times.

Example: Tarryl Clark, Democrat, House challenger
Tweet @tarrylclark Tele-Townhall describing ways we can cut the budget to reduce the
deficit for #mn06 taxpayers. #mn2010 #stribpol

This tweet is an example of how a candidate can offer a policy-centered tweet with
only 140 characters. Voters are typically not interested in too many details. They want
to feel confident that there is a plan. This tweet offers a simple message: there is a plan
and you can attend a Tele-Townhall meeting to find out more. Tele-Town Halls are a
technique for candidates to conduct large-scale telephone conference calls with constituents at low cost. The @Twitter name at the beginning of the tweet is the candidate's
name allowing the candidate to potentially build followers if this tweet was retweeted.
The hashtags are connected to the Sixth Congressional District in Minnesota in 2010,
and the *Minneapolis Star Tribune* politics.

EARMARK/PORK

The words "earmark" and "pork" were included to pick up tweets espousing any policy
position about the practice of earmarking federal funds for local spending projects. Typically, candidates are not going to use these words to paint such policies in a flattering
light. These words came, on average, a combined 0.41 times with a standard deviation of
2.07. Roughly 13% of those candidates with Twitter accounts used one of these words at
least once. Jeff Flake, a successful Republican House incumbent from Arizona used the
combination of these terms 34 times.

Example: Michael Agosta, Republican, House challenger
Tweet Read what Mr Earmarks had to say. http://fb.me/CGRUPFBZ

This is a simple tweet that clearly conveys the message that Agosta does not support
earmarks/pork. This tweet also slings mud. The link goes to a story that illuminates how
his opponent, the incumbent, is known for and proud of bringing federal funding to the
district.

ABORTION

We included the word "abortion" in our search to identify any tweets where candidates addressed abortion policy from the pro-choice or pro-life side. This was one of the most infrequently used words in our search terms. The mean use was only 0.09 and the standard deviation was 0.37. Only 6% of those candidates with Twitter accounts used this word at least once. The most frequent use of this word was only three times by three different unsuccessful Republican House challengers: Lisbeth Carter from Georgia, Ruth McClung from Arizona, and Joel Pollak from Illinois.

Example: Chris Coons, Democrat, Senate challenger
Tweet Chris Coons: "I support a woman's right to choose. . . . I think abortion should be safe, legal and rare."

This tweet is a simple example that conveys the candidate's support for the protection of the legality of abortion.

TAXES

The word "taxes" was included to pick up any tweets where candidates attempt to highlight their position on tax policy. This word came up relatively frequently with a mean of 4.48 and a standard deviation of 8.19. Approximately 73% of those candidates with a Twitter account used this word or one of its derivatives at least once. John Boehner, the future Republican Speaker of the House from Ohio, used this word 78 times.

Example: Sharron Angle, Republican, Senate challenger
Tweet Natl Taxpayers Union endorsement: "Angle a true champion for taxpayers" http://ow.ly/2Xklv Thanks, @NTU! #nvsen #tcot #dumpreid

The link goes to a press release that confirms the endorsement mentioned in the tweet. The press release discusses why Angle's tax policy would be better than the incumbent's policy. The @Twitter name tag links to their Twitter feed and the hashtags go to the Nevada Senate, top conservatives, and a discussion feed supporting the replacement of the incumbent, Harry Reid.

HEALTHCARE

We included the word "healthcare" and its derivatives to capture any tweets that purveyed the candidates' positions on healthcare policy. This search term came up 2.39 times on average with a standard deviation of 4.76. Around 55% of those candidates with a Twitter account used this word at least once. Michael Burgess, a successful Republican House incumbent from Texas, used this search term 43 times.

Example: John Larson, Democrat, House incumbent
Tweet Read @huffpost my blog post "10 Major New Health Reform Benefits Take Effect Today"http://huff.to/cbWeLB

This tweet clearly demonstrates Larson's support for the recent healthcare reform. The link goes to a blog written by Larson at *The Huffington Post*. The @Twitter name tag is for *The Huffington Post*.

GLOBAL WARMING

The words "global warming" and any related terms were included to identify tweets where candidates mention environmental policy or the science of global warming. This search term had the most infrequent use relative to all other terms we used. The mean use was 0.04 with a 0.25 standard deviation. Only 3% of those with Twitter accounts used this term at least once. Dana Rohrabacher, a successful Republican House incumbent from California used this term three times.

Example: Dana Rohrabacher, Republican, House incumbent
Tweet @AI_AGW You seem to be desperate to verify man-made Global Warming. Your complex computer data is unreliable. GIGO evidence is apparent.

This tweet is a response to a tweet by @AI_AGW where she clearly implies that global warming is not caused by humans. @AI_AGW is a Twitter bot (an account that automatically responds to postings) that was developed by Nigel Leck to try to stop what he believed was the spreading of misinformation about global warming on Twitter. The account was set to automatically reply to tweets that contain phrases associated with global warming skepticism. GIGO means "garbage in, garbage out" suggesting that scientific research confirming human contribution to global warming is based on faulty data.

TERRORISM

The word "terrorism" was included to pick up any tweets where candidates were talking about US policy as related to terrorism. This word came up 0.16 times on average with a standard deviation of 0.55. Around 11% of those candidates with Twitter accounts used this word at least once and Teresa Collett, an unsuccessful Republican House challenger from Minnesota, used it most frequently at six times.

Example: Kirsten Gillibrand, Democrat, Senate incumbent
Tweet On Sunday I anncd an $18.5 million anti-terror grant for radiation detectors around #NYC to detect dirty bomb materials http://bit.ly/b9syma

This tweet directly speaks toward support of an anti-terrorism initiative coming out of the Department of Homeland Security. The link goes to a news story describing the grant referenced in the tweet and the hashtag connects people with others tweeting about New York City.

EDUCATION

We included "education" as a search term to identify any tweets where a candidate was discussing how education policy should be addressed. The mean use of this word was 0.75 with a 2.18 standard deviation. Approximately 29% of those candidates with a

Twitter account used this word at least once. Ed Potosnak, an unsuccessful Democrat House challenger from New Jersey, used this word most frequently at 24 times.

Example: Chuck Grassley, Republican, Senate incumbent
Tweet Answered q's about Facebook & Twitter & education on this weeks AskChuck webcast Thx 4 q's http://tinyurl.com/2u38wwm
  This tweet does not directly give a position on education policy but it highlights that Grassley is attentive to the issue. Also, the link goes to a YouTube video where Grassley directly answers questions via a webcast about education policy. Interestingly, he also talks about Facebook and Twitter, confirming that he does all of his own posts.

Summary

This chapter has accomplished two goals. First, it further developed the theory being built in the first three chapters. Second, it laid a descriptive foundation for understanding much of the analysis that follows in the rest of this book. Both are essential to understanding where we are headed. Our central premise is that Twitter provides a direct conduit to the consumer, allowing them to circumvent the traditional gatekeepers. Our examination of the universe of Twitter activity, at least anecdotally, illustrated that those candidates who tended to frequently use Twitter to make campaign announcements, to attack their opponents, to illuminate their own favorable personal characteristics, and to highlight their policy positions did not seem to do well in their election bids. We will argue later in this book that this result illustrates that not all types of messaging is effective in the Twitterverse. It is more effective to try and control the flow of information by providing people with information additional to the 140 characters in a tweet. We began to see the ways they can do so, such as including links, hashtags to discussion groups, and other Twitter accounts. We will explore this more later.

  Before doing so, the next chapter further details the descriptive foundation. Specifically, we offer an analysis of the Twitter activity across party identification, race of candidate, chamber (House or Senate), and incumbency status. This analysis includes examination of differences in Twitter activity generally, and specifically with regards to our four-category typology. The results demonstrate that there is a fair amount of variation in the type of activity across different types of candidates.

5

Congress 2.0—Who's Tweeting?

In this chapter, we consider which types of candidates are tweeting the most. We measure this empirically, and consider theories that explain the volume and frequency differences. While measuring which politicians are using Twitter does not answer the broader questions about the ultimate importance of social media as a political tool, usage is important and lays the predicate for our following chapters. It is the foundational question for the supply side of our study. We begin to lay this predicate with an analysis of the total Twitter activity across the race of candidate and the chamber (House or Senate). However, our primary focus is on measures of usage across party identification and incumbency status. Party and incumbency are good indicators of the structural influence of social media in the political environment. This helps provide a way to understand and organize the role of social media beyond the individual utility of a particular candidate. More directly, we seek to show in this chapter that the social media can and is restructuring the larger partisan group dynamics of the campaign.

Empirically, the results indicate that challengers and Republicans tended to utilize Twitter with greater frequency than incumbents and Democrats. This is not inconsistent with other empirical work indicating that Republicans have tended to adopt the use of Twitter in their campaign strategies at higher rates than Democrats (Bode et al. 2011; Peterson 2012; Peterson and Surzhko-Harned 2011; Tweney 2011). There are several reasons that this might be have occurred. Republicans were the minority party in 2010 and their rapid adoption of Twitter could have been largely a product of innovation from the out-of-power group attempting to return to power (Appleton and Ward 1997; Peterson 2012). Alternatively, there could be specific characteristics of the Republican Party that make Twitter a likely and logical online technology for them to adopt. It circumvents the television and print media that Republicans often believe is biased. It also allows for the messaging of a general theme that the congressional caucus shares across districts and states. Republicans have traditionally been more cohesive and unitary in their approaches to campaigns and governance (Freeman 1986). We will explore this possibility and offer another explanation for heightened Twitter activity among Republicans below.

Additionally, we will begin to lay the groundwork for one of the primary assertions in this book: the effective use of social media contributes to a successful electoral campaign. The 2010 election resulted in many incumbent Democrats being ousted from their seats, leading to a switch in power in the House and a greatly diminished advantage in the Senate. As there are multiple variables at play, we do not claim that social media campaigning was the sole reason for this result but do assert that it was one of several important elements that resulted in this electoral outcome. In the next two sections, we begin to lay out the foundational argument here that Republicans and challengers more quickly adapted to Twitter. Then we move on to the analysis demonstrating that Republicans and challengers tended to tweet more than their respective counterparts (with additional analysis across chamber and race of candidate). This analysis includes a bivariate, multivariate, and qualitative examination of not only total Twitter activity but also of the disparities across the four-category typology developed in Chapter 4 (campaign announcements, attack/negative, personal characteristics, policy).

Motivations Behind the Use of Twitter

Twitter went online in 2006. While it was not designed particularly for politics, its relevance to campaigns and elections became apparent fairly quickly. It only took a short time for political actors to quickly convert the communication protocol to politics with significant and popular use in the campaign by 2008 (Golbeck, Grimes, and Rogers 2010). The adoption of Twitter in the campaign was likely inevitable because of its versatility and reach. At its heart, Twitter is a simple idea with broader implications. A user can send messages of 140 characters or less to other users who have decided to follow them. Upon receipt of a message or tweet, the receiving users (followers) can then distribute it to their own followers (retweet) creating a wide and divergent network of distribution.

The reach of any message is limited only by the number of the followers for a user and the willingness of those followers to retweet the message. Popular users can have followers numbering in the tens of millions, though the most popular people on Twitter are not politicians but rather celebrities like Lady Gaga or Justin Bieber. Among politicians, Barack Obama leads with over 34 million followers at this writing. Among members of Congress, the numbers of followers are more modest, in the tens of thousands for the more popular figures (TweetCongress.com 2012). The one exception is former Republican presidential candidate and current Arizona Senator John McCain, whose Twitter following is approaching 2 million at this writing. One of the most popular conservative figures on Twitter continues to be former Alaska Governor and Republican vice presidential nominee Sarah Palin, with over 900,000 followers (Twitter 2012).

The actual number of followers is important, but as noted above, not an accurate measure of influence on Twitter by itself. The reach of any message is a series of distributions. A follower of a political actor who is herself popular can redistribute the message to an audience that may be larger than the one that received the initial tweet. Organizations that receive the tweet can send it to their membership and from there the message can be distributed far and wide across the universe of Twitter users in often hard-to-follow and sometimes unpredictable ways. While disjointed on its face, the Twitter system is highly efficient and rewards clever wordplay and brevity with a fast transmission and a wide audience.

While the data clearly demonstrates that Republican candidates were more likely than Democrats to use Twitter (Bode et al. 2011; Peterson 2012; Peterson and Surzhko-Harned 2011), the reasons for such use are less clear (Tweney 2011). As Twitter is a new technology and the adoption rates are increasing dramatically, any early picture of usage can be misleading. In fact, as we have illustrated earlier, Democrats in the electorate are more likely to use Twitter to gather information, which probably means that the early adoption rate advantage Republicans have will dissipate in time. Nonetheless, evidence of higher usage among Republican office-seekers still appears to be counterintuitive. While Republicans do have a history of innovative campaign strategies such as direct mail fundraising, the Democrats were the early adopters of online technology as a campaign strategy (Gainous and Wagner 2011; Wagner and Gainous 2009). The adoption of the Internet as a viable campaign tool was a significant innovation and one in which Republicans have largely trailed.

Evidence of this trend begins as early as the early 1990s. In the 1992 presidential campaign, the Democratic ticket of Clinton/Gore used email, message boards, and discussion groups to communicate with their supporters, disseminate information, and fundraise (Smith 1994). While Republicans such as John McCain later had some success in fundraising online (Bimber and Davis 2003), the Democrats showed the major innovations in that area. In 2004, Howard Dean's presidential campaign, which reached both voters and donors through the Internet, proved to be surprisingly effective (Gainous and Wagner 2011). Dean raised over 20 million dollars from online contributions (Teachout and Streeter 2007) and organized a strong campaign through discussions, meetings, and events organized online (Trippi 2005). In the 2008 campaign, Barack Obama raised over 500 million dollars from small donations made online (Gainous and Wagner 2011). Both the messaging and the fundraising from the Obama campaign were unprecedented (Carpenter 2010; Wallsten 2010).

With such a strong advantage in technology in campaigns, the superior Twitter adoption rates of Republican candidates seem surprising. However, the adoption of Twitter by Republicans does present an interesting narrative for us to explore concerning the partisan implications of technology. The simplest explanation is one of time, position, and resources (Williams and Gulati 2011). Republicans were the minority party prior to the 2010 election and as a result they were motivated to try to integrate every possible campaign tactic into their strategy in an attempt to maximize their opportunity for success. Parties that have lost past elections are likely to innovate and adapt to improve their chances in subsequent contests (Appleton and Ward 1997; Lowi 1963). The Republicans were beaten decisively in 2008 with the Democrats, and the Democratic presidential candidate Barack Obama in particular, using online technologies to motivate supporters and gather resources. Parties must innovate to survive, so it would be expected that the Republicans would adapt to the online campaign. The initial supposition must be that that the GOP went to great lengths to catch up to the real and perceived advantages that the Democrats and President Obama had in online campaigning (Gainous and Wagner 2011; Wagner and Gainous 2009).

Beyond the attempt to simply catch up with Democrats, social media presented an alternative way to try and influence the media coverage of Congress. As is often the case with news coverage of Congress or any government institution, reporters will regularly go to leaders or spokespeople for those leaders for opinions concerning the institution (Bennett 2011; Graber 2010). A reporter is not likely to give as much, if any, coverage to a member of Congress with little authority in the chamber. Republicans who were in the minority in both chambers lacked a platform for coverage. Democrats, including the House speaker, the Senate majority leader and the especially the president, could access the broadcast media regularly. Republicans who lacked control of any branch of government were not shut out of the media, but had a more difficult time pushing stories and narratives from positions that lacked the ability to drive those ideas into the legislative arena. Social media presented an opportunity to send their message without the help of the traditional media (Peterson 2012; Shogan 2010).

Campaign Themes and the Republican Twitter Advantage

While each explanation offered above is plausible, these broad explanations are insufficient by themselves. The Republican adoption advantage is on Twitter, not in the other online technologies or protocols such as Facebook which is, at least for now, the larger social media platform. The Democrats still have a healthy advantage in most other online resources, including other social media platforms. Whether in fundraising or in the distributions of messages and information, Democrats have been particularly adroit at maximizing online campaigning and social media (Gainous and Wagner 2011; Wagner and Gainous 2009). Republicans are not absent in alternative forums, but it is in the employment of Twitter where their adoption rates and usage proved most significant. Hence, there is something about Twitter itself that is appealing to Republican candidates and officeholders.

That explanation may begin with the continual conflict over media coverage in campaigning and governance. Many office seekers, especially those in the Republican Party, perceive the media as either inattentive or biased against them. In 2010, Republican challengers often lacked the ability to easily generate news coverage. The lack of control over the levers of government meant that Republicans could not use state power to create messaging opportunities with the ease or frequency of the Democrats. Further, many Republicans considered the mediating and gatekeeping structure of the media as blocking their campaign message. The perception that the media bias works against Republicans is a well-held belief inside the party, though the evidence of such partisan bias is less clear (Graber 2010; Herman and Chomsky 2002; Kallen 2004; Sheppard 2008). Nonetheless, the belief that the bias exists is more relevant to strategies than the reality of it. For Republicans, Twitter provides a particularly useful means of disseminating a message to voters and other supporters that avoids any limiting or interpretation of the message itself. It is a social media whose focus is messaging directly to followers in short statements, making an ideal media circumvention mechanism. More directly, if one presumes that the mediator is biased, than it is logical to remove the mediator and speak directly to the electorate. In that circumstance, Twitter is a very appropriate medium.

Further, the appeal of Twitter may be as simple as the nature of microblogging and its appeal to the historical makeup of the Republican Party. Historically, the political culture of the Republican Party has been guided by a more unitary conception of representation. The construction of the Democratic coalition leads to an effort to seek benefits for various groups, but often fails to create an integrated conception of a national interest (Freeman 1986). Where the Democratic Party is often a product of the internal struggles of its constituent groups, the Republicans have been more homogenous with an approach that is more top down and focused in its policy and messaging (Freeman 1986). As a result, Republicans have been more successful at thematic branding, while Democrats comparatively seemed more disjointed in their approach. This can be advantageous for Republicans, as a focused thematic campaign is often potent as short and direct slogans work well for providing cognitive shortcuts for voters (Zaller 2004).

Twitter is an ideal campaign mechanism for political branding. It requires and rewards brevity and is easily distributed and digested by the consumer. The tradition and style of Republican messaging is more easily translated into the 140 character limit on tweets. Long before the adoption of social media, Republicans had consistently presented a more unitary and constant message to voters (Freeman 1986). The GOP has effectively applied slogans to their thematic branding with a consistent theme. Twitter provides a perfect structure to capitalize on this opportunity as it maximizes the presentation of direct and focused messaging. As a result, the move to social media, and Twitter in particular, is a logical outgrowth of the modern media environment for any politician, but especially for Republicans.

The Twitter Campaign: Old Strategies with New Technology

While Republicans may more easily adopt their themes to Twitter, we expect both parties and individual office seekers to benefit from microblogging. At the most basic level, the use of Twitter or any technology is premised on the idea that it will help win elections (Mayhew 1974). As we noted in Chapter 4, Twitter should help candidates win by making traditional campaign goals such as advertising, credit claiming, and position-taking more efficient and immediate. The usage of Twitter for just such activity, especially highlighting events, personal characteristics, and emphasizing successes is occurring with increasing frequency (Bode et al. 2011; Peterson 2012). There is already evidence that online campaign activities can have a substantial and significant effect on electoral outcomes (Wagner and Gainous 2009). If the traditional campaign strategies work and have worked for some time, there is every reason to believe the efficiency of social media in carrying out the same tasks should generate results. Twitter makes these activities more efficient, inexpensive, and immediate. Campaign messages can be tweeted to targeted audiences in seconds (Agranoff and Tabin 2011). Twitter can be used to advertise a success, claim credit for a new policy, or even respond to the actions of their opponent with great rapidity.

Prior to social media such as Twitter, advertising, credit claiming and position taking would have to occur through older, slower, and more expensive technologies such as mail or telephone. Broadly targeted messaging would be done and still is done through mass media such as broadcast television. It is a relatively slow response that requires the purchasing of time and the expensive preparation of a professional quality video. The efficiency of the Internet in the transmission of campaign ideas was illustrated by an inexpensively generated online video supporting Barack Obama in 2008 entitled "Yes, We Can." The video reached nearly four million people in a few weeks (Gainous and Wagner 2011; Wallsten 2010). It is still viewable at the time of this writing and continues to be disseminated years after its creation. Hillary Clinton, who was competing with Obama for the Democratic nomination for president in 2008, attempted to reach out using a televised town hall meeting that reached a fraction of that audience size at a much more massive cost in time and money (Rich 2008).

Direct outreach using broadcast media is time consuming, resource intensive, and expensive. Twitter is structured in a way that suits campaigns. Each tweet is limited to 140 characters. While that may be too short to have an exhaustive policy conversation, it is useful to link videos, convey slogans, organize activities, and quickly respond to events as they are happening. Messages can be targeted, repeated, and refined for greatest impact at a fraction of traditional campaign costs. As more and more people become active on Twitter, it is hard to create a plausible explanation for how it would not be an influential campaign technology. Its simplicity, efficiency, and increasing penetration make it not just useful but increasingly necessary to conduct a modern campaign.

If Twitter is being adapted to these traditional purposes, than we should see these strategies displayed in the Tweets themselves. To measure this effect we create a criterion below for how to assess whether a tweet is a being used for campaign messaging, but is also adapted to the limits and strengths of a microblogging medium such as Twitter. Our expectation is that effective Twitter use will depend on clear and direct messaging, targeted to particular audiences, but specifically targeting groups such as potential voters, volunteers, and donors. To maximize distribution we expect the tweets to directly or indirectly encourage followers to retweet the message and therefore push it beyond the first-level community of readers. To do this, the tweet will likely need an appeal or content that could garner broader interest.

Additionally, Twitter usage can penetrate outside of Twitter itself, so tweets may be targeted at media groups and journalists or even at other SNSs, particularly Facebook. Because of the limitation of 140 characters, Twitter appears to have a limited utility for refining themes and messages. However, there are ways to circumvent that limitation. Visual support including pictures or videos can be sent with the tweet. More detailed information reinforcing the theme, idea, or message can be linked. For the user, this additional information can be accessed easily with a single mouse click, or even a gesture or touch when using a touch-sensitive screen. An effective tweet can do simple messaging in 140 characters, but carry more exacting detail by directing people to additional supportive information without overwhelming the message itself. As we know that much of congressional communication does consist of the traditional activities of credit claims, advertising, and position-taking (Mayhew 1974), we expect to see all three activities, but with increased effectiveness in the Twitter environment.

Looking at the Data

Before looking at the differences across our four-category typology, we begin with a more general analysis of total Twitter activity. First, the results presented in Figure 5.1 clearly indicate that Republicans tweet overall more than Democrats. The y-axis on the graphs in this figure represents the average number of tweets in the six months leading up to the election. Thus, the mean number of tweets by Democratic candidates is approximately one hundred, and it is around 164 for Republican candidates. A t-test indicates

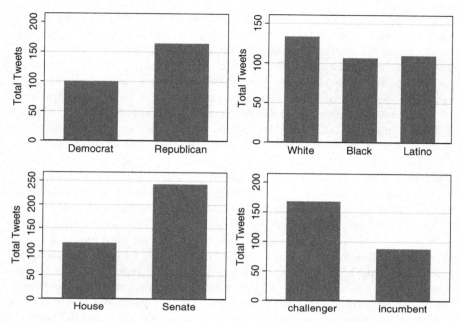

Figure 5.1 Total Number of Tweets across Party, Race, Chamber, and Incumbency.
Source: www.twitter.com.

that this difference is statistically significant ($p < 0.00$). Second, the results suggest that challengers use Twitter more frequently than incumbents. Incumbents tweeted around 88 times on average while challengers tweeted approximately 168 times on average. A t-test also indicated that this difference was statistically significant ($p < 0.00$). Given that Republicans had higher Twitter activity than Democrats in 2010 and there were more Republican challengers in 2010, it stands to reason that there would be more Twitter activity by challengers in 2010. That said, if using Twitter does actually stimulate stronger connections between candidates and constituents by allowing candidates to have a firmer control over the flow of information, then this result would suggest that white candidates are advantaged.

While not central to our larger argument that Republican challengers used Twitter more effectively in the 2010 election, looking at some other categorical differences in tweeting provides some nuance and perspective concerning the nature and usage of Twitter in the context of a campaign. Thus, we looked for differences in Twitter activity across the race of the candidate and the chamber for which the candidates were competing for a seat. The results show that whites tend to tweet more than minorities (one-way ANOVA $p = 0.02$). White candidates tweeted 134 times on average while black and Latino candidates tweeted 107 and 110 times, respectively, on average. The results also suggest that Senators' and senatorial candidates' average Twitter activity is quite a bit more frequent than that of House members ($p < 0.00$). Senatorial candidates tweeted roughly 243 times on average while House candidates only tweeted 119 times on average. This is, perhaps, a result of stronger campaign organizations with more staff to help manage peripherals and newer campaign strategies such as Twitter accounts. Greater resources are often a good indicator of the adoption of new campaign strategies, especially ones that rely on technology (Williams and Gulati 2011).

The previous chapter provided examples of tweets from each keyword to explain how and why we constructed the measures of our four-category typology of tweets. In this chapter we supplement the quantitative analysis with more qualitative examples intended to demonstrate exactly how candidates used Twitter most effectively. This is central to our premise that Republicans and challengers used Twitter more effectively in 2010. The qualitative evidence presented below offers examples of how the Republicans and challengers maximized their strategy. A direct empirical test of the advantage is in Chapter 9.

Before considering the Tweets themselves, note that we are not arguing that Democrats and incumbents were not on Twitter or were inept with their usage. Rather, we contend that Republicans and challengers simply made greater use of Twitter in their campaign strategies. Even if we hold the quality of the tweets and the strategy behind their construction and delivery constant, Republicans and challengers had an advantage in usage, distribution, and volume. Assuming tweeting matters, the aggregate effect would be magnified. Our examination of the nature of the tweets provides a more direct look and what was happening and the strategy that motivated the Twitter usage. We provide an example of an effective tweet from both a Republican and challenger for each of the four categories in our typology.[1]

The results of the differences of means tests exploring the variation in the four types of Twitter activity (campaign announcements, attack/negative, personal characteristics, policy) in the six months leading up to the election across the same independent variables contained in Figure 5.1 are presented in Table 5.1. We discuss each of the four categories individually, including the interpretation of the quantitative results and the qualitative examples. First, though, we begin with a general interpretation of the results. Republicans and incumbents tend to exhibit higher Twitter activity across all four types with only one exception. Incumbents do tend to have more policy tweets than challengers. Campaign announcements, attack tweets, and tweets that highlight the personal characteristics of the respective candidate are all directly focused on attempting to win over votes. Perhaps incumbents feel more secure and are more focused on trying to control the agenda so they can be successful in Congress, which in turn, will increase their odds of being reelected. Trying to influence the policy and maximize one's power in Congress is a well-studied behavior (Dodd 1977; Fenno 1973). Senators tended to tweet more across all four types, which is not surprising, given that they typically have stronger organizations with more staff. Finally, racial differences are only significant for attack/negative tweets and policy tweets, where whites tend to have a higher frequency of such tweets on both counts.

The detailed results from Table 5.1 provide a more nuanced view of the strategies and behaviors from office seekers using Twitter. We begin with the differences in the use of campaign announcement tweets across chamber and race of candidate. Of particular note is that the mean campaign announcements for Senators was over double that of House members, roughly 66 to 30. Another significant cross-chamber difference is that over 25% of the total tweets by Senators fell into the campaign announcement category. This commitment to the use of Twitter as a means of making campaign announcements by senatorial candidates is reflected in the relatively small standard deviation. It is actually smaller than the mean suggesting that there is not a great deal of variation around

Table 5.1 **Difference in Types of Twitter Activity across Party, Incumbency, Chamber, and Race**

	Campaign Announcements		Attack/Negative		Personal Characteristics		Policy	
	Mean	*S.D.*	*Mean*	*S.D.*	*Mean*	*S.D.*	*Mean*	*S.D.*
Democrat	26.83	37.11	13.34	28.22	9.59	13.17	6.08	9.23
Republican	41.35	55.90	31.16	59.95	13.42	16.37	11.57	15.98
p-value	0.00		0.00		0.01		0.00	
Challenger	48.59	56.35	34.02	59.56	13.79	16.64	7.91	12.65
Incumbent	15.61	24.50	7.43	17.68	8.70	11.99	10.28	14.35
p-value	0.00		0.00		0.00		0.05	
House	30.05	45.07	19.04	42.88	10.12	13.69	8.46	12.65
Senate	66.14	58.56	48.45	72.15	22.41	19.45	12.38	14.35
p-value	0.00		0.00		0.00		0.04	
White	34.73	48.47	23.04	46.43	11.39	14.34	9.06	13.18
Black	23.65	37.44	5.00	10.39	11.94	15.94	6.67	7.83
Latino	22.95	47.05	8.00	22.69	8.15	13.71	7.10	7.96
p-value	0.26		0.00		0.60		0.00	

Note: Data come from www.twitter.com. P-values represent the probability that we cannot reject the null hypothesis that the difference between the means across the dichotomous variables does not = 0, and the p-value for the race measurements is based on the chi-squared statistic derived from a one-way ANOVA test of the difference of means.

the mean. More directly, most senatorial candidates are using Twitter to make campaign announcements.

Campaign announcements are one of the simplest usages for an SNS like Twitter. The prevalence of this type of tweet for Senators suggests that while Senators and their staffs realized that Twitter was important and could be useful, and they had the resources to create and keep active an account, they had a limited understanding of its utility. However, that is likely to change. In the early adoption of the Internet as a campaign vehicle, web pages tended to be only electronic announcements or billboards before the greater interactive options were understood and applied (Gibson and Ward 1998; Wagner and Gainous 2009; Ward and Gibson 2003). There will likely be a similar pattern with Twitter. When it comes to the race of the candidate, there are no statistically significant differences. Black, Latino, or white candidates were no more or less likely to use Twitter to make campaign announcements.

Of primary interest to us are the differences across partisanship and incumbency. It is clear in these data that both Republicans and challengers were far more likely to be using Twitter to make campaign announcements. On average, Republicans made around 15 more campaign announcement tweets than Democrats and challengers made around 33 more than incumbents. Both of these differences are statistically significant and the standard deviations were not that much larger than the means across any of these categories, suggesting there was not a great deal of variation around the mean. We contended that challengers (most were Republicans in 2010), being the minority party, were compelled to use every means available to become the majority party (Peterson and Surzhko-Harned 2011). Twitter fits this bill. It is an additional avenue to reach voters. Republicans and challengers were hungry for victory and utilized the opportunity structure, which includes social media.

Next, just as we did in Chapter 4, we offer some qualitative examples of campaign announcement tweets. The difference here is, first, that we tried to pick examples that we believe were particularly effective use of Twitter. We began to develop arguments for what makes a tweet effective in the descriptions of the qualitative examples offered in Chapter 4 and further illuminated the theory behind it in this chapter. To summarize our argument, we list the characteristics of an effective tweet here: (1) The message is clear, (2) It is resource centered (attempts to attract voters, money, or volunteers), (3) It offers the potential for the tweet to reach a wider audience, (4) It connects to other SNSs, particularly Facebook, (5) It directs people to additional supportive information, and (6) It credit claims, advertises, or takes a position.

Second, because our primary interest throughout the use of these data for the rest of the book focuses on the diverging use and effectiveness across party and incumbency, we select a tweet from a Republican, one from a Democrat, one from an incumbent, and one from a challenger. We do this, in this order, for each category. This means that there will be 16 examples in this chapter. We describe how each tweet reflects the broader four category typology and illuminates how partisanship and incumbency may have been shaping the use of Twitter in the 2010 congressional election campaign. Clearly we are not suggesting that Democrats and incumbents did not effectively use Twitter, as we will provide examples of how both have done so, but as evidenced in the description of Table 5.1, Republicans and challengers did it more often.

CAMPAIGN ANNOUNCEMENT

We begin with four examples from the campaign announcement category:

1. Have you heard about our Merlin Froyd for Congress We-Need-You-At-This-Meeting Meeting? We need you there! . . . http://fb.me/sJQ3tWTY (Merlin Froyd, R-CA)
2. Saturday is our big march and rally against the Sunrise Powerlink, to be h Lake Park in Lakeside. . . . http://fb.me/HOOJdhDt (Raymond Lutz,
3. rt @stxherry John Faulk is running against Sheila Jackson Lee and nee in this poll http://ht.ly/2ldDf #TX 18 PLZ RT! (John Faulk, R-TX)
4. Johnny will be in Columbus on Monday for a GOP Rally! Event d on.fb.me/bf57BX #gapolitics #gagop #tcot (Johnny Isakson, R-GA)

It is difficult for a single tweet to satisfy all six of our criteria for being classified as an effective tweet, but we tried to find tweets that met several of them for the examples we use here. The first from Merlin Froyd satisfies five of our criteria with a simple straight-forward statement. It is stated clearly, it is resource centered in that it reaches out to attract voters and potential volunteers, it connects people to his Facebook account with the link, the Facebook post has a link to his campaign web page so it directs people to additional supportive information, and finally, it advertises the candidate (Mayhew 1974).

The next tweet by Lutz does all the same things but it also manages to take a position against the Sunrise Powerlink, a high-voltage power transmission line that would bring power to San Diego County. The next tweet by Faulk (challenger) is a retweet originating from @stxherry, which immediately connects all of the @stxherry followers with Faulk's Twitter feed, so it connects to a wider audience. It also connects to a wider audience by using the hashtag #TX. It is a clear statement that tries to attract voters and does so by showing that another tweeter likes him. The link goes to a poll that is intended to show which candidates are representing conservative voters best, directing people to additional supportive information. Finally, Faulk requests that people please retweet, which would help him reach an even wider audience (PLZ RT). The final tweet exampled above by Isakson (incumbent) satisfies all six criteria.

ATTACK/NEGATIVE CAMPAIGNING

The next category in our typology, attack/negative tweets, also exhibits some interesting differences. Before moving to the differences across party and incumbency, we note the differences across chamber and race of candidate. Notice in Table 5.1 that the same pattern regarding campaign announcement tweets is evident across chamber; senatorial candidates were considerably more likely to employ such a strategy, but also notice that the differences across race of candidate are significant here. White candidates were substantially more likely to go negative than black or Latino candidates. The standard deviation for Latino candidates is quite high relative to the mean. This is driven by the 107 attack/negative tweets coming for Ilario Pantano, a Republican House challenger from North Carolina. The differences across partisanship and incumbency when it comes to using Twitter to go negative are quite clear. First, Republicans, again, are considerably more likely to use Twitter in this way as well. Their average number of attack/negative tweets is well over double that of Democrats. That said, the differences across incumbency are even starker. Challengers tended to go negative nearly five times as often as incumbents, on average. Perhaps this is a product of context. The public mood (Stimson 1999) was swinging against incumbents, presenting the opportunity for challengers to go negative. Twitter simply offered an additional vehicle for this strategy.

We offer four examples below of what could be considered effective attack/negative tweets according to our criteria. Again, we present one from a Republican, one from a Democrat, one from challenger, and one from an incumbent (in that order):

1. More than 80 liberal organizations starting to attack. Please help us! http://bit.ly/9bhtpM #AZ #AZ01 #azgop #icon #tcot #gop #hhrs (Paul Gosar, R-AZ)
2. RT @whitehouse: Fact checking Rep. Boehner's bogus attacks on the economy. 37 consecutive tweets coming. Just kidding: http://bit.ly/9MNgT7 (Nancy Pelosi, D-CA)

3. Jerry McNerney Brings Home Borrowed Pork; Saddles US With Debt—NewsWeek http://tumblr.com/xv2mdrl5t #CA11 #tcot #ca47 (David Harmer, R-CA)
4. DEBATE @nanhayworth 5-minute long defense of Tea Party extremism http://tinyurl.com/2eqknpr #ny19 (John Hall, D-NY)

Again, we evaluate these tweets based on our six criteria. The first, by Gosar, does a good job of presenting a clear and concise message that uses the word liberal, which conservatives tend to use as a negative. On top of that, it attacks while accusing liberals of attacking. It is resource centered in that it seeks help. It also provides a link that directs people to his campaign website that offers additional information about the content of the tweet. It, at least indirectly, takes a position against the direction liberals seek. Finally, it offers the potential for reaching a wider audience and generating new followers with the inclusion of multiple hashtags. The next example, a tweet from the former Speaker of the House Pelosi, is quite a biting attack, accusing the future Speaker of the House Boehner of being dishonest. It uses humor to catch followers' attention with a clear message that is intended to stimulate the base by attacking a Republican leader. It also provides a link to a supportive story, and is a retweet coming from the White House, which connects to a wider audience and offers credibility. The same can be said about this tweet concerning position-taking. Pelosi clearly takes the position against the Republican leader.

The final two examples of attack/negative tweets come from a challenger, Harmer, and an incumbent, Hall. Harmer presents a clear message that his opponent is contributing to US debt by supporting pork legislation. This clearly could be considered position-taking (Mayhew 1974), the tweet reaches out to wider audience by including multiple hashtags, and it is resource centered in that it is trying to push voters away from his opponent. Additionally, the tweet connects people to Tumblr, another SNS that is a blogging platform allowing users to post text, images, videos, links, quotes, and audio. So the tweet simultaneously connects to another SNS and provides supporting information. This tweet satisfies all six criteria. The final example by Hall satisfies most of our criteria for an effective tweet. It is fairly clear and resource centered, trying to push voters away from Tea Party ideas by characterizing them as extreme. This could also be an attempt to mobilize the base, which is already opposed to the Tea Party platform. It attempts to connect to a wider audience by using hashtags, it provides additional information by linking to a video, and it takes a position against the Tea Party agenda.

PERSONAL CHARACTERISTICS

Next, we move on to analyzing the differences in Twitter activity across party, incumbency, chamber, and race of candidate when it comes to tweets about candidate-centered personal characteristics. The results presented in Table 5.1 suggest some significant differences, but the magnitude of differences is not as large as that of campaign announcements and attack/negative tweets. That said, consistent with those other results, senatorial candidates were significantly more likely to have tweeted about their own personal characteristics. The differences across the race of candidates were not significant. Finally, and central to the argument asserted in this book, Republican candidates as well as challengers were more likely to employ this strategy to communicate with their constituents. Republicans tweeted about their own personal characteristics approximately thirteen times on average and Democrats were slightly lower at approximately ten times. Challengers tweeted about their personal characteristics about fourteen times while incumbents only did so about nine times over the six-month period leading up to the election.

As we have for the other categories of tweets, we offer four examples below of tweets where candidates mentioned personal characteristics about themselves. Again, we offer one from a Republican, one from a Democrat, one from a challenger, and one from an incumbent:

1. Last Friday at the Thompson Boxing event in Corona CA. I was awarded with a lifetime achievement award for my work ... http://fb.me/uScS0oxc (Larry Andre, R-CA)
2. Did you vote for Chuck Grassley in the past? Voting Roxanne Conlin this year? Tell the @BoldProgressives here: http://bit.ly/bKobS9 DM Iowa (Roxanne Conlin, D-IA)
3. Even NPR is calling the election for us. We are taking nothing from granted and will be working hard for every vote. http://n.pr/aHvezd (Jesse Kelly, R-AZ)
4. TX AGFUND says Congressman Marchant brings "much-needed conservative voice" to halls of Congress. News http://t.co/bAZnN5r via @AddThis (Kenny Marchant, R-TX)

In our qualitative examination of the personal characteristics tweets, we noticed that the candidates seemed less likely to connect to other information and use hashtags. Perhaps this is a result of the nature of these tweets. They are not announcements and may be aimed at a more targeted audience. The first two tweets, one by a Republican and one by a Democrat, both present clear messages that are aimed at attracting voters by painting the candidates' personal characteristics in a positive light, hard-working in the first and progressive in the second. The first does so by presenting a positive image of the candidate (winning an award) and the second actually asks voters to go vote for the candidate in an online poll. This online poll can be seen as a way to connect people to more information. Presumably, Conlin believes she will come out ahead in the poll. The first connects to Facebook through the link and the second connects to a wider audience through adding the progressive @Twitter name, tapping into a wider audience. Both are clearly advertising.

The second two tweets, one by an incumbent and one by a challenger, are also good examples of effective tweets. They both present clear resource centered messages intended to attract voters by highlighting positive personal characteristics, hardworking in the first and conservative in the second. The first presents additional information that is particularly persuasive because conservatives often tend to think of NPR (National Public Radio) as a liberally biased news source. The second connects potential voters to supplemental information and tries to reach a wider audience by including the TX AGFUND (Texas Farm Bureau Friends of Agriculture Fund), and it uses the @AddThis application, which is a content-sharing and social insights platform designed to increase followers, drive viral traffic, connect to other social media platforms like Facebook, and provide analytics into the user's audience activity. Both of these tweets are advertising merits of the respective candidates.

POLICY

The results presented in Table 5.1 show significant differences in the frequency with which candidates tweeted about policy across all of the categories explored here. The results are consistent with the others (campaign announcements, attack/negative, and personal characteristics) in that senatorial candidates tend to tweet about policy more than House candidates. Also, white candidates tend to tweet more about policy than black and Latino candidates. The results also indicate that both Republicans and challengers were more likely to tweet about policy. That said, consistent with the general results for the policy category presented in Chapter 4, the means are not very high across any of these categories. Policy tweeting is not that prevalent. The standard deviations are all relatively low as well. The distributions are all largely centered around the mean.

Again we offer four examples from this category:

1. The Texas Model: Low Taxes + Low Regulation = Job Creation http://t.co/2qv1gNq via @AddThis (Kenny Marchant, R-TX)
2. Who can you trust in DC? I helped make AR 2nd in the nation for pre-school education http://bit.ly/blQhEL #ar02 #ar2 (Joyce Elliot, D-AR)
3. Midterm report card from @vanityfairmag highlights @bquayle writings and his denial of global warming. http://bit.ly/ajXIdF (Jon Hulburd, D-AZ)
4. Red ink alert: federal budget deficit exceeded $1 trillion for 2nd straight year http://bit.ly/9J2nos #hhrs #tcot #gop (Mike Coffman, R-CO)

These four examples of policy tweets all satisfy our criteria well. Each presents a clear message that seeks to reach out to voters presenting the candidate's policy positions in a positive light. They all provide supplemental information that is supportive of each respective candidate. Each tries to broaden the audience in different ways. The first uses @AddThis, which again helps to reach more followers and is connected to the candidate's other social media platforms. The second and fourth tweets include hashtags. Finally, the third links up to others' Twitter feeds, including Hulbard's opponent, which could be an attempt to siphon off Quayle's support. Finally, they each meet Mayhew's (1974) description of typical congressional behavior. They all take positions and the second one claims credit, a tactic that is less frequent than advertising and position-taking, based on our observations.

Modeling Candidate Twitter Activity

This analysis is complemented with a series of multivariate models designed to estimate the relationship between the aforementioned independent variables along with two more controls (district competitiveness and campaign spending differential)[2] to determine which, if any, of the above identified relationships are spurious. We model the total number of tweets, the number of campaign announcement tweets, attack/negative campaigning tweets, tweets highlighting personal characteristics, and tweets centered on policy. Because this analysis relies on negative binomial regression[3], we include the incident rate ratios, or the odds of the rate increasing or decreasing where the rate is defined as the number of times a candidate tweets, in our interpretation. Just as we did in Chapter 2 with the Pew data, we also replaced the missing values here using multiple imputation. There were forty-six out of the 884 cases where vote totals in the previous election were not reported or there was not a Senate election (483 which had Twitter accounts). The imputation model was simple: it included only those variables that had missing values (the winner's vote total in the previous election, the loser's vote totals in the previous election, the total vote for the candidate in 2010, and political experience).[4]

The partisan differences identified in Table 5.1 hold up in the multivariate results presented in Table 5.2. Republicans are clearly more likely to tweet across all types. Controlling for alternative explanations does not account for this observed relationship. According to the incident rate ratio estimates, the magnitude of the effects is not small in absolute terms either. In fact, Republican candidates tweeted approximately 1.60 times more than Democratic candidates. Republicans tweeted 1.34 times more than

Table 5.2 **Models of Candidate Twitter Activity**

	Total Tweets	Campaign Announcements	Attack/ Negative	Personal Characteristics	Policy
Republican	0.47***	0.29***	0.78***	0.40***	0.77***
	(0.10)	(0.11)	(0.16)	(0.12)	(0.12)
Incumbency	−0.53***	−1.10***	−1.46***	−0.38***	0.44***
	(0.10)	(0.11)	(0.17)	(0.11)	(0.12)
Chamber (Senate)	0.69***	0.82***	1.02***	0.91***	0.39*
	(0.18)	(0.20)	(0.29)	(0.20)	(0.25)
White	−0.17	−0.09	0.21	−0.33**	−0.29*
	(0.13)	(0.15)	(0.22)	(0.15)	(0.16)
Distr Competitive	−0.16	−0.38**	−0.55***	−0.15	0.01
	(0.15)	(0.16)	(0.18)	(0.17)	(0.19)
Spend Differential	0.20	0.28	0.23	0.08	0.33
	(0.19)	(0.22)	(0.31)	(0.22)	(0.23)
Constant	4.14***	2.84***	1.72***	1.59***	1.25***
	(0.22)	(0.25)	(0.35)	(0.24)	(0.26)
Pseudo R^2	0.01	0.03	0.03	0.01	0.02
N	483	483	483	483	483

Note: Data come from www.twitter.com and the Federal Elections Commission. Table entries are negative binomial estimates with associated standard errors in parentheses. ***p < 0.01, **p < 0.05, *p < 0.1.

Democrats to make campaign announcement tweets, 2.19 times more to post attack/negative tweets, 1.50 times more to tweet about personal characteristics, and 2.16 times more to tweet about policy-related issues. These results lay the foundation for the analysis in Chapter 9, where we will focus on how well this activity worked in actually garnering votes for Republicans.

We will also be focusing in Chapter 9 on the differential effect that Twitter campaigning had for challengers as opposed to incumbents. Before doing so, it is again important to look at the varied degree to which challengers and incumbents are using Twitter to campaign and in what ways they are using it differently. The results here confirm the bivariate results presented in Table 5.1, ceteris paribus. Challengers tweeted more than incumbents, made more campaign announcement tweets, were more likely to go negative, and were more likely to tweet about personal characteristics, but incumbents were more likely to tweet about policy-related issues. The incident rate ratio estimates indicate that challengers tweeted 0.59 times more than incumbents. They tweeted 0.33 times more than incumbents to make campaign announcements, 0.23 more to make attacks or go negative generally, and 0.68 times more about personal characteristics, but incumbents tweeted 1.56 times more than challengers about policy. Taken altogether, the differences across incumbency are not as large as those across partisanship. That said, they nonetheless not insignificant. With the exception of policy tweeting, challengers clearly attempted to utilize Twitter more. Perhaps incumbents tweeted more about policy because they were involved in policymaking more than their counterparts.

The results for chamber hold up, ceteris paribus, across all the models. Apparently, senators' higher frequency of tweets is generally not accounted for by the combination of the other control variables in the models. In fact, the magnitude of the effect is fairly large. Senatorial candidates tweeted approximately 2.00 times more than House candidates overall, 2.27 times more to make campaign announcement tweets, 2.77 times more to post attack/negative tweets, 2.47 times more about personal characteristics, and 1.48 times more about policy-related issues. Concerning race, there are some interesting changes. First, the relationship observed in Table 5.1 suggesting that white candidates were more likely to go negative dissipates to insignificance when introducing the controls. Next, when adding the controls it appears that whites are less likely to tweet about their personal characteristics (IRR = 0.72). Interestingly also, it appears that whites are less likely to tweet about policy-related issues (IRR = 0.75) when holding all other variables at their means. This is in the opposite direction of the bivariate results. As described above, we also included the additional controls, district competitiveness and spending differential. We thought it was important to test the premises that those in competitive districts may be more likely to use Twitter to try to secure an advantage and that those who have less money may be more likely to use Twitter because of the low cost. These hypotheses did not generally pan out. Only district competitiveness is significant and only in the campaign announcements and attack/negative tweeting models. The results suggest that both campaign announcement and attack/negative tweeting decrease as the margin gets larger (IRR, respectively = 0.69, 0.58). This makes sense. Simply, candidates are likely less compelled to employ these strategies when they are in noncompetitive races.

Summary

This chapter has built the theoretical and empirical foundation for much of the congressional Twitter analysis that follows. We began to develop the theoretical argument here for why both Republicans and challengers were more likely to utilize Twitter as an avenue for campaigning. The results in this chapter have provided clear evidence that they both tended to use Twitter more to make campaign announcements, to attack their opponents or go negative generally, to tweet about personal characteristics that present them in a positive light to potential voters, and to tweet about policy-related issues. We will argue later that this heightened use may also be reflected in how they used Twitter to control the flow of information and that controlling this flow may be the way to actually influence voters.

Before getting to this analysis and theory building, we move back to an exploration of the demand side of SNS use. Specifically, we explore whether the use of SNSs within the voting public can stimulate social capital. Is heightened SNS use associated with the propensity to join groups and with increased political participation? The results presented in Chapter 6 suggest that the answer to both these questions is affirmative.

6

Public Opinion 2.0—The New Social Capital

There is a large body of work on the importance of digital media on political participation in the political science and communication literature. Most of the research supports a positive relationship between technology and political participation, though there are some variances in the literature concerning the strength and consistency of this relationship (see Barber 2001; Bimber 1998; Bode 2012; Bonfadelli 2002; Boulianne 2009, 2011; Delli Carpini 2000; DiMaggio et al. 2004; Gainous and Wagner 2011; Gainous, Marlowe, and Wagner 2013; Gibson, Lusoli, and Ward 2005; Hendriks Vettehen, Hagemann, and Van Snippenburg 2004; Kittilson and Dalton 2011; Krueger 2002, 2006; Norris 2001; Pasek et al. 2009; Polat 2005; Shah, Kwak, and Holbert 2001; Tolbert and McNeal 2003; Valenzuela, Park, and Kee 2009; Wagner and Gainous 2009; Ward, Gibson, and Lusoli 2003; Weber, Loumakis, and Bergman 2003; Xenos and Moy 2007). Shah et al. (2005) model data from a panel study to illustrate that online media helps to foster political discussion and as a result influence civic participation. Bakker and de Vreese (2011) find that use of the Internet correlates with political participation, but frequency of use does not. Nonetheless, the general consensus is that increased use of these digital media technologies results in greater degrees of engagement by the users in the political sphere, though the effect is mediated by the users' interest and willingness to discuss politics (Bimber and Copeland 2013; Cho et al., 2009; Gainous, Marlowe, and Wagner 2013; Shah et al., 2005, 2007; Xenos and Moy 2007).

Some scholars have suggested that the relationship is likely to grow with the evolution in the use and increased penetration of the digital media (Cho et. al., 2009; Gainous and Wagner 2011; Xenos and Moy 2007). We agree and posit that social media is part of that new online shift. Previous work has explored whether online social media has the potential to stimulate social capital and political participation in the process (Bode 2012; Conroy, Feezell, and Guerrero 2012; Gainous and Wagner 2011; Gainous, Marlowe, and Wagner 2013; Gil de Zúñiga, Jun, and Valenzuela 2012; Pasek, More, and Romer 2009; Valenzuela, Park, and Kee 2009). We seek to build on this literature in this chapter with the empirical addition of the incorporation of Twitter effects. While most previous research has primarily been aimed at addressing whether Internet use can stimulate social capital and political participation in the process, to our knowledge, only the work of Gil de Zúñiga, Jun, and Valenzuela (2012) has explored whether SNS use facilitates activity in offline civic groups. Group level effects are essential to knowing whether SNS use can stimulate social capital. Many studies that explore the link between SNS use and political participation assume that an observed positive relationship is theoretically explained by social capital. Simply, participation goes up because SNS use stimulates social capital. Putnam's (1995a, 1995b, 2000) theory of social capital is founded in the idea that social capital is generated through the interaction between people in groups. While Gil de Zúñiga, Jun, and Valenzuela (2012) identify a positive relationship between SNS use to gather news and an index of civic participation, their five-item index contains only one item that taps respondents' proclivity to join groups. It is here where we attempt to build on their work, and those abovementioned, by looking specifically at the link between SNS use and offline group activity as well as the link between SNS use and political participation—both voting and online participation.

Further, we focus our attention on the implications. Particularly, we argue that those who gather political information via SNSs are more likely to participate, meaning that an opportunity is provided for candidates to benefit electorally if they can effectively campaign using SNSs by controlling the flow of information. By participating in and influencing the content and tone of the information, political actors can shape their friends'/followers' dispositions, generating support, or at least crystallizing it among those who are predisposed to favor them. The evidence presented in this chapter indicates that those who use SNSs such as Facebook, MySpace, and Twitter are more likely to join groups, and this likelihood is increased for those who use these sites more. The results also indicate that those who use SNSs such as Facebook and Twitter to gather political information are more likely to participate in political activities online (gather information about candidates, sign petitions, contribute money, etc.). Before moving to the results, we detail how Putnam's (1995a, 1995b, 2000) theory of social capital can be extended to theoretically explain these results.

Bowling Leagues versus Bowling Online

Technology has had a significant effect on the way that people engage with each other and the society in which they live. It is not just a change in how we engage and interact with one another, it is a shift in the relation of a person to the greater society and even a substantive change in the private and public spheres in that society. For social scientists, these kinds of shifts are difficult to anticipate, measure, and evaluate. Major technology shifts can cause some degree of uncertainty with traditional measures and indicators. For example, if one was looking to measure interpersonal relations through social gatherings, the invention of the telephone likely made the familiar units of analysis less reliable. Social media is another significant development in this area. The expansion and intensification of SNS use is significant even by Internet growth standards (Hoge 2009). The myriad of social media and the incalculable number of networks subsequently created have produced an environment that allows individuals to build relationships, network, and even create a sense of community in ways which differ substantively from the past. The nature and quality of this networking are clearly different from traditional face-to-face networking, and it is difficult to explain and measure as an element of the political and civic environment.

Political scientists have tried to account for the Internet and its role in building a political community. Boulianne (2009) conducted a meta-analysis of various studies that examined the effects of the Internet on civic-mindedness and political participation. Her results, which incorporated most studies published and unpublished at the time, did find a positive Internet effect. Nonetheless, the number of actual measures and studies of networking through the Internet is rather limited but rapidly growing, especially when focused on the effect of online social networking on political participation. The dearth of research is understandable considering how new most SNSs are and the relatively recent movement of people to use them. The limited research available with empirical examinations has suggested a relationship between SNS use and political participation/civic engagement in the United States (Bode 2012; Conroy, Feezell, and Guerrero 2012; Gainous and Wagner 2011; Gainous, Marlowe, and Wagner 2013; Gil de Zúñiga, Jun, and Valenzuela 2012; Pasek, More, and Romer 2009; Valenzuela, Park, and Kee 2009). We build on the theoretical framework of this research, extending it to a larger look at how the use of SNSs is changing group formation and political participation in the aggregate.

While the application of the Internet and online social media to civic engagement and participation is new, the study of the influences on engagement and participation are not. There is a well-developed body of literature suggesting that social capital results from the engagement and interconnectedness between people (Bourdieu 1986; Coleman 1988, 1990; Putnam 1995a, 1995b, 2000). Social interaction and the resulting bonds between people are strongly correlated with civic engagement (Brehm and Rahn 1997; Shah 1998). Not all social networking is the same, as the influence of social interaction on political participation is a product of the amount of political discourse that occurs inside the social networks (Klofstad 2007, 2009; McClurg 2003). The type of social capital is important, and there are differences between social capital that is built through political interactions and social capital that is not (Lake and Huckfeldt 1998). If the building of social capital occurs in civic groups that meet in person and that in-person group formation is declining (Putnam 2000); then the obvious subsequent question is whether social capital can developed through online interaction such as SNSs use.

This is also an area of limited, but not unknown, research. Early studies have shown a relationship between SNS use and social capital (Ellison, Steinfield, and Lampe 2007; Gil de Zúñiga, Jun, and Valenzuela 2012; Valenzuela, Park, and Kee 2009) as well as civic engagement/political participation and online networking (Bode 2012; Conroy, Feezell, and Guerrero 2012; Gainous and Wagner 2011; Gainous, Marlowe, and Wagner 2013; Gil de Zúñiga, Jun, and Valenzuela 2012; Pasek, More, and Romer 2009; Valenzuela, Park, and Kee 2009). Bode (2012), in particular, theorizes and estimates how specific types of behavior within online networks may stimulate participation, but only briefly addresses how the effects of these exchanges may be contingent on their political relevance. The studies are all restricted to some degree by temporal limitations. Social media is being rapidly adopted, so early measures are likely not capturing the larger and developing effect. Even more recent measures and research would almost certainly miss the influences of the massive increases in Twitter use. Further, even if some of this is captured, it is difficult in only one or two election cycles to account for other intervening or antecedent causes.

In this chapter we do not attempt to answer all of the questions concerning the nature of social media's influence on political participation. A more certain model would clearly include multiple election cycles occurring after the adoption of social media had become fairly ubiquitous. Nonetheless, there are still patterns to observe in the nature and usage of social media that can provide guidance concerning what is occurring and what the future might hold. To explore these patterns we consider and measure whether SNS use is generating politically relevant social capital among online social network-ers. More particularly, if group level activities are what build social capital, we consider whether the use of SNSs results in a greater likelihood to form or join groups. If SNS use is generating more group formation, or even simply a greater likelihood of joining a group, there are interesting implications. Users of SNSs could actually spread the in-fluence of their network offline and into the local civic or political groups to which they belong.

Additionally, we look directly at whether there are measurable relationships between SNS use and political participation. Does SNS use correlate with greater degrees of po-litical participation? Does the correlation hold when controlling for attentiveness and partisanship? We subset the measures and look to see if there are familiar patterns across race, age, income, and ethnicity. Individuals with a higher socioeconomic status (SES) are more likely to benefit from technology (Gainous and Wagner 2007). Rather than creating a benefit for all users, the advent of online social networking may exacerbate traditional cleavages in political participation because the social capital built by using these sites is not qualitatively equal across the "have" and "have not" divide. Before moving to the analysis, we proceed with a discussion of social capital theory, incorpo-rating the Internet and new media into that paradigm.

Digital Relationships as Social Capital

Relationships between people are the glue of any society. For a society, especially a de-mocracy, to function, scholars have theorized that a citizen's political participation is a product of their investment or connection within a society and with the people around them (Putnam 1995b). The investment into those relationships generates social cap-ital, which is a flexible and generally inclusive term describing the value of the bonds created around an individual. A more direct definition of social capital is the networks, norms, and trust and the way they help to make life's endeavors more efficient (Schuller 2000). When people invest in their communities and in relationships with their neigh-bors, they are more willing to bear the burdens of political participation, as they see themselves as part of a larger community. The absence of those relationships leads to a person becoming disconnected and nonparticipatory in the society and government. More directly, social capital is an acknowledgment of value in association, society, and civic engagement.

Prior to the large increases in social media, much of social capital and the relation-ships built in society were described in terms of direct, or in-person, interactions be-tween people. Most of these interactions were in groups that had some component of civic engagement. Everything from a bowling league to a traditional service organiza-tion fit within the definition (Putman 1995b). The logic of this construct is clear. By engaging in face-to-face interaction with other citizens, we learn the skills of negoti-ation, tolerance, and creative problem solving that are essential to the functioning of democracy (Putnam 1995b, 2000). The creation of the general societal norm of reciprocity is the key. Reciprocity produces trust and community; trust and community stimulate political participation. Scheufele and Shah (2000) integrate this relationship, arguing that social capital is built through social interaction by generating personal life satisfaction, social trust, and civic and political participation.

Many of the measures of social networking rely on face-to-face interactions and have not adequately accounted for the changes ushered in by digital networks. Much of the work on social capital (Putnam 2000; Scheufele and Shah 2000) is based on measuring the number or frequency of face-to-face interactions or offline group participation. The implication is that the declining in-person interaction should lead to spiraling lower social capital. Relying solely on measures of the physical interactions of people to account for civic engagement and social capital omits interaction through digital networks. The previous indicators and measures used to test civic and social engagement did not anticipate the degree that people would move so many of those activities online. Finding civic engagement at a bowling alley or service club is increasingly difficult. The production of social capital has moved in large part to online communities from the fixed locations where it was produced in preceding decades (Bode 2012; Ellison, Steinfeld, and Lampe 2007; Gainous and Wagner 2011; Gil de Zúñiga, Jun, and Valenzuela 2012; Pasek, More, and Romer 2009; Valenzuela, Park, and Kee 2009).

Hence, traditional models of civic engagement are missing much of the digital interaction, unless the measure of social engagement is broadened to include the online environment. Yet scholars are and should be wary of a false equivalency. More directly, do social networking websites provide a benefit similar to in-person engagement and therefore replace to some degree the declining face-to-face interactions? Anecdotally, the initial evidence is supportive. People increasingly communicate and interact through SNSs such as Facebook and Twitter. People can respond to each other and engage in political discussions at least as energetic and contested as those that occur in face-to-face meetings. At least as far back as 1994, online discussion forums were popular spots for political conversation and organization. One group "alt.politics.Clinton" received approximately 800 postings each day during the height of the presidential contest between Bill Clinton and George H. W. Bush (Smith 1994).

As a result, these new online communities have the potential to counter or perhaps even reverse the effect of traditional social capital decline on political participation by replacing the missing interactions measured by scholars such as Putnam (1995a, 1995b, 2000). While scholars of social capital and more traditional measures of civic engagement are not sure of the weight to be given to online communities, they are now including online measures. Putnam's inclusion of craigslist.com as an example of a thriving (virtual) community in his edited work *Better Together: Restoring the American Community* (Putnam, Feldstein, and Cohen 2003) is an acknowledgement that Internet networking can play an important role in community-building. Mossberger, Tolbert, and McNeal (2008) do not look directly at the influence of SNSs on political participation, but they do find evidence that chat room participation is positively correlated with the propensity to vote. Their findings are supportive of the notion that a politically relevant social capital can be built online. Yet these admissions and conclusions are still focused on familiar indicators or traditional online behaviors. They do not account for the penetration and influences of the SNSs themselves. The effect of SNSs may be more influential because the networking sites are more pervasive and regularly used as compared to a static website, unappealing discussion board, or an often confusing chat room.

SNSs such as Facebook are just now being studied, but there is increasing evidence suggesting they have the potential to generate social capital, though often in small or limited samples. Ellison, Steinfeld, and Lampe (2007) used a student sample to demonstrate the intensity with which students use Facebook. They found that the extent of the emotional connection to Facebook, and the degree to which it was integrated into their life, was related to the foundational elements of social capital, including bridging and bonding. Valenzuela, Park, and Kee (2009) also used a student sample to present evidence that Facebook use can stimulate social capital, though the magnitude of the effect in their data was not large. Pasek, More, and Romer (2009) used a large random sample of young people and found that social capital is developed online. Interestingly, they note site-specific differences that influence the degree to which social capital is generated. Bode (2012) similarly uses a student sample to measure different types of online social capital that may be built from using Facebook. She finds there is a relationship between such use and online and offline political participation. Gainous and Wagner (2011) use both student data and population data to demonstrate that online networking does stimulate participation, but their measure broadly defines online networking to include components other than SNSs. Perhaps the most direct and convincing evidence of the efficacy of SNSs as social capital builders is provided by Gil de Zúñiga, Jun, and Valenzuela (2012). Their study suggests that the extent to which people use SNSs to keep up with political news, public issues, and information about their community positively predicts social capital as measured by an index of whether they feel intimate in the community, share community values, talk about community problems, feel connected, and help resolve problems and watch out for community members.

A real-world measure of the potential for SNSs to perhaps stimulate social capital and participation in the process was conducted during the 2010 midterm elections in an attempt to quantify the influence of networks of friends on Facebook (Bond et al. 2012) on the choice to vote. The authors conducted an experiment in which certain Facebook users were shown a nonpartisan "get out the vote" message on their news feeds during election day. Included in the message was a reminder about the election, a clickable "I Voted" button, polling place information, and a counter showing users who had voted along with pictures of the user's friends who had reported voting. The authors also used control groups with no reminders, or with a reminder that did not include information on their friends. The results showed that the people who received the message with pictures of their friends were the most likely to vote (Bond et al. 2012). The finding suggests that not only are traditional network influences alive on the Internet, they can be scaled to great effect.

SNSs: The Opportunity Structure

While there is empirical support for a positive relationship between SNS use and political participation, that is only part of a larger narrative. Equally important, political groups are formed online and those groups can have influence on policy and elections. This was evidenced as early as 1994 when then House Speaker Thomas Foley was driven from office in part due to the efforts of a political action committee that was organized online (Browning 2002). Howard Dean's early success in the run-up to the 2004 Democratic presidential primaries was fueled by his campaigns efforts to organize supporters and potential supporters through online forums. Dean was also able to effectively convert online engagement into offline activity by organizing meetings, rallies, and even coffee discussions through online discussion boards (Trippi 2005). Not only did it help him raise money, it created enthusiasm and connected Governor Dean to an active, passionate, and engaged citizenry that worked for him largely as volunteers. The well-known liberal advocacy group Moveon.org also got its start as an Internet movement. Moveon.org was an email discussion group that started a petition to oppose the impeachment of then-President Bill Clinton in 1998. Today, it continues to be based online and organizes citizens on behalf of progressive candidates, while raising millions of dollars to influence elections and policies (McNally 2004).

It is in the group formation and maintenance that the power of social media and the Internet may be most significant. If the Internet and SNSs in particular are bringing people together in not just social groups, but political ones, there is a large potential for the creation of social capital. Interestingly, there is also a great potential for political actors to influence people and policy as well. It is far harder for a campaign or politician to reach out to every important group and attend their meetings. Even if they are able to do so, they may fail to reach the elements of that group or organization that miss the actual meeting. However, a political actor online can interject themselves directly into the conversation between group members and their network of friends and acquaintances. They can influence members of the group and those members can then bring that influence to physical meetings of the group.

If social media is encouraging group formation and membership, then the potential for influence is greater than that of the face-to-face interaction. Effective communications through SNSs will filter down into the various groups. Those who gather political information via SNSs are more likely to participate, and this means that an opportunity is provided for candidates to benefit electorally, if they can effectively campaign using SNSs by influencing the flow of information. Controlling the flow of information will shape their friends'/followers' dispositions, generating support, or at least crystallize it among those who are predisposed to favor them. All of this can occur outside the traditional media and avoid the gatekeeping function of newspapers or television news. It is a new world of engagement, but the engagement is still there.

Modeling Social Capital

We introduce another study conducted by the Pew Internet & American Life Project in 2010 called the Social Side Survey.[1] This survey is similar to the post-election survey conducted by Pew used in Chapters 2 and 3 (and also this chapter) but it focuses on social media, and particularly on people's propensity to join civic groups and their behavior in those groups. This makes these data ideal for examining whether social media use actually stimulates social capital, if we accept the premise that heightened participation in civic groups is reflective of, or builds, social capital.

The Social Side Survey included the same two indicators of SNS use that were included in the post-election survey we used in Chapters 2 and 3. We, again, constructed an additive index of these indicators and called it *SNS/Twitter Use*: (1) Please tell me if you ever use the Internet to do any of the following things. Do you ever use the Internet to use a social networking site like MySpace, Facebook or LinkedIn?, and (2) Please tell me if you ever use the Internet to do any of the following things. Do you ever use the Internet to use Twitter? These two items were statistically significantly related ($p < 0.001$). Our primary dependent variable for the analysis using these data, *Propensity to Join Groups*, is also measured using an index. This index comprised of twenty-seven items that attempted to tap people's membership/participation in a variety of civic groups/organizations ranging from community groups or neighborhood associations to sports or recreation leagues, from veterans groups or organizations such as the American Legion or VFW to literary, discussion, or study groups, from travel clubs to labor unions. See the appendix for a description of all twenty-seven items that were used to construct the index ($\alpha = 0.79$).

Before moving on to a multivariate model of the propensity to join groups, the bivariate relationship between SNS use and the propensity to join groups is displayed in Figure 6.1. There is a clear pattern here. The more likely respondents were to use social media, including Facebook, MySpace, LinkedIn, and Twitter, the more likely they were to join groups. While this relationship is statistically significant ($p < 0.001$), the magnitude is not large ($r = 0.12$). Thus, it is entirely possible that this relationship will dissipate, or at least be accounted for, when introducing controls into the model. We estimate a Poisson regression model of the propensity to join groups as a function of SNS

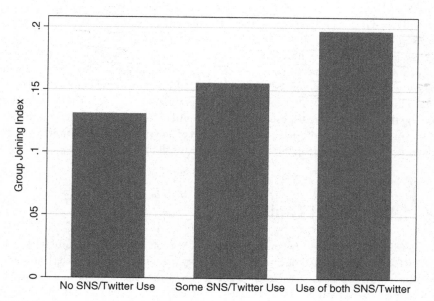

Figure 6.1 SNS Use and Joining Civic Groups. Source: 2010 Pew Internet & American Life Project Social Side Survey.

Table 6.1 **Model of the Propensity to Join Groups**

	Estimate	*Standard Error*	*p-value*	*IRR*
SNS Use	0.33	0.19	0.09	1.40
Internet Use	0.03	0.02	0.20	—
Partisanship Strength	0.06	0.09	0.48	—
Age	0.21	0.10	0.03	1.24
Education	0.23	0.08	0.00	1.26
Income	0.13	0.09	0.15	—
Black	0.21	0.19	0.27	—
Latino	0.02	0.23	0.93	—
Asian	−0.25	0.46	0.59	—
Female	0.02	0.12	0.85	—
Constant	−3.47	0.38	0.00	—
Pseudo R^2	0.03			
N	1781			

Note: Data come from the 2010 Pew Internet & American Life Project Social Side Survey. Table entries are Poisson regression estimates. IRR is the incident rate ratio.

use, Internet use, partisanship strength, age, education, income, race, and gender.[2] The results indicate that the relationship is robust (Table 6.1).

In fact, the incident rate ratio derived from the Poisson regression estimate suggests that every one unit increase in SNS use increases the number of groups people have joined by 1.4 times. This is significant, considering that the incident rate ratios for one unit increases in the other significant variables in the model age and education are both smaller at 1.24 and 1.26, respectively. We must note that the relationship between SNS use and joining groups may be recursive. People who were likely to join groups may be more likely to use SNSs. That said, we include the controls in this model to simultaneously assure that our predicted effects are not spurious and to help account for the possibility of endogeneity. Simply, the controls help assure that the causal direction is in the hypothesized direction. By including them, we avoid creating dependence between the error term and the rest of the variables in the model. That said, even if there is reason to expect a recursive relationship, our theory and conclusion is not adversely impacted. People who use SNSs are more likely to be civically engaged and participate in the political process, which makes them more susceptible to the influence of elites who are using this medium to control the flow of information. Therefore, it does not matter which way the causal arrow runs, it only matters that those who are more likely to join groups are also more likely to use SNSs. These people are also probably more likely to participate in the process. The next set of analyses confirms this expectation.

SNSs and Political Participation

The next set of models is based on the post-election data gathered by Pew. We estimate three separate ordered-logit models of online political participation. Our measure of *Online Political Participation* is an index constructed from seven items inquiring about respondent's use of the Internet to participate in political activities (see the Appendix for exact wording). These activities include using the Internet to contribute money to a candidate, look for information online about candidates' voting records or positions on the issues, volunteer for a campaign, share photos, videos, or audio files that relate to the campaign, send email related to the campaign, organize or get information about in-person meetings to discuss political issues in the campaign, or take part in an online discussion, listserv, or other online group forum such as a blog related to political issues or the campaign ($\alpha = 0.67$).

Again, we model this outcome as function of general SNS use relying on the index described in Chapter 3 (and replicated in this chapter using the Social Side data) but also as a function of the indices of *Political SNS Use* and *Political Twitter Use* from the items described in Tables 2.1 and 2.2 and used in the models in Chapter 3. We estimate three separate models to assess the independent effects of general use, political use of Facebook and/or MySpace, and political use of Twitter while controlling for general Internet use, attentiveness to public affairs, partisanship strength, age, education, income, race, and gender. Again, the operationalization of all these controls is included in the appendix.

The results presented in Table 6.2 suggest clearly that those who use SNSs generally and also to gather political information are more likely to participate politically online. Again, this relationship may be recursive, but that is not an issue for our theory. It only matters that there is a relationship, ceteris paribus. Consistent with the models of the propensity to join groups, the odds ratios for these ordered-logit estimates indicate that all types of SNS use have a larger effect on online political participation than most of the other controls in the models. The models suggest that a one unit increase in political attentiveness increases the odds of being higher on the online political participation index by 3.51 times in the model including only general SNS use and other controls (Model 1), by 2.23 times in the model including only political SNS use (Model 2), and by 1.99 times in the model including only political Twitter use (Model 3). Partisanship strength is only significant in Model 1 (the general SNS use model), estimating a negative relationship (significant only at the 0.10 level) suggesting that those who are stronger partisans are 0.82 times less likely to participate online.

Age is only significant in Model 2 (the political SNS use model), estimating a positive relationship indicating that a one unit increase in age on the ordinal scale increases the odds of participating online by 1.31 times. Next, education is significant in both Model 1 and Model 2, suggesting that a one unit increase in education increases the odds of participating online by 1.08 and 1.29 times, respectively. Income is only significant (at the 0.10 level) in Model 2, suggesting there is an increase in the odds of participating online for those who have higher income (1.16). Finally, race is largely insignificant with the exception that the political Twitter use model (Model 3) suggests that Latinos are 0.38 times less likely to participate online than whites which are

Table 6.2 **Modeling Online Political Participation as a Function of SNS/Twitter Use**

	Model 1	OR	Model 2	OR	Model 3	OR
SNS Use	0.25**	1.29	—	—	—	—
	(0.11)					
Political SNS Use	—	—	0.67***	1.95	—	—
			(0.06)			
Political Twitter Use	—	—	—	—	1.04***	2.81
					(0.22)	
Internet Use	−0.00	—	0.00	—	−0.01	—
	(0.02)		(0.02)		(0.06)	
Attentiveness	1.26***	3.51	0.80***	2.23	0.69***	1.99
	(0.08)		(0.10)		(0.25)	
Partisanship Strength	−0.20*	0.82	−0.17	—	0.10	—
	(0.11)		(0.15)		(0.40)	
Age	0.14	—	0.27**	1.31	0.21	—
	(0.09)		(0.12)		(0.26)	
Education	0.32***	1.08	0.25***	1.29	0.53	
	(0.07)	.	(0.10)		(0.28)	
Income	0.08	—	0.16*	1.16	0.01	—
	(0.08)		(0.09)		(0.28)	
Black	−0.23	—	−0.18	—	−0.19	—
	(0.19)		(0.28)		(0.48)	
Latino	−0.24	—	−0.12	—	−0.96*	0.38
	(0.20)		(0.26)		(0.56)	
Asian	−0.57	—	−1.01**	—	−1.86	—
	(0.38)		(0.52)		(1.26)	
Female	0.02	—	−0.19	—	0.07	—
	(0.11)		(0.13)		(0.33)	
Pseudo R²	0.12		0.15		0.18	
N	1583		1138		149	

Note: Data come from the 2010 Pew Internet & American Life Project Post-Election Survey. Table entries are ordered-logit estimates (threshold values suppressed) based on respondents who use the Internet at least occasionally for Model 1, who use SNSs for Model 2, and who use Twitter for Model 3, with associated standard errors in parentheses, and odds ratios (OR). ***p < 0.01, **p < 0.05, *p < 0.1.

the reference category (0.10 level). The differences in the effects of the controls across models are a function of different subsamples of the data. Largely Models 1 and 2 predict the same effects but the Twitter model varies greatly in predicted effects and sample size. The variation is perhaps a result in the variation of who uses Twitter described in Chapter 3 but is most likely simply a result of the smaller sample size.

As mentioned above, the relationship between SNS use and online political participation is significant and positive across all three models. Not only are each of the indicators, general SNS use, political SNS use, and political Twitter use significant, but the odds ratios are relatively large. First, in Model 1, the estimate suggests that every one unit increase in general SNS use raises the odds of increasing on the online political participation index by 1.29 times. This is the second highest odds ratio of the significant variables in the model. Next, in Model 2, the estimate indicates that every one unit increase in political SNS use increases the odds of being higher on the online political participation index by 1.95 times. This is, again, the second highest odds ratio in this model. Finally, in Model 3, every one unit increase in political Twitter use predicts a 2.81 increase in the odds of being higher on the online political participation index. This is the largest odds ratio of the significant variables in the model. Taken altogether, it is clear here that SNS use, generally and for political purposes, has a rather consequential effect on political participation.

Summary

This chapter builds on and extends earlier theory suggesting that social media has the potential to build social capital. The real empirical contribution here is that we identify a positive relationship between SNS use and the propensity to join groups. This brings us to the core of Putman's (1995a, 1995b, 2000) theory of social capital because his entire argument was centered on the decline in participation in civic groups. Most research on the effects of SNS use has centered on whether it stimulates political participation (Bode 2012; Gainous and Wagner 2011; Gainous, Marlowe, and Wagner 2013; Pasek, More, and Romer 2009; Valenzuela, Park, and Kee 2009). The results in this chapter confirm these earlier results. However, that group formation and maintenance correlates with SNS use presents a larger narrative (see also Gil de Zúñiga, Jun, and Valenzuela 2012). If those who gather political information via SNSs are more likely to participate, an opportunity is provided for candidates to benefit electorally by using SNSs to control the flow of information with the intent of being the beneficiary of this heightened participation.

This finding puts us both consistent with and at odds with analysis and theory that proposes a large democratizing effect from the Internet and social media. Our findings support the notion that these new technologies are increasing participation. The Internet does remove the barriers allowing some who would otherwise lack a voice to speak in the public sphere. It creates a place to both allow and motivate political participation. However, we do not hold to the notion that this participation must result in greater democratization as some scholars have suggested (see Barber 2001; Barber 2003; Corrado and Firestone 1996; Hagen and Mayer 2000; Lupia and Sin 2003). Nor does social media necessarily mean the shifting of power away from political actors to the public. The participation itself has value, but the social media platform presents pitfalls as well. Using an SNS allows more people to speak, but it also presents a useful opportunity structure for the most effective and organized actors to not just speak louder but also to control a message and direct it through organized and receptive channels of political communication.

Interestingly, the potential for the distribution of information or opinion that is demonstrably false increases as well. Social media has great potential to misinform for political gain. An easy example of this is the is a vast amount of information disputing President Obama's birth in Hawaii and multiple active networks of people and groups that are fertile ground for its dissemination (Mann 2012). Without the moderating effect of the media's watchdog role, there is little to deter political actors or their agents from taking advantage of the opportunity structure that social media presents. In fact, the inability or unwillingness to do so will likely translate into an electoral disadvantage. While the traditional media may fact-check social media information, the penetration of those traditional sources of media, as well as the trust in them, is declining. We are only now seeing the beginning of the likely free-for-all that online campaigning through social media will be.

The next chapter begins to explore how candidates can use SNSs, Twitter specifically, to attempt to control the flow of information. We explore how candidates attempt to do so by providing links to news stories, endorsements, and blogs that present them in a favorable light.

The narrative that we began developing in Chapter 5 is extended in this next chapter. The evidence is clear that challengers and Republicans did a better job of controlling the flow of information with their use of Twitter in the 2010 elections.

7

Congress 2.0—Controlling the Flow
of Information

The importance of social media in the political sphere is based in part on how we consume and understand information. In previous chapters we have set forth a theoretical foundation for our premise that the use of SNSs will have a substantial and significant effect on the nature and structure of our political discourse. We base our proposition on the essential structure of how people obtain and understand political information. Peoples' attitudes are made up of an average of the range of relevant considerations they may have (Zaller 1992). Since the world and the information environment are not static, people are constantly updating their assessments of politics, policy, and political figures based on the information they receive. This ongoing progression, referred to as online processing, can be influenced by the nature, magnitude, and scope of the information as they sample it from external sources (Lodge, Steenbergen, and Brau 1995; Lodge 1995). As a result, what people know and understand about politics is based on the types, frequency, and point of view of the news and analysis they consume and how they reconcile it with their worldview and predispositions.

Substantial studies on this cognitive process have been the focus of major research (Lodge 1995; Zaller 1992). A substantial piece of the impact of a new media format such as social media is placing it in our current understanding of the cognitive process. We need to consider how social media can alter the process people engage in when deciding which information they will consume and how they will view it. This process is based on an understanding of the psychology of forming beliefs and worldviews. It is also based in part on comprehending the media environment in which people are learning and consuming information. The latter is fertile ground for research. Media politics is its own subdiscipline and has been frequently studied (Bennett 2011; Graber 2010; Prior 2007). Tendencies toward misinformation, infotainment, profit-driven content, commercial influences, and structural biases are prominent outcomes of the mass media model (Bennett 2011).

Social media supplies a paradigm-changing element to the system. Using SNSs to obtain information presents a very different dynamic. The consumption of information is interactive and occurs inside networks of friends and acquaintances. As we discussed in previous chapters, this type of information distribution has some increasingly measurable effects on participation, polarization, group formation, and levels of knowledge. The age of the mass media and its significant pathologies are not over, but rather a new distribution channel is available, which brings its own implications, both positive and negative.

Many of the influences we have discussed in earlier chapters are important measures of this new and perhaps novel public sphere. However, they are only a portion of the larger influence of SNS use. All speak, to some degree, about the needs and wants of the information consumer and putting that consumer in some control of their content. As we observed, this can cause important changes to what is consumed and how it is understood.

However, the rise of SNSs and their growing use has a larger importance beyond the consumer. It is an opportunity structure for political actors. As we have argued, the SNSs are an information distribution channel that are open to anyone and allow interactive communication outside the purview of the modern media. Consider that for much of our history, political communication was based on utilizing an often-expensive method of mass information distribution such as a printing press or later a radio or subsequently television broadcast. One of the key limiting factors for political actors was the limited ability they had to use these channels and the mediating effect of the owners of them. With SNSs, the channel is unmediated, the messages are unrestrained in number or frequency, and the distribution is limited only by the rapidly increasing scope and penetration of the Internet and social media.

Earlier we examined how politicians were using this new medium, focusing in particular on Twitter. In this chapter we are going to consider more specifically the nature of the information flow and the means by which politicians can use Twitter to manipulate the scope and direction of the information being given to followers and different networks of people. We will look at why Twitter creates such a strong environment for message control and how political actors can take advantage of that structure to reinforce preexisting views as well as to signal to their followers how they should understand and consider information. Too much of the focus of the work on social media assumes that the individual consumer is the new content editor. We suggest that the consumers' power is far more illusory. Increasingly clever campaigns help the consumer come to conclusions, though effective online campaigns worked increasingly through ascertainable networks of like-minded friends and acquaintances.

This chapter will make an argument that is two-fold. First, a theory will be developed asserting that use of the Twitter tools described above may serve candidates who are trying to control the flow of information better than simply using simple 140 character or less tweets that fit into the four-category typology developed in Chapter 4. Second, we further develop the argument that Republicans and challengers did a better job of controlling the flow of information in this election cycle but suggest an alternative argument to those presented in Chapter 5. We contend that it is possible that Republicans and challengers by circumstance happened to be on the popular side of the information flow, and Twitter provided the perfect opportunity for them to capitalize on these information control tools as a means to further crystallize their support.

This theoretical development is followed by some descriptive analysis exploring the distribution of use across partisanship, incumbency, chamber, and race identifying that Republicans, challengers, senators, and white candidates tended to use these tools more frequently. We then present qualitative data that provide more examples of how these Twitter tools were used (links, @Twitter names, and hashtags) in particular by Republican challengers. Finally, we conclude with a multivariate model demonstrating that Republicans, challengers, and Senators tended to use these tools of information control more frequently, ceteris paribus.

Information Control and Social Media

One of the great media misconceptions held by many Americans is the idea that there is an absolute objective means to report information. Ironically, even attempting to generate news that is divorced from politics or somehow objective creates its own type of bias (Bennett 2011). In every system, there are advantaged parties and disadvantaged ones. When print media was dominant, the most advantaged were the ones that owned the press or could afford to purchase space. In the television age, resources were still an advantage, but visual appeal became important as well. In the Internet age, we would like to believe that infinitely expanding the channels of information distribution created an open and perhaps even democratic media environment. The inherent openness of the Internet leads to a somewhat optimistic view of the future (Allison 2002). However, the removal of the media owners from a dominant position in the distribution network is not necessarily a panacea. The new system, like all previous systems, creates opportunity structures that can be advantageous for some (Riker 1986). It is never a question of whether a system can be exploited, it is a question of who will be in position to do it.

Perhaps the biggest influence of the social media may well be in the shifting of power in the political communication sphere, not from the media to the individual, but from the media to various politicians and political interests. It is in the elevation of the political actors to the role of unmediated information provider that the most lasting and substantial effect may be occurring. Twitter is a new medium that candidates can use to provide and influence the considerations being evaluated by users/potential voters. In doing so, they can circumvent the traditional media—the normal gatekeepers. People are choosing, but it is the political actors that are often doing the speaking. As a result, social media appears to provide open communication with limitless choices, but in escaping the media's filtering, the SNSs have provided a fertile ground for the political actors to drive and influence content.

The early adopters are biggest beneficiaries so far. The narrative that became evident in Chapters 4 and 5 persists in the data here. Challengers and Republicans did a better job of controlling the flow of information with their use of Twitter in the 2010 election cycle. Chapters 4 and 5 laid the foundation for understanding the ways candidates may use Twitter to campaign. It was there that we started to build the empirical foundation for how candidates may have used Twitter in the 2010 election cycle in an attempt to control the flow of information. We did so by highlighting how they may have used links, @Twitter names, and hashtags in their tweets to secure support. Some of the same strategies that we have traditionally seen members of Congress use, such as advertising, credit claiming, and position-taking are evident (Mayhew 1974). However, they are done with no mediation and with increased frequency, targeted to specific audiences with the advantage of requiring few resources and no substantial costs. Twitter maximizes all of the traditional strategies with unprecedented efficiency, speed, and responsiveness.

Since Twitter makes it relatively easy to reach networks of supporters without having to meet journalistic standards of accuracy or even relevance, candidates have unprecedented control of their message and messaging. With such levers on information distribution, candidates are able to control the flow of information by providing links to types of news, endorsements, and blogs that present them in a favorable light. For some users who obtain most or even all of their information from social media, the influence of political actors can be determined. The idea of living in a bubble of one type of information is no longer theoretical, it is an obtainable reality. It is also a reality that people are creating around them, without necessarily understanding its existence. It is in this bubble that opinions can be reinforced and contrary information excluded or eliminated.

While these networks are problematic in the area of accuracy, there are other concerns as well. Significantly, SNSs are a media reality readily exploitable by political actors who will integrate into the network and cater to the predispositions of its users. Yet it is not solely message control, which would alone be paradigm shifting. It is messaging in a targeted way toward populations and networks with readily ascertained predispositions. Followers of particular people or groups are cognitively receptive to information tailored to their predispositions. For example, a network of liberal activists is fertile ground for messaging on income inequality or alleged threats to the social safety net. As people are uncomfortable when confronted with information that is not consistent to their predispositions, they order themselves online into groups and networks with very real and consistent patterns or beliefs and understandings. These patterns of networks online are the inadvertent effect of human psychology and the desire to avoid cognitive dissonance or any general discomfort. Challenging information causes discomfort. Agreeable information sources are preferred, because they prevent the user from experiencing discomfort by helping them avoid exposure to any contrary information which could cause confusion or doubt.

A prime example of this trend was in the 2012 US presidential election. Conservatives and conservative political actors discarded the weight of the polling information that suggested a narrow but persistent lead favoring President Obama and redirected their followers using social media to blogs, media, and other postings that were said to report polling without media bias (Morris 2012). Many tweets directed conservatives to Unskewed.com, a website that purported to fix polls by weighting them with greater numbers of Republican voters. Other tweets simply confirmed that the polls in general were wrong with a reference to supporting websites. The election results, which were largely consistent with the disparaged media and public polling, surprised many conservatives, including the authors of some of the websites championing their incorrectly adjusted polling (Benson 2012). This type of cueing through the social media is possible because it plays on the inherent distrust in the media by conservatives. The organization of people ready to believe that the media intentionally favors one political party already exists. The exploitation of that network is relatively simple as a result. The social media can play a significant role in creating or reinforcing predispositions like this as long as the politicians and political interests continue to self-interestedly drive content consistent with such a narrative into targeted elements of the SNSs.

Not only is Twitter ideal for this type of messaging, the tools inside Twitter are useful in fine-tuning the message and its audience. A tweet can be personalized inside these networks, making it more likely to be read and more carefully directed. Candidates can respond directly to one person, but with a public message. This message would have the @Twitter name of the individual in it. A retweet would also have a @Twitter name in it. This is a way for the candidate to appear concerned about an individual with very little resource cost. Politicians, or their staff can respond directly to constituents or can pass on positive information that was generated from somewhere else. An @Twitter name can also be included in a tweet to link into the followers of another Twitter user that tends to be favorable toward the candidate. Taken altogether, including an @Twitter name is an effective method to help define and control the flow of information.

The name is important, but a more significant organizing tool inside Twitter is the hashtag. Political actors may use hashtags to direct content and emphasize particular facts or points of view. This is a particularly important means of controlling the flow of information. As described earlier, hashtags are when a user includes the # symbol to mark keywords or topics in a tweet. People use the hashtag symbol before relevant keywords in their tweet to categorize those tweets, making them identifiable in a Twitter search. Hashtagged words that become very popular are often categorized as "trending topics." These are topics that are immediately popular rather than topics that have been popular for a while or on a daily basis. They can cue people to the most important breaking news stories from around the world. They can also suggest or signal to a person to how they should understand the information and its relative importance. A hashtag has many uses but is a particularly convenient or even shorthand way to insert an opinion into an otherwise neutral statement. Political actors can do this to the stories relevant to congressional candidates, or to generally trending topics that can be made relevant to a particular point of view. More directly, candidates can try and marshal or influence the flow of information by using hashtags that connect their tweets into popular groups and/or topics.

As a campaign and political tool, Twitter has much to recommend it. It is unmediated, immediate, and able to be targeted at important groups with little cost. The Twitter conventions including links, hashtags, and user names are useful for directing information and reinforcing messaging. In the Twitter universe, the sophisticated political actors are the advantaged users.

Republican Challengers Controlling the Flow: The Descriptive Evidence

The quantitative analysis in this chapter is based on counts of the number of times candidates had linked information in their tweets (counted by checking to see if the tweet contained "http"), included @Twitter names (counted by checking to see if the tweet included an @ symbol), and hashtags (counted by checking to see if the tweet included a # symbol). After doing counts for each candidate, we also constructed separate measures to gauge the frequency with which candidates were using these means of controlling the flow of information by calculating the percentage of their total tweets comprised of each respective means (http, @, #). We simply divided the number of times each candidate used one of these tools, respectively, by the total number of tweets. This means that it was possible for the percentage of use of these tools to be higher than 100%. This outcome is possible because many candidates are using links, @Twitter names, or hashtags, more than once in a given tweet. We chose to measure it this way because including more of these tools in a single tweet should have a greater effect on the control of the flow of information and connect followers to a wider audience. This practice was quite common as we saw from the qualitative data presented in Chapters 4 and 5. For the analysis in this section we, first, plot the frequency of this percentage for each outcome. Next, we explore the number of times candidates used each of these tools across party, incumbency, chamber, and race.

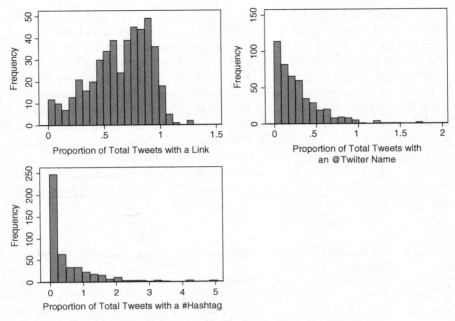

Figure 7.1 Distribution of the Percentage of Information Control Tweets.
Source: www.twitter.com.

The first observation that can be made from the distributions displayed in Figure 7.1 is that generally speaking these tools seem to be used quite frequently. Notice that the proportion of the X axis often exceeds 1.[1] The results illustrate that most candidates have a very high proportion of their total tweets containing links to other information. In fact, the modal outcome was 60% and the mean is around 65%, suggesting that generally most tweets included a link. This is a significant result because providing a link to information that paints the candidate in a favorable light may be the most effective way of using Twitter to control the information that followers have cognitively accessible to form an opinion about the candidate. While the distribution of candidates having tweets with a @Twitter name in them was tilted toward 0, this was nonetheless still a quite frequently used tool. On average around 29% of the total tweets by candidates contained an @Twitter name. Again, remember that this number is higher than the actual number of tweets containing an @Twitter name because we divided the total number of tweets by the total number of @Twitter names in those tweets, but nonetheless it reflects that this is a fairly common practice. This means that there are over a quarter of the instances of the use of an @Twitter name relative to the total number of tweets. Finally, the distribution of total tweets with a hashtag was also titled toward zero, but nonetheless, hashtags were not used infrequently. On average, the calculation of number of uses of a hashtag divided by the total number of tweets was around 52%. Again, many of them had multiple hashtags, suggesting that candidates were trying to connect constituents to multiple streams of information simultaneously.

Next, we examine potential differences in the types of candidates who use these different tools for controlling the flow of information. As described above candidates did so quite frequently. In fact, Tim Griffin, a successful Republican challenger for a House seat in Arkansas included 1,311 links in his tweets and he also included an astonishing 4,399 hashtags. While Sean Bielat, an unsuccessful Republican challenger for a Massachusetts seat in the House included an @Twitter name in his tweets an astonishing 2,136 times, Griffin also had a sizable number of @Twitter names at 378. These two candidates were certainly tweeting more than most but as demonstrated in earlier chapters and in the above results, they were not alone and there does appear to be a pattern emerging of who is most likely to both tweet and use certain tools.

The results in Table 7.1 clearly indicate that Republicans and challengers are more likely to seek to control the flow of information via Twitter by including links, replies, and hashtags than their respective counterparts. In fact, the mean number of tweets

Table 7.1 **Information Control via Twitter across Party, Incumbency, Chamber, and Race**

	http		@		#	
	Mean	S.D.	Mean	S.D	Mean	S.D.
Democrat	60.67	79.08	31.39	56.02	55.07	130.11
Republican	117.65	157.92	72.14	195.32	177.86	476.55
p-value	0.00		0.00		0.00	
Challenger	114.53	158.23	66.85	184.30	178.60	463.20
Incumbent	58.27	63.28	33.68	70.25	40.95	84.30
p-value	0.00		0.01		0.00	
House	80.50	125.79	46.05	142.94	100.18	358.73
Senate	162.10	133.47	100.31	169.95	259.57	341.38
p-value	0.00		0.01		0.00	
White	91.31	125.35	53.87	144.71	124.29	376.38
Black	70.94	114.84	22.44	43.60	69.76	210.80
Latino	58.70	81.08	85.25	311.40	50.05	160.44
p-value	0.06		0.00		0.00	

Note: Data come from www.twitter.com. P-values represent the probability that we cannot reject the null hypothesis that the difference between the means across the dichotomous variables does not = 0, and the p-value for the race measurements is based on the chi-squared statistic derived from a One-way ANOVA Test of the difference of means.

including a link or @Twitter name is around twice as much for Republicans relative to Democrats (approximately 118 to 61 and 72 to 31, respectively) and over three times as many hashtags are included in Republican tweets relative to Democrat tweets (178 to 55). The pattern is much the same across incumbency. Challengers were also around twice as likely as incumbents to include a link or @Twitter name (approximately 115 to 58 and 67 to 34, respectively) and over four times as many hashtags are included in challenger tweets relative to incumbent tweets (179 to 41). Finally, Senators and white candidates are generally more likely to do all of these things with one exception. The data suggest that Latino candidates were more likely to use @Twitter names.

Republican Challengers Controlling the Flow: The Qualitative Evidence

Perhaps one of the most subtle ways that candidates can use Twitter to control the flow of information is to include @Twitter names. As described earlier, this provides candidates the opportunity to reach a wider audience by potentially connecting them with the followers of the user with the @Twitter name they included. And by including their own @Twitter name, it makes it easy to build new followers if this tweet is retweeted. People can simply click on the candidate's @Twitter name and then choose to become a follower. We provided many examples of such in Chapters 4 and 5 but provide another here to be clear about what we are measuring in this chapter and why we are measuring it. Because we will continue to build on our argument that Republican challengers more effectively capitalized on the use of Twitter in the 2010 election cycle, we provide an example here of how such a candidate used this tool, and presumably increased his control over the flow of information.

We use Tim Griffin again as our exemplar here. He retweeted the following tweet: Today I voted for: @griffincongress @markdarr @Keet4Arkansas @Boozman4AR jeremy hutchinson and the best of all @David_J_Sanders. He really got the maximum use of the inclusion of @Twitter names. First, the tweet includes his @Twitter name (@griffincongress). Next, it includes the @Twitter names of several prominent Republican candidates from Arkansas including Mark Darr, who had a successful bid to be the lieutenant governor, Jim Keet, an unsuccessful gubernatorial candidate, John Boozman, a successful candidate for the U.S. Senate, and David J. Sanders, who is in the Arkansas House of Representatives but led an unsuccessful bid for state senate. The inclusion of all these candidates is clearly intended to put Griffin in with a group that he believed would be viewed favorably by the audience he is trying to reach. Finally, this retweet originated from a voter who had taken advantage of early voting in Arkansas. By including this fact, Griffin could potentially stimulate early turnout among others. Our data cannot tell us if this in fact worked, but we do know that he won the election as a challenger.

Hashtags are another way that candidates can guide or control the flow of information. We highlighted the use of hashtags in Chapters 4 and 5 but will dig deeper, empirically, here. Before moving on to a quantitative analysis of the use of hashtags, we provide examples below of some of what we consider to be the effective use of hashtags by

Republican challengers in this election cycle. Again, we focus on Republican challengers because as the quantitative analysis in previous chapters has suggested concerning
other uses of Twitter and in this chapter concerning the use of hashtags, Republicans
and challengers tend to use this tool more often. Note that we include three broad types
of hashtags in this list: (1) those that tap into a broad, perhaps national or at least state-
wide, audience, (2) those that reach a race/election specific audience, and (3) those
that are centered on an idea or policy. We think that those who try to do all of these, not
necessarily in a single tweet, are the most effective. Here is a list of particularly pointed
and effective hashtags (some were already highlighted in Chapters 4 and 5):

#TCOT: The creators of this hashtag characterize themselves as "the twitter hashtag for
following top conservatives on twitter." This hashtag came up quite frequently. For
this reason, it is a great strategy for candidates to include it in their tweets. If it is
coming up frequently, there will be great numbers of Twitter users both checking
it and including it in their tweets. This provides tremendous opportunity to reach
a wider audience. It also attaches Republican candidates to an idea (conservatism)
that is popular among their potential voters.

#TeaParty: The Tea Party was quite a popular movement among conservatives during
the 2010 congressional elections. Thus, any connection to the Tea Party was likely
beneficial for many conservative candidates. This also provides opportunity to reach
a wider audience.

#GOP: This is a general hashtag that will connect the candidate to broader discussion
going on related to the Republican Party.

#ILSen: This is a hashtag that refers to the Illinois Senate. We cited examples of similar
hashtags in Chapters 4 and 5. The idea here is that people doing searches about the
Senate (for Illinois in this case) under this hashtag will find tweets discussing issues
related to the state's Senate delegation, election, or campaign. The interesting thing
here is that candidates from both sides of the aisle may be using this hashtag, so
actual debate and competition for voters can happen in the discussion under these
type hashtags. This makes it important for candidates to use these hashtags so that
they do not lose this battle for voters.

#AZGOP and **#AZRIGHT:** These are two examples of hashtags referring to the Arizona
Republican Party and right-leaning or conservative ideas/people from Arizona.
While the previous hashtag for the Illinois Senate is open to the left and right, this
hashtag seeks to create a more homogenous discussion. Like the Tea Party and Republican Party hashtags described above, these hashtags connect the candidate to
discussions/groups that the candidate is targeting, but unlike those, these are even
more targeted, specifically aimed at potential voters from the candidates' home state.

#AZ01: This is another hashtag from Arizona. It refers to the First Congressional District of Arizona. This is clearly specific to that district and race. Again, this provides
opportunity for the candidate to compete for followers, voters, and attention. It is
key to include hashtags such as this because it directs one's supporters to the discussion falling under this hashtag. The more followers pointed in this direction the
more likely they are to post in the discussion. This can help a candidate to dominate the discussion, or at least the distribution or supporters/opponents, under this
hashtag.

#SOCIALSECURITY: This is clearly a hashtag aimed at discussions centered on social security, an extremely salient issue. While this issue is of particular importance to seniors who are not as likely to be tweeting, it is also relevant to people in their 40s and 50s, who are likely voters and also represent a large share of users who gather political information via Twitter (see Table 3.2). Using a hashtag about a policy issue allows the candidate to feed its followers into the discussion. This can help win over other tweeters who are already in the discussion. A candidate can also use an issue hashtag when they believe they are on the winning side, or more popular side, of the issue. Finally, we think it is good practice to create hashtag discussions centered on issues where the candidate knows they are on the winning side. Altogether, candidates did not seem to use issue hashtags frequently, and most candidates who were tweeting did not use such hashtags. We think this is a missed opportunity to directly control the flow of information. They could use the hashtag discussions to post more information through links that painted the candidate or candidate's position in a favorable light. Perhaps we will see more of this as candidates become more Twitter-savvy.

The final Twitter tool we discuss in this chapter that candidates have at their disposal is the inclusion of links. We think this is probably the most effective way that candidates can control the flow of information and circumvent the gatekeepers in the traditional media. Remember that our primary theoretical assertion is that Twitter provides an opportunity structure that is well-suited for both candidates on the supply side and voters or consumers on the demand side. Consumers tend to want information that reinforces rather than challenges their predispositions avoiding the potential for cognitive dissonance or any resulting discomfort. Candidates want their votes so they are inclined to want to provide them with supportive information. Consumers choose to follow those candidates for whom they are supportive and those candidates then provide them with information that reinforces their predispositions. Twitter facilitates this exchange. Providing links to news stories that are supportive of the candidate allow consumers to gather information without discomfort and builds support for the candidate.

We provide an example of a linked news story in Figure 7.2. This story was linked in a tweet that came from David McKinley, a successful House challenger from West Virginia. The tweet read: So why should I vote for David McKinley for the House of Representatives when he has promised to vote for tax cuts . . . http://fb.me/KYIxFSJY. The link was shared from Facebook and came from the website of the local newspaper in McKinley's district, *The Parkersburg News and Sentinel*. This story is an opposite of the editorial page story (op-ed) and is clearly using a biting sarcastic tone. Its intention is to come from the conservative take on a liberal voice. The story offers a series of traditional conservative critiques of liberal policy (e.g., calls it socialist, big spending, sending jobs overseas, big government). Then it asks the question, "Why should I vote for David McKinley for the House of Representatives?" and replies with standard conservative talking points (e.g., he'll cut taxes, support small business, oppose the national health care bill, and oppose Democrat leadership). The link to this story is a perfect example of how a candidate can provide his followers with information that reinforces their predispositions. The supportive consumer could read this and experience no discomfort.

So why vote for David McKinley?

September 28, 2010

Parkersburg News and Sentinel
Save | ⬜ SHARE ▪ ▪ ▪

A huge out-of-control government is necessary if we really want a socialist government that redistributes wealth. We need a government that spends money we do not have so they can raise taxes to give it to those who really do not want to work or those who live in other countries, because we really don't deserve all we have. We want a government that keeps spending out of control so our children and grandchildren will be so far in debt their standard of living will be less than ours, allowing the rest of the world to catch up. We want a government that rams socialist health care bills down our throats because they know what is best for us. We want a government that will significantly increase our energy costs by passing an energy bill and sending (oil and coal) jobs to other countries that need to grow and raise their standard of living. We want a government that does not support capitalism and the free market because the American dream is an old-fashion idea just for greedy hard-working folks that want to make life better for themselves and their families. We want a government that passes a stimulus bill to give our money to union pension funds, and groups like ACORN, and does not create jobs but puts money into the hands of folks that will keep the present leaders in control. We want a government that will take over our automobile, banks, and insurance companies because the government is so much more efficient and fair in managing industries, just look at Cuba and other third world countries.

So why should I vote for David McKinley for the House of Representatives when he has promised to vote for tax cuts and support small businesses to grow jobs, who will vote against any increase in taxes that raise energy costs and drive jobs out of West Virginia. He will vote to repeal health care, to stop excessive spending and balance our budget. He will oppose the Obama administration efforts to transform America from a free market society based on the Constitution to a socialist one.

If you vote for David McKinley you will be voting against Pelosi, Oliverio, Obama, and Reed – the ones who will transform this great country into a socialist nightmare. It's your choice and this election may be your last!

Fred Dailey

St. Marys

Figure 7.2 Linked News Story/Controlling the Flow of Information.

Republican Challengers Controlling the Flow: The Multivariate Evidence

Finally, we provide the results of the multivariate analysis. We modeled the number of times each candidate included, respectively, a link, an @Twitter name, or a hashtag as a function of party, incumbency, chamber, race (white dummy), district competitiveness, and spending differential.[2] The story here does not significantly change from that being told in Table 7.1 and earlier chapters. Challengers and Republicans appear more likely

Table 7.2 **Models of Information Control via Twitter**

	http	IRR	@	IRR	#	IRR
Republican	0.65***	1.91	0.81***	2.25	1.00***	2.72
	(0.11)		(0.14)		(0.21)	
Incumbency	−0.51***	0.60	−0.53***	0.59	−1.16***	0.31
	(0.11)		(0.14)		(0.21)	
Chamber	0.69***	2.00	0.61**	1.85	0.98***	2.66
	(0.22)		(0.26)		(0.34)	
White	−0.14	—	−0.05	—	−0.05	—
	(0.14)		(0.19)		(0.26)	
District Competitiveness	−0.20	—	−0.10	—	−0.12	—
	(0.17)		(0.21)		(0.27)	
Spending Differential	0.23	—	0.47	—	0.40	—
	(0.19)		(0.32)		(0.43)	
Constant	3.60***	—	2.89***	—	3.26***	—
	(0.24)		(0.33)		(0.43)	
Pseudo R^2	0.02		0.01		0.02	
N	483		483		483	

Note: Data come from www.twitter.com and the Federal Elections Commission. Table entries are negative binomial estimates with associated standard errors in parentheses. IRR are the incident rate ratios. ***$p < 0.01$, **$p < 0.05$, *$p < 0.1$.

to use each of these methods of controlling the flow of information (see Table 7.2). This relationship endures even when controlling for chamber and race, and the introduction of controls for district competitiveness (the absolute value of the difference between the loser and winner in that district in the previous election divided by 500 thousand) and campaign spending differential (the absolute value of the difference between the candidates divided by 10 million). Chamber is the only other significant variable in any of the models, suggesting that use of each of these means of controlling the flow of information increases is more predominant for senators.

Because these models are negative binomial regressions, we include the incident rate ratios. Republicans' number of links is, on average 1.91 times higher than Democrats' number of links. Their number of @Twitter names is 2.25 times higher than Democrats and their number of hashtags is 2.72 times higher. These are relatively large differences. While not as large, the incident rate ratios associated with the estimates for the effects of incumbency are also meaningful. Incumbents' number of links is, on average 0.60 times lower than challengers' number of links. Their number of @Twitter names is 0.59 times lower than challengers and their number of hashtags is 0.31 times lower. The incident rates for chamber are also quite large. The model estimates that senators have 2 times more links in their tweets than House members, 1.85 times more @Twitter names, and 2.66 times more hashtags.

Summary

This chapter further developed our theory on how social media can be used as a tool to help candidates control the flow of information. Further, the empirical groundwork demonstrating that both Republicans and challengers seem to be employing such strategies with more frequency was extended in this chapter. Clearly both are more likely to include links to external information, to include @Twitter names, and to include hashtags in their tweets. This finding holds up ceteris paribus. Altogether this chapter is building toward our primary theoretical and empirical result in Chapter 9 that indicates the types of information control tools described in this chapter are the most effective at garnering votes and that Republicans and challengers benefitted more from the use of these tools than their respective counterparts.

Before moving to the analysis in Chapter 9 of the effectiveness of the tools described in this chapter, we revisit the demand side of the information flow by exploring the implications of heightened social media consumption on public opinion. If we are correct that citizens prefer gathering political information via SNSs because it allows them to avoid information that challenges their predispositions and that politicians are providing them with such information, essentially circumventing traditional information gatekeepers, then we should expect to see some attitudinal effects. In Chapter 8, we, first, develop our theory that explains why heightened SNS use should lead to attitude extremity, and second, empirically evidence this relationship across a series of varied political attitudes.

8

Public Opinion 2.0—The Direct Conduit

Much of the early chapters in this book have been used to establish a framework for how social media fits into the larger political sphere. We have provided descriptive evidence suggesting, first, that a sizable portion of the public use social media to gather political information, and second, that many members of Congress use social media to disseminate political information. We have approached the use of social media from the requirements of both the political actors on the supply side and the SNS users on the demand side to create a structure that documents how information flows through these modern online social networks. We have yet to test and measure the larger implications for the political sphere of this new kind of online social network.

In this chapter, we remedy this absence by conducting an in-depth exploration of the attitudinal implications of SNS use. We return to our foundational premise that politicians are able to circumvent traditional gatekeepers through the use of SNSs, and that this strategy is effective because their constituents are open to one-sided information flows due to their desire to avoid cognitive dissonance or any discomfort that may arise from exposure to information that challenges their predispositions. In this chapter, we build on the findings from Chapter 2, where we presented a model supporting the premise that those who prefer one-sided information were more likely to gather political information through social media. Here we examine whether increased consumption of political information through social media results in crystallized and more extreme attitudes. Subsequently, we test the effects of this attitude extremity and whether it promotes political participation.

Understanding how people organize and understand the information they consume is an area of considerable study in political science. There are two dominant theoretical perspectives focused on how people obtain and process information. Both approaches were outlined in earlier chapters, but we will expand that analysis here. The first approach is to understand that individual attitudes are made up of the averaging of considerations that people have cognitively accessible (Zaller 1992). Alternatively, people keep a running tally of their views and these considerations are constantly being updated based on the information available to them (Bizer et al. 2006; Hastie and Park 1986; Lodge and Taber 2000).

SNSs provide an opportunity structure for politicians to have a more direct role in providing the information for either model. Using SNSs, people can avoid the filter imposed by the traditional media gatekeepers as well as avoid having their preferred flow of information juxtaposed against ideas, facts, or beliefs that are inconsistent with their own and would otherwise cause them discomfort. This is a particularly desirable outcome for both the politician and their constituents. The politician wields more influence by replacing traditional media as the sources of information, and the consumer avoids cognitive and affective discomfort by allowing a more visceral approach to guide them in favoring certain networks of information. We develop this theory further in this chapter by considering how these cognitive models work together to explain information processing and public opinion, and how this translates in the online environment.

The empirical tests in this chapter are based on the data from Pew Research. The empirical results presented here are fairly direct and not complex. They indicate that those who consume more political information via SNSs have more extreme attitudes. As we have theorized that consumers wish to avoid information that challenges their predispositions, this is what we would expect to find. Further, this self-selection of information may be facilitated through social media by political candidates who presumably build support while effectively stimulating the push toward more extreme attitudes. If those with more extreme attitudes are more likely to participate in the political process, then those who use SNSs more frequently should be more likely to politically participate as well. The results confirm this expectation. Thus, not only is the opportunity provided for candidates to help shape potential voters' attitudes, but social media provides the opportunity to stimulate actual support at the voting booth.

Social Media: One Side Is Enough

Zaller (1992) argues that the considerations people rely on to form opinions largely come from the media, and the balance of the information flow from the media can be characterized by how tilted it is to the left or the right. He suggests that the popular media consists primarily of two information flows: one from the left, or liberal, side and one from the right, or conservative, side. The relative distribution of the flow has varied across time. When there were few media outlets, the information flow was two-sided, representing both views so as to appeal to the large, diverse audience. In the modern media age with multiple cable networks, the information flow is increasingly one-sided as it appeals to a very specific audience (Prior 2007).

More than even cable news, social media presents a unique opportunity for candidates to provide potential voters with a one-sided information flow. This view is an extension of our initial views of the role of the Internet in information distribution. In our earlier work, we proposed that the Internet in general creates multiple one-sided information flows (Gainous and Wagner 2011). We presented evidence that people who preferred one-sided information were more likely to gather political information via the Internet, were more likely to gather information from one-sided sources,[1] and that those who gathered more information from one-sided sources were more likely to participate politically (Gainous and Wagner 2011). The addition of the increasing use of SNSs is a natural theoretical extension of this approach. Social media simplifies the gathering of one-sided information for consumers because they can self-select who and what to follow just as cable television made it easier for selectivity of partisan-biased news (Arceneaux and Johnson 2013; Prior 2007) and the Internet in general makes self-selection easier (Bimber and Davis 2003). Likewise, candidates can capitalize on this opportunity by providing information to networks of consumers, already organized by their predispositions, that fits into their preexisting political views.

Before detailing our explanation of the relationship between ideological information flows, it is important to clarify Zaller's (1992) treatment of information flows. He begins his examination by exploring one-sided communications. He uses survey data from the American National Election Studies to demonstrate that contextual changes in the flow of information correlated with shifts in public opinion. Specifically, his evidence showed that the generally one-sided (negative) coverage of elite discourse surrounding the Iran-Contra scandal in the 1980s corresponded with decreasing evaluations of President Reagan. The data indicated that public opinion became more polarized as elite discourse, as covered in the popular media, became more partisan or ideological. Zaller proposes that the stability of public opinion is largely a product of the balance of information flows. He contends that, in most cases, there exists not a one-sided flow, but rather a dominant message and a countervailing message. His theory suggests that people's resistance to the dominant message is shaped by the relative intensities of the messages. Further, that people's own personal characteristics such as ideological predisposition, political awareness, and values condition their receptiveness to both the dominant and countervailing message (Zaller 1992).

In our previous work, we argued that the Internet disrupts the two-sided information flow for individuals, making the resistance to dominant or countervailing views unnecessary because of the ease in self-selecting the media information on the Internet (Bimber and Davis 2003); one-sided information can be selected at virtually no cost (Gainous and Wagner 2011). There may still be a two-sided information flow in traditional media outlets, but the Internet allows people the opportunity to tune to the side they prefer. Social media maximizes the ability to select information by predisposition and preference. Social media creates multiple one-sided information flows, including a liberal one and a conservative one, providing people the freedom to select which information and viewpoint to consume. This we posit creates two basic sequential premises: (1) SNSs allow people to choose whom to friend/follow, and (2) SNSs serve as a *selective* political news/information aggregator. As people can choose who and what to follow, their personalized SNSs will provide political news and information for them in a central location that compiles it from multiple sources biased to their views. The SNS, as a selective aggregator, essentially provides individuals with one side of the information flow, the side that conforms to their predispositions.

The power of social media rests largely in the networks that people join and construct. The building of these social networks online is fairly straightforward. SNSs allow people to choose whom to friend/follow. As a result of this fact, people likely tend to friend/follow others with whom they are familiar and comfortable and who usually share their point of view. This is a behavior which is consistent with a large body of literature suggesting that people employ selectivity when choosing news information to consume (see Arceneaux and Johnson 2013 for a complete review). As they are motivated to avoid being exposed to information that challenges their predispositions, people seek out networks with information consistent with their preexisting beliefs (Festinger 1957; Fischer et al. 2005; Fischer, Schulz-Hardt, and Frey 2008; Frey 1986; Sears and Freedman 1967). As a result, people are essentially drawn toward attitude-consistent news (e.g., Garrett 2009a, 2009b; Garrett, Carnahan, and Lynch 2013; Iyengar and

Hahn 2009; Iyengar et al. 2008; Mutz and Martin 2001; Stroud 2008, 2011). We have no reason to expect selectivity to be different when deciding which information to consume via social media.

The underlying reasons that motivate people to seek out attitude-consistent information generally are based in part on human nature. A hedonic motivation exists to seek out pleasure and avoid pain. This idea is threaded through the basic motivational assumption theories across all areas of psychology (see Higgins 1997). Theories of emotion in psychobiology (e.g., Gray 1982), conditioning in animal learning (e.g., Mowrer 1960; Thorndike 1935), decision-making in cognitive and organizational psychology (e.g., Dutton and Jackson 1987; Edwards 1955; Kahneman and Tversky 1979), attitude consistency in social psychology (e.g., Festinger 1957; Heider 1958), and achievement motivation in personality (e.g., Atkinson 1964), all use this basic premise as a lens from which to make sense out of observations. If we accept the premise that people are compelled to seek out pleasure and avoid discomfort, it makes sense that they would tend to read, follow, and engage in exchanges with those people who share their point of view. It is also reasonable to believe that such behavior would continue in the social media where it can be more easily accomplished.

The application of this approach to information consumption online is more limited. While there is limited research regarding the motivations for political information consumption via social media, a fair amount of evidence about Internet discourse in general is consistent with the approach that people are using motivated reasoning that involves seeking attitude-consistent information. They are also avoiding attitude inconsistent information on the Internet as well. For instance, the research focusing largely on chat rooms and general online discussion forums has suggested that the Internet provides echo chambers where like-minded people are exposed to one-sided arguments that reinforce their initial predispositions (Davis 1999; Hill and Hughes 1998; Sunstein 2002; Van Alstyne, Marshal and Brynjolfsson 1995; Wilhelm 2000; Wojcieszak 2006; Wojcieszak and Mutz 2009).

When given the chance, people will organize themselves into smaller units that share some degree of political or ideological consistency. The evidence suggests that "birds of a feather flock together." We contend that SNSs may facilitate this process, with greater magnitude, because of the popularity of sites such as Facebook and Twitter. While it is true that people are exposed to a variety of perspectives via their lists of friends/followers, people are often selective about whom to actually pay attention. They will even remove themselves from networks that consistently post information that causes discomfort. This will become more important when we discuss how social media websites organize News Feeds and further explicate the use of EdgeRank (mentioned in Chapter 2) by Facebook as a means of connecting people with the people they interact with the most.

Not only can people ignore the postings from friends and followers who do not share their point of view but they may also choose to simply eliminate those who disagree with them from their SNS profile. The following Facebook status update is a piece of anecdotal evidence to suggest that this practice takes place: "Going on an 'un-friend' rampage. . . . I might have to be tolerant of your views in real-life, but I don't need to subject myself to your stupidity on social media. Goodbye!"[2] Unfriending is simply a practice where people can remove people from their list of friends on Facebook. They may also choose to hide people's postings from their News Feed, which does not eliminate them from one's list of friends but it prevents their postings from showing up. There is no way to judge how common these practices are without surveying, but the frequency of unfriending/hiding is not as important as one would think. Increasingly, the SNSs are sorting your information for you based on your preferences so that unfriending is not always necessary to avoid the postings of those who have a different point of view. On Facebook, EdgeRank essentially keeps most of them out of one's News Feed, as the algorithm quite efficiently picks up on the information and people you like and brings them to you.

The efficiency of the SNSs in organizing information to suit one's preferences creates a much tailored news channel for the user, allowing SNSs to serve as personalized news aggregators. More directly, SNSs serve as a *selective* political news/information aggregator. It is reasonable to expect that the political news or information that citizens consume is largely determined by the available options. Since the advent of the Internet, the breadth of options has considerably broadened, and social media serves as a tool that selectively aggregates these options for consumers. Not only do SNSs serve as echo chambers because people selectively choose who to follow, but they also structure what information people are exposed to for the same reason.

It is quite common for Facebook and Twitter users to post news stories. In the same way that our earlier evidence indicated that congressional candidates tend to post news stories that painted them in a positive light, citizens are likely to post news stories that share their point of view. This makes individuals' SNS pages serve as a sort of news aggregator but one that tends to be biased. The postings themselves are part of the information flow that each user creates for themselves and can fairly regularly prune if they choose. Users can very easily ignore the postings originating from friends/followers who do not share their point of view.

There is a fair amount of research on news aggregators, but the assertion that SNS pages can, in effect, fill this same role is a novel assertion on our part. Most popular news sites on the Internet are owned and operated by the same major conglomerates that run the major television and print outlets along with news aggregators (Freedman 2006; Prior 2007; Sparks 2000; Stanyer 2008). These news aggregators do not produce their own content. They, essentially, compile material from other news agencies. Much of the content is drawn from traditional outlets. While this is convenient for users, this type of news delivery on the Internet is static and beyond the user's control. Online news aggregators have done little to change the content of information that people acquire as it is all still sourced from traditional outlets (Gainous and Wagner 2011).

In a news aggregator website, we would expect a typical two-sided information flow as opposed to two one-sided flows from the left and right (Gainous and Wagner 2011). This is largely based on journalists from traditional outlets trying to maintain some kind of "objectivity" consistent with a code of journalistic ethics. Management and ownership also generally prefer this approach so that they may reach a wider audience (Bennett 2004). Social media, as a news aggregator, changes the content of information to which people are exposed because the users are the gatekeepers. They can select stories that are tilted toward their predispositions, from any kind of information source online, including blogs, videos, and even websites created to push a political viewpoint. They can even self-select one-sided information from major outlets. Editorials from major

outlets are generally either liberal or conservative, as can be seen clearly with their candidate endorsements (Druckman and Parkin 2005; Kahn and Kenney 2002).

Research has suggested that the Internet enables people to avoid broader surveys
of the news for increasingly specific and focused distributions and analysis of an issue
(Tewksbury 2005; Tewksbury and Rittenberg 2008). This kind of *specialization,* the
desire for news and information focused on one smaller issue lends itself to one-sided
information flows. Focusing on them is made even easier for the consumer by social
media. If they are able, people tend to focus their attention on specific topics (Tewksbury and Rittenberg 2008) and they can connect with people who share interests in
similar topics. The whole idea of SNSs contributing to specialization as a news aggregator is facilitated by two factors: (1) on Facebook and Twitter, people choose who to
follow, and (2) on Facebook, the EdgeRank algorithm facilitates self-selection, even if
that was not the user's goal.

The argument that people intentionally choose one-sided information is likely to be
unpopular. The desire to be seen as open-minded or moderate is a consistent mindset
among Americans (Fiorina and Abrams 2009). We suspect that arguing that people want
one-sided information itself would cause discomfort among users and relegate us to the
bottom of some networks or out of others. Interestingly, SNSs are solving that problem
for users by self-selecting one-sided information for them. On Facebook, EdgeRank
works with user behavior to construct a more palatable News Feed. People both choose
who to friend and which postings to read from those whom they choose. The EdgeRank
algorithm then determines which friends with whom one most frequently interacts. This
is judged by what posts one reads or whose pages one views. Facebook then organizes a
user's News Feed so as to favor posts from people with whom the user has shown interest.

The process is essentially based on the use of an affinity score, a weight, and a time
decay calculation to determine who ends up in one's News Feed. Affinity is based on actions taken by the user such as clicking on postings, liking, commenting, tagging, sharing, and friending. Each of these actions is then assigned a weight based on the level
of interactivity (e.g., clicking "like" is weighted less than posting an actual comment).
Finally, those actions that happened more recently are weighted more.[3] Thus, if one is
most likely to interact with those who share their point of view, then those who share
their point of view are most likely to end up on one's News Feed. This means that the
News Feed serves as a selective news aggregator that may also lead to specialization because of shared interest in issues.

The online information universe is more complex than many people understand.
Social media make it easier for people to select information that is consistent with their
predispositions because they can choose who and what to follow. Even users who would
avoid such behavior are pushed to it by social media outlets such as Facebook, which
uses algorithms to infer what people's preferences are by monitoring who and what they
follow. In the end, people are increasingly provided with information that better fits
their preferences than would occur from a standard news aggregator, or an even more
random distribution, or a simple chronological distribution of their friends' postings.
SNSs serve the role of a news aggregator, but more selectively than other websites have
performed in the past.[4] The remaining question centers on understanding the attitudinal
implications of this phenomenon. We address this below by further detailing how the
consumption of one-sided information should lead to more extreme political attitudes.

Social Media, Information Gathering, and Attitude Extremity

In the previous section, we argued that social media helps to create a one-sided information flow. In this section, we address the attitudinal consequences of such a media environment. In doing so, we will detail our cognitive model which relies heavily on existing models: the Receive-Accept-Sample Model (RAS) and the Online Processing Model (OPM) (Lodge 1995; Lodge, McGraw, and Stroh 1989; Lodge, Steenbergen, and Brau 1995; McGraw, Lodge, and Stroh 1990; Zaller 1992; Zaller and Feldman 1992).[5] Using these approaches, we theorize that people's attitudes are based on the information they have cognitively available at any given moment in time, and much of this information comes from the media. We further posit that the self-selection of information online, after the selection of who and what to follow has been made, is based both on memory (RAS), and the processing of information, best described as a summation of a running tally of that information (OPM). We are mostly concerned with how the one-sided flow of information coming from social media shapes these attitudes. If people are consuming one-sided information, their attitudes will reflect as such.[6] Below we describe both models, discuss how the two models can be merged,[7] and then elucidate on how this shapes our expectations regarding the effects of social media.

Taber (2003) eloquently describes the memory-based model asserted by Zaller and the online model asserted by Lodge and his colleagues (Lodge, McGraw, and Stroh 1989; Lodge, Steenbergen, and Brau 1995; Lodge 1995). What is so important about Taber's (2003) description of these models to our approach is that he asserts that they are not inconsistent with each other, that the literature's frequent presentation of these models as competing is both inaccurate and unproductive. We concur with his interpretation and will outline why below after describing each of the models. Before doing so, we briefly outline the history behind the development of these models, as it is critical to a full understanding of how they explain the nature of attitudes and the implications of online social media.

The baseline assumption of all political attitudinal models is that people develop and maintain political attitudes. While the possibility that this is not true may seem unlikely, scholars of public opinion are well aware that this idea is central to the development of our understanding of political public opinion. The argument was never really about the possibility that attitudes were nonexistent, but rather it was about the possibility that many people, particularly those who were not attentive to politics and public affairs, did develop any consistent attitudes concerning many political issues (nonattitude). This belief was evidenced by the instability of opinion in surveys and by the lack of constraint or consistency shown between people's various attitudes (Converse 1964). It took nearly 30 years for scholarship to offer explanations of attitude instability that became widely accepted alternatives.[8] It is from this base of research that information processing models such as RAS and OPM were developed.

Both RAS and OPM assume that people hold actual reasoned attitudes. The real distinction between the two is centered on how they treat people's reliance on long-term memory to form opinions. The RAS model and other memory based models assume that people do not simply retrieve and report attitudes from memory, but rather they construct an attitude from the range of considerations that they can draw from their long-term memory at the time they are being prompted to report some kind of attitude (Martin and Tesser 1992; Tourangeau, Rips, and Rasinski 2000; Zaller and Feldman 1992; Zaller 1992). Zaller and Feldman (1992) assert that people are drawing from a range of considerations that may come into conflict, and this explains survey response instability. The model suggests that people are weighing the pros and cons of a given position based on stored memory and formulating an opinion (Taber 2003). Alternatively, the OPM suggests that "citizens spontaneously extract the evaluative implications of political information as soon as they are exposed to it, integrate these implications into an ongoing summary counter or running tally, and then proceed to forget the descriptive details of the information" (Lavine 2002, 227). The largest distinction between the models is how people store and draw information from memory. Either people are making a running tally and summing across those considerations that are relevant at the time (OPM), or they are using long-term stored memory to make a judgment (RAS).

Taber (2003) argues that these two models are not necessarily inconsistent. He suggests that memory-based models are typically seen as more applicable to complex attitude objects (e.g., multidimensional issue positions) and online models being more applicable to simpler objects like candidate evaluations. His argument is that researchers have picked unrealistic extremes to demonstrate the variance in applicability of these models. Simply, concerning the OPM, he contends that it is unrealistic to believe that people would not have the necessary ingredients in their long-term memory to weigh the evaluative implications of new information (Taber 2003). Essentially, these models assume that stored information is forgotten or at least not accessible on the spot. Concerning memory-based models, he argues that it is also unrealistic to believe that people "refrain from all evaluation of information at the time of exposure; such an organism would have no ability to resist persuasion or otherwise maintain beliefs through time" (Taber 2003, 453). We agree with Taber that a far more plausible theoretical explanation of people's evaluative process is found in hybrid models of these two perspectives (see Hastie and Pennington 1989; Sherpenzeel and Saris 1997). These hybrid models suggest that the online process may create evaluative tags or short-term heuristics and the degree to which long-term memory considerations shape one's opinion may be contingent on how strong these tags are (Lavine 2002).

So what does this mean for how people process new information coming from their social media exposure? We posit that people's attitudes are made up of the mix of considerations that people have and these considerations are also a mix of both long-term memory such as values, party identification, and personal experience and short-term memory consisting of recent experience such as new stories and conversations with others about a topic. As a result, information coming from and through social media is influenced in two ways. From the RAS, we would posit that long-held positions will be influential in the selection bias that people will bring online. The choice of what information to consume is likely shaped by predispositions rooted in long-term memory. These more stable considerations will help determine the social network that a person creates or joins. The OPM model informs more of the daily activity people will engage in through social media. It will have its strongest impact through developing immediate attitudes, which will affect the running assessment that an individual has about political actors or policies. The influence that this new information has on one's overall attitude will depend on how strong the tag is relative to the stored long-term memory for relevant considerations (Lavine 2002).

Lavine (2002) asserts that one of the reasons issue attitudes may become more online (OPM) as opposed to memory-based (RAS), is that they are at the center of the debate where they are subject to regular updating. We agree and contend that once people are using the Internet, social media provides a mechanism to push people toward more online processing. It provides a direct conduit for information at the center of national debate. In fact, as we have seen in previous chapters, candidates facilitate the dissemination of this information focusing on a range of issues and attitude objects. That said, we believe that the degree to which this new information affects people's overall summaries is contingent on their initial predispositions, both because they will self-select information that is consistent with their long-term predispositions and the overall effect of new information on their running tallies is shaped by the bias of the new information (and stored information) they are consuming.

Taken altogether, the memory-based model (RAS) likely determines people's self-selection of who to follow and what information to consume. People have a long-term memory that determines their party identification and ideology and these factors shape who and what people follow. Once this selection is made, however, new information about issues relevant to current discourse shapes opinion and is likely explained by the OPM. People keep a running tally of information and SNSs can feed this running tally, determining how people sum up their attitudes. Based on the above, consuming information via SNSs may not have as large an effect on long-term predispositions such as ideology or party identification but could have a much greater impact on positions at the center of current political discourse. The Pew data allow us to test these premises. We have data on ideological extremity and data on attitudes about the Tea Party and the federal government in general, two topics at the center of the debate in the 2010 elections.

If people are conducting a running tally of information and which information they consume is based on long-term predispositions, additional information introduced into the ongoing tally should continue to push people's attitudes toward the existing bias. Simply, people are consuming one-sided information based on their predispositions and when this information is added to the existing information, the result is crystallization of the bias. Thus, heightened information consumption via social media should lead to more extreme attitudes.

Attitude Extremity and Political Participation

The preceding two sections established, first, that social media helps create a one-sided information flow, and second, that, theoretically, the attitudinal consequence should be a push to more extreme attitudes at the individual level. In this section we address the behavioral consequences, arguing that those with more extreme attitudes are more likely to politically participate. Thus, the one-sided flow that SNSs facilitate as selective news aggregators may have a normative consequence that many Americans value and appreciate: civic engagement. This is consistent with the social capital argument presented in Chapter 6, that heightened social media use stimulates political participation, but for an entirely different reason. We outline in this section why someone with a more extreme attitude should be more likely to politically participate.

Our previous research argued that the consumption of one-sided information via the Internet would stimulate political participation because it would lead to more extreme attitudes, and those with extreme attitudes are more likely to participate (Gainous and Wagner 2011). We did not test whether the consumption of one-sided information actually did stimulate attitude extremity or whether that extremity was associated with the propensity to participate. Rather, we demonstrated that those who sought out one-sided information were more likely to vote. Here we test both of these premises, but rely largely on the same theoretical framework with the extension to social media. The social media is largely a one-sided information flow, and we will show below how the consumption of one-sided information should stimulate participation.

While we contend that social media will ultimately alter the internal calculus concerning why people politically participate, we do not reject the well-developed literature centered on the socioeconomic drivers of political participation. There are several schools of thought among this literature. Verba, Schlozman, and Brady (1995) organized these separate schools into what they called the *civic volunteerism model*. This model classifies the different influences on participation into three distinct categories: (1) personal characteristics, (2) group effects, and (3) political attitudes. Concerning personal characteristics, political scientists argue that income and education help develop the skills and orientations that facilitate the ability to engage the system (Nie, Junn, and Stehlik-Barry 1996; Verba, Schlozman, and Brady 1995) and that other personal characteristics such as gender (Norris 2002) and race (Leighley and Vedlitz 1999; Verba et al. 1993) may also stimulate political participation. As argued in Gainous and Wagner (2011) and in Chapter 6 of this book, the Internet and particularly social media may create a group effect that encourages political participation by building social capital via social networking (Putnam 1995a, 1995b, 2000; Putnam, Feldstein, and Cohen 2003). Our earlier work proposed that one-sided information flows via the Internet stimulated political participation by influencing political attitudes such as partisan attachment and ideology (Gainous and Wagner 2011). We extend and revise this premise here by building on our argument that, because of partisan and ideological predispositions, people who consume information through SNSs are likely to have crystallized and more extreme attitudes, and as a result of these attitudes, they are more likely to participate.

As described earlier, people's predispositions are likely shaped by the flow of information they consume or are exposed to through social media. Social media is disrupting a two-sided information flow at the individual level for the consumer, resulting in the consumption of a one-sided flow. If this is occurring and causing the crystallization of attitudes, people should be less likely to be ambivalent or confused about issues or candidates. Rather, exposure to the one-sided flow likely encourages satisfaction with the side being positively presented and dissatisfaction with the opposing side (Gainous and Wagner 2011). Such satisfaction and dissatisfaction can encourage participation (Dalton 2006). Those satisfied may vote to continue the government's current direction and those dissatisfied may vote to change it. Dalton (2006) presents direct evidence that ideological extremists and strong partisans are more likely to participate politically. If social media consumption can crystallize attitudes leading to more extremity and these attitudes are a predictor of participation, then the inherent transitive property tells us that social media consumption should stimulate political participation. This suggests that in addition to the evidence presented in Chapter 6, suggesting that there is a direct relationship between social media consumption and participation (through the building of social capital), there is another way that social media consumption can encourage political participation. We model these effects below.

Modeling the Effects of SNS Consumption

The analysis that follows has three distinct components. First, we examine the bivariate relationship between the use of social media to gather political information and attitude extremity in general. Second, we examine how well this relationship holds up and whether the effect of political SNS use varies across specific attitudes ceteris paribus. This latter part of the test allows us to make inferences about whether the mechanism of influence is best explained by a memory-based model or online model. Third, we test whether attitude extremity has a positive relationship with political participation, again ceteris paribus. For the first test, we look at the relationship between the Guttman scale of the political use of SNSs used in Chapter 2 and an attitude extremity index using a graphical display (including an interpretation of the descriptive results). For the second set of tests we model, in five separate models, ideological extremity, Tea Party awareness, support for the Tea Party, anger with the federal government, and the attitude extremity index as a function of the Guttman scale of political SNS use, Internet use in general, partisanship strength, age, education, income, race, and gender. For the final tests we model both online political participation and voting (see the Appendix for operationalization),[9] in two separate models, as a function of the attitude extremity index, political attentiveness, partisanship strength, age, education, income, race, and gender.

For political SNS use we rely on the Guttman index described in Chapter 2. The index incorporates the use of both Facebook and Twitter to gather political information without the loss of cases because only people who used the SNSs were asked whether they used it to gather political information. Theoretically, we believe that the combination of Facebook and Twitter use would increase the effects, but dropping all the cases unless they had used both would bias the results. Thus, the Guttman approach provided a suitable solution.

The Pew data offer four suitable measures of attitude extremity. The first is a five-point indicator of ideology ranging from very liberal to very conservative. We folded this scale to measure ideological extremity. Those who are on the poles of the scale are grouped together in the highest response category. Those who claim to be liberal or conservative but not at the extreme are in the middle response category, and those who are moderate are in the lowest category. Second, we measured awareness of the Tea Party using a question that asked how much respondents had heard about the Tea Party (nothing at all, a little, a lot). While this is not inherently a measure of attitude extremity, we contend that the measure has validity since the Tea Party is on the extreme right of the American political spectrum, and if people are gathering more information via SNSs, then they are being exposed to more one-sided information. This is certainly the weakest of our indicators of attitude extremity, but due to the fact that there are limited possible indicators of attitude extremity in these data, we decided to include it and let readers see the relationship.

Next, we included a folded four-point scale of gauging how strongly people agree with the Tea Party. Those who strongly agreed or disagreed with the Tea Party were grouped together, and those who simply agreed or disagreed were grouped together. This creates a measure of attitude extremity about the Tea Party. Finally, we have a measure of anger with the federal government ranging from basically content, to frustrated, to angry. This is a three-point ordinal scale that did not need to be folded. Our contention is that angry is more extreme than basically content, and frustrated is somewhere in between. Finally, we construct an index of these four items to create a measure of overall attitude extremity. Each of the items were rescaled to range between 0 and 1 and then added together.

The graph in Figure 8.1 plots where those below the mean on the political SNS and Twitter Guttman scale fall on average on the attitude extremity index against where those who are above the mean fall. Additionally, there is a reference line for the mean attitude extremity for the full sample (0.50). This allows us to see if there is a general bivariate positive relationship between SNS/Twitter political use and attitude extremity. The pattern is clear. Those who use SNSs such as Facebook and Twitter to gather political information generally possess more extreme attitudes across the four indicators we used here. The mean on the index for those below the mean on the SNS/Twitter use scale was about 0.49 and it was about 0.54 for those above the mean.[10] Thus, those who use social media less frequently are only slightly below the mean attitude extremity (0.50) and those who use it more frequently are considerably above the mean attitude extremity. This relationship was highly significant (p < 0.001). This does not necessarily

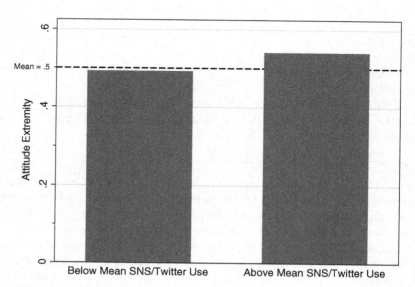

Figure 8.1 Political SNS/Twitter Use and Attitude Extremity. Source: 2010 Pew Internet & American Life Project Post-Election Survey.

mean that there is a causal relationship between the two. That said, a multivariate model would provide support to this argument.

While the descriptive results presented in Figure 8.1 are informative, they do not tell us if the observed positive relationships hold up in the face of alternative explanations. We turn to multivariate models to test for such. The results here, as presented in Table 8.1, are clear. Using SNSs and Twitter to gather political information has a significant positive effect on attitude extremity across all these items, with the exception of the folded ideology scale, ceteris paribus. This provides evidence that the effect that gathering information via these outlets has on attitudes is likely best described as an online process. It is not likely that ideology, a memory-based value, would fluctuate as new information is being obtained and processed. That said, we do not think this means that memory-based assessments have nothing to do with the process. People tend to self-select the people and the issues that they follow according to their memory-based predispositions. Thus, the availability of the information that is being cognitively processed online is conditional on one's self-selection, which is guided by a memory-based evaluation.

The magnitudes of the various effects presented in Table 8.1, are worth noting. While holding party identification, race, income, and education constant, the Guttman scale increases the odds of being higher on the awareness of the Tea Party indicator by 1.35 times, on the folded agreement with the Tea Party indicator by 1.14 times, on the anger with the federal government indicator by 1.15 times, and finally, on the attitude extremity index by 1.21 times. It is important to remember that models are estimating these results while holding alternative explanations of attitude extremity constant. As evidenced in Table 8.1 several of those alternative explanations are significant. We controlled for general Internet use (same operationalization as previous chapters) because we want to make sure that the observed effect was consistent for the average Internet user and that it was not only for those who have heightened Internet use in general. There was only a positive and significant relationship between this variable and awareness of the Tea Party.

The next control, and perhaps most the important one because it directly addresses the most significant alternative explanation of attitude extremity, is partisanship strength (operationalization is included in the Appendix). We suspect that stronger partisans, Democrat or Republican, would tend to have more extreme attitudes. The results generally confirm this expectation. The relationship is insignificant only in the awareness of the Tea Party model and is negative in the anger with the federal government model. This latter result is clearly a product of the variance of Democrats and Republicans with regards to general ideological support for government as a solution to problems. Liberals tend to be more supportive and conservatives are less supportive (see Gainous 2012).

Finally, we held constant a series of demographic indicators to assure that the observed effect could not be explained away by group attitude differences. Age was positively related to awareness of the Tea Party and anger with the federal government. Education was positively related to awareness of the Tea Party. Income was negatively related to the folded ideology scale and positively related to awareness of the Tea Party. Blacks and Asians tended to have less anger with the federal government and extreme attitudes generally. Latinos were less aware of the Tea Party. Finally, females were less ideologically extreme, aware of the Tea Party, and had less extreme attitudes generally.

Table 8.1 **Models of Attitude Extremity**

	Ideology Folded	Odds Ratios	Aware Tea Party	Odds Ratios	Agree Tea Party Folded	Odds Ratios	Anger Federal Government	Odds Ratios	Attitude Extremity Index	Odds Ratios
Pol SNS/Tw	0.08	—	0.30***	1.35	0.13**	1.14	0.14***	1.15	0.19***	1.21
	(0.05)		(0.06)		(0.06)		(0.05)		(0.05)	
Internet Use	−0.02	—	0.05***	1.05	0.02	—	−0.01	—	−0.01	—
	(0.02)		(0.02)		(0.03)		(0.02)		(0.02)	
Partisanship Strength	0.59***	1.81	0.09	—	0.39**	1.48	−0.29**	0.75	0.44***	1.55
	(0.12)		(0.12)		(0.17)		(0.12)		(0.14)	
Age	−0.03	—	0.69***	2.00	0.12	—	0.33***	1.40	0.08	—
	(0.08)		(0.08)		(0.13)		(0.08)		(0.11)	
Education	0.04	—	0.48***	1.61	0.16	—	−0.11	—	0.11	—
	(0.07)		(0.07)		(0.11)		(0.08)		(0.09)	
Income	−0.15**	0.86	0.37***	1.44	−0.02	—	0.07	—	0.00	—
	(0.07)		(0.08)		(0.12)		(0.11)		(0.09)	
Black	−0.25	—	−0.21	—	0.02	—	−0.72***	0.49	−0.62**	0.54
	(0.20)		(0.19)		(0.30)		(0.21)		(0.26)	
Latino	0.10	—	−0.49***	0.61	0.01	—	−0.14	—	−0.20	—
	(0.18)		(0.19)		(0.37)		(0.21)		(0.30)	

Table 8.1 (continued)

	Ideology Folded	Odds Ratios	Aware Tea Party	Odds Ratios	Agree Tea Party Folded	Odds Ratios	Anger Federal Government	Odds Ratios	Attitude Extremity Index	Odds Ratios
Asian	-0.22	—	-0.43	—	-0.41	—	-1.18***	0.31	-0.84*	0.43
	(0.35)		(0.35)		(0.58)		(0.40)		(0.46)	
Female	-0.28***	0.76	-0.34***	0.71	-0.01	—	-0.15	—	-0.36***	0.69
	(0.10)		(0.11)		(0.15)		(0.12)		(0.13)	
Pseudo R²	0.02		0.10		0.02		0.02		0.01	
N	1583		1583		811		1583		811	

Note: Data come from the 2010 Pew Internet & American Life Project Post-Election Survey. Table entries are ordered-logit (threshold values suppressed) and logit estimates (constant estimate = –2.00, S.D. = 0.58, p = 0.00) based on all Internet users (except for the Agree Tea Party Folded where only cases who responded affirmatively to being aware of the Tea Party were used because the others were filtered out of this question by Pew), with associated standard errors in parentheses, and odds ratios.

***p < 0.01, **p < 0.05, *p < 0.1.

Table 8.2 **Modeling Political Participation as a Function of Attitude Extremity**

	Online Participation	IRR	Vote	OR
Attitude Extremity	0.85**	2.34	1.51***	4.57
	(0.44)		(0.52)	
Attentiveness	0.59***	3.27	0.17	—
	(0.11)		(0.13)	
Partisanship Strength	−0.12	—	0.12	—
	(0.19)		(0.22)	
Age	0.07	—	1.25***	3.48
	(0.14)		(0.17)	
Education	0.11	—	0.30**	1.35
	(0.13)		(0.13)	
Income	−0.01	—	0.22	—
	(0.13)		(0.14)	
Black	−0.02	—	0.02	—
	(0.34)		(0.35)	
Latino	0.04	—	−0.23	—
	(0.38)		(0.42)	
Asian	−0.29	—	−0.29	—
	(0.72)		(0.58)	
Female	0.12	—	−0.04	—
	(0.18)		(0.20)	
Constant	−3.55***	—	−3.07***	
	(0.69)		(0.72)	
Pseudo R^2	0.06		0.12	
N	811		811	

Note: Data come from the 2010 Pew Internet & American Life Project Post-Election Survey. Table entries are Poisson estimates in the online participation model and ordered-logit estimates in the vote model based on respondents who use the Internet at least occasionally and were aware of the Tea Party, with associated standard errors in parentheses, and incident rate ratios (IRR)/odds ratios (OR). ***$p < 0.01$, **$p < 0.05$, *$p < 0.1$.

The final evidence we present in this chapter is contained in Table 8.2. It is here where we test if attitude extremity is a stimulant for political participation. The previous results in Table 8.1 indicated that gathering political information via SNSs such as Facebook and Twitter leads to more extreme attitudes. Thus, if attitude extremity stimulates participation, the transitive property would suggest that heightened use of SNSs to gather political information would stimulate political participation. We already know this to be the case from the results presented in Chapter 6, but the two-step process presented here provides a test of whether there is also an intervening variable.

The results indicate that there is a positive and significant relationship. There is a strong relationship between attitude extremity and the propensity to participate online and to vote. In fact, the incident rate ratio derived from the Poisson regression estimate suggests that every one unit increase in attitude extremity increases the number of political participatory acts people claimed to have done by 2.3 times. Likewise, the voting model estimate suggests that a one unit increase in attitude extremity increased the odds of voting by 4.57 times. The control variables across the models were largely unrelated to the outcomes with the exception of positive relationships of attentiveness in the online participation model[11], age in the voting model, and education in the voting model. We are not particularly concerned about the general insignificance of the controls. We primarily have them in the model to assure that the observed effects are consistent while holding these variables constant. Many of them are actually significant when the models are estimated without creating subsamples for those who were asked all of the questions used to make the attitude extremity and online participation indices.

Summary

This chapter built a theoretical model for understanding why heightened social media use is likely to lead to attitude extremity. The model is built around the idea that people self-select the people and issues to follow based on avoiding the discomfort that may result from exposure to information inconsistent with one's predispositions. This guides the information to which consumers are exposed, and as a result shapes the information they use to form an opinion. In addition, we suggested that this process was likely guided by both ideas and views established in long-term memory and through an online cognitive process. People self-select based on ingrained long-term predispositions and then process new information through a running tally. We then provided empirical evidence that heightened SNS use to gather political information was predictive of attitude extremity on issues that would be centered in current election discourse. It was not predictive of ideological extremity, a likely long-term ingrained predisposition.

Finally, we built a theoretical model suggesting that those with extreme attitudes (as a result of heightened use of social media to gather political information) are probably more likely to participate in politics. We presented empirical evidence to support this proposition. Those with more extreme attitudes were both more likely to participate in political activities online and more likely to exhibit offline participation in the most traditional sense, by voting. It is on this final point where the next and final empirical chapter of this book expands the analysis. We test in the next chapter whether those candidates who capitalized on the opportunity to control the flow of information via Twitter tended to do better in the election.

9

Congress 2.0—Tweeting for Support

To this point, we have considered the impact of social media on individual behavior from both the demand and supply side. We theorized how the increasing use of SNSs can affect the political sphere, and why shifting the nature of political communication can lead to larger changes in the political process. In this chapter we will bring much of this discussion to its logical conclusion and answer, as far as possible, the critical question of causality. More directly, describing the growing use of SNSs is only the initial step. Here we look to answer the larger puzzle as to whether congressional candidates' tweeting activity generates measurable positive results in an election. In previous chapters, we established a theoretical explanation of why we believed the answer to this question would be affirmative. We posited that social media allows political actors to form a direct conduit to the minds of the American voters, controlling the flow of information and garnering support in the process. Below, we will measure whether our proposition holds up in our data.

Measuring the impact of technology on electoral outcomes is a difficult task. In any given year there are a number of variables that affect the outcome of an election. Isolating technology, especially a particular form of technology such as social media, sufficiently to make causal statements can at times be an overreach. Our previous scholarship considered the effects of the Internet, and specifically candidate websites, on election outcome (Gainous and Wagner 2011; Wagner and Gainous 2009). We were able to control for the standard drivers of outcomes and measure the impact of successful websites on voting results. Our findings were largely positive and significant, though with partisan differences (Wagner and Gainous 2009). We apply much of that theoretical framework here, and create an expanded paradigm to understand the role and implication of social media in the political sphere.

While we will test the broad notion of how the use of Twitter impacts political outcomes, we have a more substantial goal in this chapter. Not all political communication on Twitter is the same or even has the same purpose. To account for these differences, we parse the use of Twitter to provide a greater insight into what works, and what does not, for political actors attempting to influence electoral outcomes. In Chapters 4 and 5 we explored Twitter activity using our four-category typology (campaign announcements, negative tweeting, personal characteristics, and policy tweets). We added to this approach in Chapter 7, where we examined Twitter activity that we characterized as attempting to control the flow of information through the inclusion of approaches such as links, @Twitter names, and hashtags. In this chapter, we test if standard campaign tweeting or information control tweeting provide better electoral outcomes for the users. Our findings illustrate that even well before more universal adoption, the power and importance of SNS use is significant and growing, and that controlling the flow of information is paramount.

Listening Online: The Public Mood in 2010

One of the reoccurring trends in our data has been the advantage of challengers and Republicans in the use of Twitter demonstrated in the 2010 data. We have also shown repeatedly that both groups tend to tweet more across all categories. This is clearly in part to the out-of-power status of both groups and their attempt to lessen the often over-whelming incumbency advantage in American elections (Ansolabehere and Snyder 2002). Since this pattern is durable in our data, we further explore that pattern by test-ing whether the effect of tweeting on the share of the vote garnered varies across incum-bency, when holding party constant. This should provide a more direct answer to the partisanship puzzle. Though it is worth noting that partisan advantage can be fleeting, as both sides are able to adjust in subsequent elections. Sometimes the changes can occur fairly rapidly. When we examined the 2006 midterm election, the Democratic advan-tage online was evident, though mainly a product of campaign websites (Wagner and Gainous 2009; Gainous and Wagner 2011). The adoption of Twitter by the GOP in our current data was a remarkably quick response.

We will more comprehensively consider the findings and results of our measures later in this chapter, but the immediate answers show a complex story in the adoption of social media to the campaign. The initial results suggest that information control tweeting has a positive effect and campaign tweeting actually has either no effect or, under certain conditions, a negative effect. Interestingly, the partisan advantage does hold up, though only marginally. The positive effect of information control tweeting is slightly more reliable for Republicans. Finally, the results indicate that information control tweeting works better for challengers and that this effect is independent of party. Simply, challengers who tweeted more often to control the flow of information got larger shares of the vote, on average, whether they were Republicans or Democrats. Information control tweeting, even when controlling for standard influences on elec-tion outcomes, is significant. Taken altogether, we can say, using our data, that those who try to control the information flow through Twitter have more positive results in the election.

While the effect of this Twitter use does hold up independently, it cannot be di-vorced from the election context, which helps explain both its usage and importance. Information control tweeting has an effect independent of party, but with the results from Chapter 7 suggesting that Republicans tended to do more to control the flow of information via Twitter in 2010, the benefit they received, in the aggregate, was larger. Why such an advantage to the GOP in 2010? Context is relevant. The Democrats con-trolled Congress and the executive entering the election. Twitter was a particularly useful tool to access a public mood (Stimson 1999, 2004) driven by groups, such as the Tea Party, and other people outside the standard party networks who were dissatis-fied with the then-current government. The mood was shifting to favor both challengers and Republicans at the time, making voters more receptive to the flow of information coming from those candidates. They capitalized on this opportunity by taking advantage of social media, especially Twitter.

While we would contend that effective use of social media can always aid a campaign, the political environment of 2010 created an opportunity structure that made Twitter more useful for the challengers. Many individuals were not pleased with the performance of Congress, bringing its approval rating to a then-record low (Jones 2010). As a result, they were open to the flow of information coming from challengers who opposed the policies of the sitting president and the congressional majority. This environment was particularly friendly to Republicans as both houses of a very unpopular Congress were controlled by the Democratic Party. Republican challengers were able to capitalize on the opportunity structure created by the combination of the political climate and conduit to voters that is Twitter. As there was a not a similar large-scale receptivity for the message from the politicians on the wrong side of the information flow, they were forced to rely on Twitter more predominantly to employ standard campaigning tactics. This approach had a less positive result. In 2010, Republicans were able to take back the House and nearly eliminate the Democratic majority in the Senate.

Does the Internet Stimulate Electoral Success?

One of the most difficult aspects of any discussion of social media and SNSs like Twitter is to avoid overstating the effect. There are two foundational questions at the heart of this discussion. First, does the Internet, with its often impersonal digital communication in and of itself present a large influence in the political understandings that people develop? More directly, where does what we read and see online fit into the creation and maintenance of our political views and attitudes? Second, has the adoption of social media reached a large enough saturation point to matter? Even if social media is an effective tool, are there enough users to affect electoral outcomes? We posit that the answer to these questions is yes.

While discussions of technology and its influence can create a more complex lens from which to view an election, it does not change the underlying foundations of how and why people vote. The tools that political actors use to reach us may shift, but the factors that motivate us to participate in the political system are largely constant. In recognizing this, we are not contending that the changes and influence of the Internet and social media are insignificant but rather that social media, and Twitter in particular, add a new procedural lens and some novel variables to include in the more familiar participation equation. Election turnout and political participation in general is still a personal decision that relies in part on individual-level assessments of the costs of participating, the closeness of the election, and one's perceived influence on the outcome (Barry 1970; Downs 1957; Riker and Ordeshook 1968; Tullock 1967). People with more limited resources and education are less likely to participate. This explains in part the disparity in levels of participation for different groups in society and particularly explains differences between socioeconomic groups (Verba et al. 1993).

The use of SNSs has an influence on this underlying participation equation. SNSs lower the cost of acquiring information on candidates and issues for the voter. It also is a much less expensive way for the candidates and political groups to reach potential voters with a message or relevant information. As challengers often lack the resources that incumbents have available to them, the ability to campaign through social media is a particularly appealing approach, as the reach of the Internet is vast, targeted, and relatively inexpensive. Hence, we would expect a larger reliance on SNSs from challengers who can only marshal limited resources. Interestingly, the resource puzzle actually increases the move to a social media-based campaign. A candidate may prefer to use traditional means and method of campaign but simply not have the resources to do so. Standard large media outreach often involves buying time on television, a significant drain on campaign resources (Graber 2006), especially in larger markets.

The result is that campaigns on the Internet are an alternative that allows competition where limited resources might have provided none. The social media campaign allows for easier outreach and education of the voters at a fraction of the cost of traditional media. From both the campaign (supply side) and the voter (demand side), the cost is minimized, and the potential exchange far more substantive, as the Internet can hold significantly more information and is interactive in scope. However, the larger question is not one of cost, but effectiveness. Is this online campaign a viable alternative to the traditional media campaign? Do politicians generate a greater response by lowering the cost of information delivery and engaging the electorate using a considerably less costly means such as Twitter? While we do not claim that this online interaction is a total replacement for the traditional campaign techniques (at least not yet), we do assert that the campaigning through social media can and will affect campaigns and turnout.

SNSs may lack the broad, instant audience of a broadcast commercial, but they have advantages that television lacks. SNSs allow the campaign to access voters through targeted appeals. Candidates can provide voters with more information that might otherwise be impossible to disseminate. They can reach voters that traditional campaign advertising might otherwise miss, especially in an age of splintered consumption of traditional media. A well-tailored social media appeal should be able to put a focused, directed, and targeted appeal to the voters with limited costs. If well-executed, a series of messages through social media networks can drive an idea, influence issue understanding, and effectively reach and motivate voters to support a candidate at the polls. A social media presence then becomes not a replacement for older campaign strategies but an important explanatory variable for electoral success in any current or future campaign. Early evidence has supported such a proposition (Gainous and Wagner 2011). We show further support in our measures below.

The chief limitation on any measure of this impact is the still limited reach and penetration of social media. It does not matter if a social media appeal is inexpensive, persuasive, and targeted if the audience is too small to matter. As a result, the effectiveness of using SNSs as a means for information control and distribution will be highly dependent on the penetration of a particular SNS on the Internet and in the electorate overall. This factor allows for significant variability, as even the best designed social media appeals are electorally insignificant when they are not widely seen and distributed. Scholars have already argued for blunted effects based on the digital divide or the inability of some Americans to access the Internet (see Gainous and Wagner 2007; Mossberger, Tolbert, and Stansbury 2003).

Nonetheless, this seems a largely temporal limitation. As technology gains greater penetration and voters increasingly use the Internet to access information, the significance of the Internet as a campaign tool should continue to grow. In truth, the effects of SNS use on the campaigns in our measures are likely conservative because the data are taken from 2010, one of the earliest uses of social media in a campaign. As we have already noted, the growth rates of SNS use are staggering, even by Internet growth standards. Hence the audience for leading SNSs such as Facebook and Twitter is likely to be larger each subsequent election cycle, increasing their importance, reach, penetration, and power to drive news and issue comprehension. Later networks are likely to be well-established and far larger in size, and with greater durability. More directly, the fact that social media is significant even now tells us that the potential importance of social media going forward is likely to be massive.

Yet no matter the numbers in our statistical model, no one can plausibly argue that Twitter users alone reshaped the election in 2010. Twitter reached nearly 150 million users in the United States in 2012, but with nearly 35 million accounts created just in 2012, it had a far smaller footprint in 2010 election cycle (Semiocast 2012). As a tool, its reach is large, but hardly comprehensive. However, it is a mistake to isolate an SNS and suggest that its influence is solely in the number of immediate users. An SNS's influence is likely as part of a larger information strategy that influences the importance of particular political issues and shapes how people place that information in their understanding of both campaigns and governance. The mistake is to believe that the influence of any social media ends at the computer screen. While political actors can push their thoughts and views to others online, the flow of information does not cease at the end of the online network. People will take what they have learned online with them into their daily activities. In this sense, the online learning cannot be divorced from the offline learning.

Scholars have already shown that the public will learn political information as a by-product of their daily activities (Popkin 1994). This is likely to occur both online and offline. Voters develop an affinity toward like-minded opinion leaders in media and in personal interactions, and they share those beliefs with friends, family, and co-workers. Information and understandings learned online will be shared through normal modes of participation and communication. The dissemination of these ideas may begin online, but the public deliberation likely occurs simultaneously, both in and out of the online network, pushing the power of social media far beyond the initial pool of followers or friends on the SNS. A humorous video, or a serious story, is discussed and shared with online and offline friends, helping to create opinions and understandings of the news. In some sense, just being friends or family with a person who uses social media makes one part of the larger network that can be influenced by online content and message shaping. Everything from the important political issues to evaluations of a candidate's competency and sincerity are moving through these combined networks, shaping and influencing political attitudes and opinions.

What makes social media so useful for political actors is that it presents a very powerful means to interject oneself into preexisting networks of friends and family that are far harder to target and reach with a broadly framed mailer or television advertisement. Social media creates an opportunity to capitalize on the flow of information in the intimacy of a social network. If the information is effectively constructed it will encourage the members of the network to distribute it, making the information more likely to be considered than if it were from a stranger. Once the message is inside the broader social networks that everyone has developed over time, the smaller scope of the online network becomes less relevant.

In the right political environment, SNSs are an opportunity for people who are on the right side of the public mood/flow of information to easily provide information to which people are already receptive. As a result, there should be a stronger relationship between electoral success and information control tweeting for those who are on the right side of the flow (i.e., Republicans and challengers in 2010). Candidates are simply trying to direct consumers to the preferred flow of information. Those candidates who are on the wrong side of the information flow do not have as much opportunity to direct consumers to a preferred flow, and thus they may be more likely to rely on Twitter for standard campaigning tactics. We would expect such an approach to be beneficial, though with a smaller effect. When the political environment favors one side of the information flow, the alternative view is likely being pushed against greater resistance. This does not mean the effort is useless but rather more difficult to accomplish.

Estimating Opportunity Capitalization

We estimate a series of models of candidate vote share here, and again rely on district/state-level data combined with the Twitter content data. As we are seeking not only the larger impact of Twitter, but how different uses affect outcomes, the focus of these measures are on the effects of what we call *standard campaign tweeting* and *information control tweeting*. We constructed two separate indices. The first, standard campaign tweeting, is based on the summed counts of the four types of tweeting we identified in the analysis in Chapter 4 and examined in Chapter 5 (campaign announcement tweets, attack/negative tweets, tweets about personal candidate characteristics, and policy-based tweets). The second, information control tweeting, is based on the summed counts of the types of tweets identified in Chapter 7 (tweets with links, @Twitter names, and hashtags).[1] We make this distinction based on the idea that these two categories are two qualitatively different ways that candidates utilize Twitter. One is simply a fairly blunt campaign information tool, and the other is more about trying to direct users to the preferred flow of information and analysis.

We estimate twelve separate models. For clarity, and to make the results more readily comprehensible, we have organized the twelve into three sets of models. The first set examines the effects of information control tweeting and standard campaign tweeting on vote share across party identification by estimating separate models for Republicans and Democrats. This separation serves a few functions. First, ordinary least squares regression assumes that the error from one observation is independent of the error from another observation. Because the dependent variable is a percentage, the values of vote share for Republicans are plainly not independent of those for Democrats. As a result, combining them in the same model would be problematic, as it would violate the independence assumption. The second reason is substantive, rather than methodological.

It allows us to test our contextual hypotheses concerning the partisan advantage, which has been fairly consistent in our data, favoring the volume and perhaps the effectiveness of the use of Twitter by Republicans. This set of models, as well as the other two sets of models, are also estimated separately for the full sample, and then only for those candidates who had a Twitter account. This allows us to determine if those who are tweeting are faring better at the polls than those who are not. We can also measure if how much candidates are tweeting matters, and if the approach to Twitter they are using matters. Next, we follow the same process for the same reasons across incumbency. Finally, we estimate an interactive model to test if information control tweeting works better not just for Republicans and challengers but also for the combined category of Republican challengers.

Specifically, vote share is modeled as a function of information control tweeting, standard campaign tweeting, district competitiveness, spending differential, political experience, and the total number of candidates in the models across party identification.[2] The models across incumbency conform to the same specification except incumbency is replaced with a Republican dummy variable. The final set of models, designed to estimate the potential conditional influence of incumbency and party identification on the effect information control has on vote share, includes an interaction term between incumbency and information control tweeting. These interactive models are estimated for both Democrats and Republicans. This essentially creates a three-way interaction without the complication of interpreting a multiplicative term that has three variables. We can simply look to see if the two-way interaction behaves differently across partisanship.

Each of the control variables was included in the models because the extant literature suggests they are important in explaining candidates' share of the vote. They must be included to assure that our estimated effects are not spurious. First, district/state competitiveness helps determine the electoral success of both incumbents and challengers (see Breaux and Gierzynski 1991; Koetzle 1998; Welch and Hibbing 1997), so it must be included. Campaign spending is also included as evidence indicates that it can influence electoral success (Erikson and Palfrey 1998; Green and Krasno 1988). We include a measure of political experience, as it is well settled that it can be an important factor contributing to electoral success (Abramowitz 1991; Bond, Covington, and Fleisher 1985; Jacobson 1992; Krebs 1998; Squire 1989). Finally, we included the number of candidates in each race, as vote share is plainly diminished simply as a mathematical byproduct of having more candidates and as a result of greater campaign competition (Holbrook and Tidmarch 1993; Krebs 1998).

The first set of results in Table 9.1 indicate that the effect of information control tweeting is significant and positive for both Republicans and Democrats, but the estimated effect is more reliable for Republicans.[3] Again, it is important to remember that the results in Chapter 7 suggested that Republicans were considerably more likely to employ these tactics (Table 7.2). That said, it may not be their heightened use of these tactics that explains the more reliable estimate. Rather, as previously noted, the public, at large, may just have been more receptive to the Republican flow of information. So the context at the time may explain this divergence. Nonetheless, while the statistical significance is less reliable for the Democrat models, the estimated effect is larger. The model estimates a 0.11 increase in vote share in the full sample Democrat model for an increase of 1,000 total links, @Twitter names, and hashtags a Democrat used.[4]

Table 9.1 **Effects of Campaign Tweeting and Information Control Tweeting on Vote Share across Party Identification**

	Full Sample		Twitter Users	
	Republicans	Democrats	Republicans	Democrats
Info Control Tweeting	0.03**	0.11*	0.04**	0.10*
	(0.01)	(0.06)	(0.02)	(0.06)
Campaign Tweeting	−0.12	−0.22	−0.24**	−0.19
	(0.09)	(0.19)	(0.10)	(0.20)
District Competitiveness	−0.04	0.07***	−0.05*	0.06***
	(0.03)	(0.02)	(0.03)	(0.02)
Spending Differential	0.01	−0.01	−0.00	0.01
	(0.02)	(0.02)	(0.03)	(0.02)
Incumbency	0.21***	0.17***	0.15***	0.17***
	(0.02)	(0.01)	(0.02)	(0.02)
Political Experience	0.03***	0.04***	0.03***	0.03***
	(0.01)	(0.01)	(0.01)	(0.01)
Total # of Candidates	−0.05	−0.12**	0.07	−0.06
	(0.05)	(0.05)	(0.06)	(0.06)
Constant	0.44***	0.37***	0.43***	0.35***
	(0.02)	(0.02)	(0.02)	(0.02)
R^2	0.50	0.55	0.44	0.55
N	451	431	225	218

Note: Data come from www.twitter.com and the Federal Elections Commission. Table entries are ordinary least squares regression estimates with associated standard errors in parentheses. The full sample models incorporate all candidates including those without Twitter accounts and the Twitter users models include only those candidates with Twitter accounts. The models are estimated separately for Republicans and Democrats to avoid violating the independence assumption of OLS. ***$p < 0.01$, **$p < 0.05$, *$p < 0.1$.

The model estimates a 0.03 increase for Republicans in the full sample. The results for the sample of candidates with Twitter accounts are similar. The model estimates a 0.10 increase in vote share in the Democrat model for an increase of 1,000 total links, @ Twitter names, and hashtags used and a 0.04 increase for Republicans.

Next, standard campaign tweeting is largely unrelated to electoral success as measured by vote share in these models. This is not surprising given that we do not think there are enough Twitter users for the campaign tactics used here to sway enough voters to change the outcome of an election, much less even to affect the percentage of total votes. Again, we do not assert that the positive effect of information control tweeting is solely the result of winning over votes, but rather it is reflective of candidates who are on the right side of the information flow using Twitter to capitalize on this opportunity. Notice the significant, and quite large, negative effect of standard campaign tweeting (−0.24) in the Twitter users model for Republicans (this variable was also divided by 1,000). This was a bit unexpected but does not detract from our theory that controlling information via Twitter shapes opinion and behavior. The likely reason for this result is that those candidates who are on the wrong side of the information flow do not have as much opportunity to direct consumers to a preferred flow, and thus they may be more likely to rely on Twitter for standard campaigning tactics. In addition, and perhaps more importantly, those candidates who are trailing, or lack exposure and financial resources, are likely using Twitter to try to attract attention to their campaign. As a result, candidates who are using Twitter for standard campaign tactics may be those who are more likely to lose in the first place. Simply, candidates who are trailing are compelled to try to generate interest in their campaign and detract interest from the opposing candidate using the most cost-efficient methods available. Twitter fits this bill.

The results of the control variables for the models in Table 9.1 are also worth noting. First, the results of district competitiveness are mixed. It is significant and positive in the model of Democratic candidates for the full sample and for the Twitter users only model. The estimate indicates that for every one unit increase in district competitiveness (remember in Chapter 5 that the absolute value of this variable is divided by 500 thousand to make the interpretation of the estimates clearer), there is a 0.07 increase in vote share in the full sample and a 0.06 increase in the Twitter users only model. As the value for district competitiveness gets larger the competitiveness is less because the margin is greater. Thus, Democrats did worse than other Democrats if they were in a district that was won by a large margin in the previous election. Interestingly, the relationship is negative in the Republican Twitter users only model ($p < 0.10$), indicating a 0.05 decrease. This means that Republican Twitter users tended to do better than other Republicans if they were in a district that had a large margin of victory in the previous election. There were no real surprises with the other control variables with the exception that spending differential had no influence. Incumbents tended to garner a larger vote share as did those candidates with more experience. Finally, the total number of candidates in the race was only significant in the full sample model for Democrats.

The results presented in Table 9.2 provide, perhaps, a bit more convincing evidence in support of our story that both Republicans and challengers were provided an advantaged opportunity to use Twitter to capitalize on the flow of information at the time. While the reliability of the information control tweeting estimate was weaker for Democrats in the models in Table 9.1, it is not significant at all for incumbents in the models in Table 9.2. Simply, incumbents who tried to control the flow of information through Twitter were not successful electorally. On the other hand, challengers who tried to control the flow of information through Twitter clearly had electoral success. This result is consistent with what we should expect based on the existing political environment and the receptivity of the public to a particular flow of information. The public mood was swinging against the incumbent Congress, providing a perfect opportunity for challengers to capitalize on this opportunity, using Twitter as one tool to do so.

The full sample estimate for information control tweeting is slightly less reliable ($p < 0.10$) than the Twitter users only estimate, so for every additional information

Table 9.2 **Effects of Campaign Tweeting and Information Control Tweeting on Vote Share across Incumbency**

	Full Sample		Twitter Users	
	Challengers	Incumbents	Challengers	Incumbents
Info Control Tweeting	0.02*	0.07	0.04***	0.02
	(0.01)	(0.05)	(0.02)	(0.05)
Campaign Tweeting	0.01	−0.59***	−0.11	−0.44**
	(0.08)	(0.20)	(0.10)	(0.20)
District Competitiveness	−0.04**	0.33***	−0.02	0.39***
	(0.02)	(0.04)	(0.02)	(0.07)
Spending Differential	0.01	−0.05*	0.01	−0.03
	(0.02)	(0.03)	(0.02)	(0.03)
Political Experience	0.07***	0.01**	0.07***	0.01
	(0.01)	(0.00)	(0.01)	(0.01)
Total # of Candidates	0.01	−0.16***	0.05	−0.06
	(0.04)	(0.05)	(0.06)	(0.07)
Republican	0.07***	0.10*	0.08***	0.07***
	(0.01)	(0.01)	(0.01)	(0.01)
Constant	0.33***	0.56***	0.33***	0.53***
	(0.02)	(0.02)	(0.02)	(0.02)
R^2	0.21	0.34	0.23	0.35
N	470	414	263	181

Note: Data come from www.twitter.com and the Federal Elections Commission. Table entries are ordinary least squares regression estimates with associated standard errors in parentheses. The full sample models incorporate all candidates including those without Twitter accounts and the Twitter users models include only those candidates with Twitter accounts. The models are estimated separately for incumbents and challengers to avoid violating the independence assumption of OLS. ***$p < 0.01$, **$p < 0.05$, *$p < 0.1$.

control tweet (divided by 1,000) vote share increased by 0.02 units for candidates who tweeted relative to all candidates whether they tweeted or not. In the Twitter users only model, not only is the estimate more reliable ($p < 0.01$), but the magnitude of the effect is also larger. For every one unit increase in information control tweeting, the model estimates a 0.04 increase in vote share among candidates who tweeted. Thus, it is not only tweeting that matters but also those candidates who used Twitter a specific way tended to be more successful electorally. We see a similar narrative with standard campaign tweeting that we saw in the Twitter users only model in Table 9.1. This time though, standard campaign tweeting is negative and significant in both the full sample model

and the Twitter users model for incumbents. We believe the same theoretical explanation we offered for the result in Table 9.1 holds true here. Incumbents were simply not
on the right side of the flow of information and as a result were not able to use Twitter
to capitalize. As a result, they used Twitter more often to employ standard campaigning
tactics, and as we already know, many incumbents lost in 2010, and thus their vote share
tended to be lower, on average, than challengers' share of the vote.

The control variables in these models, again, provide some contextually revealing results. District competitiveness is negative in the challengers models (only significant in
the full sample model) and positive in the incumbents models. Unsurprisingly, incumbents did better in districts with a larger partisan margin in the immediately past election. Conversely, and again only significant in the full sample model, challengers did not
do as well when the election was tight in the previous cycle. This too meets with our
expectations.

Political experience has a positive effect in all the models, except the Twitter users
model, where it is insignificant. This is an interesting result. It suggests that among those
incumbents who use Twitter, those with a large amount of political experience did not
do well in the election. Clearly, this is a product of the public mood swinging against
incumbents, even those with considerable seniority. The total number of candidates was
only significant and, as expected, negative in the full sample model for incumbents. Finally, Republicans tended to do better than Democrats regardless of how the sample
was partitioned. While challengers in general did well, in the aggregate Republicans
were more successful, as they gained a significant number of seats.

The series of additive models in Tables Table 9.1 and Table 9.2 make it clear that
information control tweeting benefited Democrats, Republicans, and challengers.
However, the effect was marginally more reliable for Republicans. The importance of
informational control types of tweeting is evident when considering the main effects
and controls in the models in Table 9.3. The main effects for the information control
indicator are positive and significant across all four models when holding incumbency
at 0 (challengers). Interestingly, the model actually performs better, and there are much
more reliable information control indicators, when the interaction is added to the
model as compared to the models in Table 9.1. In addition to the findings provided in
Table 9.2, these models continue to support our proposition that challengers tended to
be on the beneficial side of the information flow. SNS use allows political actors to reach
and direct people with a predisposition to hear the provided information. The relationship is reflective of their heightened use of Twitter to connect potential voters to their
preferred flow of opinion, analysis, and information.

The benefits of Twitter use for challengers remain durable in our models. The interactive models in Table 9.3 provide evidence that the positive effect of information
control tweeting for both Republicans and Democrats is stronger among those who
were challengers. In fact, this effect is plotted in Figure 9.1, and what becomes apparent
is that the effect is positive for challengers from both parties. The effect is negative for
incumbents. Some of this is clearly driven by the electoral context. It is important to
remember that the 2010 election was a particularly positive year for challengers. Interestingly, the interactive line is stronger for the full sample, indicating that the positive
effect of information control tweeting for challengers relative to the negative effect for

Table 9.3 **Interactive Effect Information Control Tweeting and Incumbency**

	Full Sample		Twitter Users	
	Republicans	Democrats	Republicans	Democrats
Info Control Tweeting	0.03**	0.15**	0.05***	0.14**
	(0.01)	(0.06)	(0.02)	(0.06)
Incumbency	0.22***	0.18***	0.17***	0.19***
	(0.02)	(0.02)	(0.02)	(0.02)
Campaign Tweeting	−0.11	−0.22	−0.23**	−0.18
	(0.09)	(0.19)	(0.10)	(0.19)
District Competitiveness	−0.04	0.07***	−0.05*	0.06**
	(0.03)	(0.02)	(0.03)	(0.02)
Spending Differential	0.01	−0.01	0.00	0.01
	(0.02)	(0.02)	(0.02)	(0.02)
Political Experience	0.03***	0.04***	0.03***	0.03***
	(0.01)	(0.01)	(0.01)	(0.01)
Total # of Candidates	−0.04	−0.12***	0.08	0.07
	(0.05)	(0.05)	(0.06)	(0.06)
Info Control X Incumbency	−0.09*	−0.19***	−0.10*	−0.20**
	(0.05)	(0.08)	(0.06)	(0.08)
Constant	0.44***	0.36***	0.42***	0.35***
	(0.02)	(0.02)	(0.02)	(0.02)
R^2	0.51	0.56	0.45	0.57
N	451	431	225	218

Note: Data come from www.twitter.com and the Federal Elections Commission. Table entries are ordinary least squares regression estimates with associated standard errors in parentheses. The full sample models incorporate all candidates including those without Twitter accounts and the Twitter users models include only those candidates with Twitter accounts. ***$p < 0.01$, **$p < 0.05$, *$p < 0.1$.

incumbents is even stronger when comparing Twitter user incumbents to non-Twitter user incumbents. This means that while those candidates who used Twitter to control the flow of information did better at the polls than those candidates who were less likely to use Twitter in that manner, their advantage over those who did not use Twitter at all was even greater. The findings illustrate that the effective use of Twitter was important for electoral outcomes. Those who were on the right side of the public mood, the challengers, effectively used Twitter to control the flow of information and had a superior outcome at the polls relative to their incumbent counterparts.

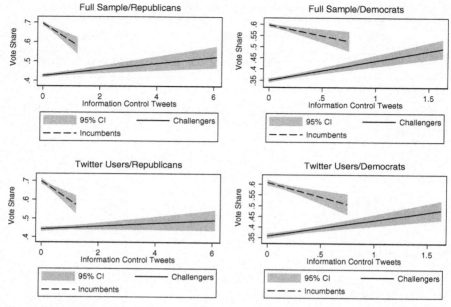

Figure 9.1 Effect of Flow of Information Tweeting across Incumbency. Source: www.twitter. com and the Federal Elections Commission.

Summary

In this chapter we took the framework we constructed to explain how social media, and Twitter in particular, is likely to affect electoral outcomes, and applied it to the real world example of the U.S. election in 2010. This chapter was intended to put our theoretical assertions to an empirical test. While much of the book has demonstrated descriptively and inferentially many of the implications of the congressional use of Twitter, this chapter gets directly at what is perhaps the most pressing question: What is the relationship between electoral success and Twitter use? It is a practical question that draws us back to the most basic reason that we study SNS use and Internet politics in general. Does any of it matter?

Part of the larger challenge of such a measure is considering if there is a large enough social media penetration to make its advantages in distribution, control, and cost significant. We contended herein that while we do not believe that there are enough Twitter users and followers of candidates to make Twitter campaigns alone the driving force behind election outcomes, we do propose and assert that candidates can use Twitter to capitalize on the opportunity to guide the flow of information in a campaign and that effort can affect outcomes. Our findings are supportive of this proposition. The evidence illustrates that those candidates who use information control approaches to Twitter are the candidates who have greater electoral success. This is true even when controlling for more typical predictors of winning campaigns. This means in the 2010 congressional elections both Republicans and challengers were able to capitalize on this opportunity more effectively.

Perhaps the largest concern we had in building our model was not that the relationship between SNS use and electoral success was untrue but rather our measure might have been an election cycle too soon. The growth rates of social media are very high, but 2010 was only the first year of a somewhat large-scale adoption of this technology for political purposes. The number of users of social media in 2010 is likely to be but a small fraction of the people engaging with politics and political groups online in future election cycles. Just looking at the millions more users that have come online between 2010 and 2012 is staggering (Semiocast 2012). Nonetheless, we theorized that the effects of such an open and unfettered information outlet would not be limited solely to people online. We know that information and political understandings are very much learned and transmitted in everyday life no matter where the ideas originated (Popkin 1994). Further, 2010 presented an interesting test case for us. If the relationship proved to be significant in the smallest adoption election cycle, the likelihood is that the importance of social media as a growing concern in the political sphere would only be increasing in subsequent years. If it matters when only some of the voters are online, there is a sizable potential for a more massive impact in future years with closer to universal adoption.

The next and final chapter summarizes the theoretical and empirical contributions of this book. While we make these reflections, we also try to place all these results in a larger context to help us understand what we believe the future of social media holds for politics. This contextualizing includes significant discussion about the use of social media in the more recent 2012 U.S. elections.

10

Social Media Tomorrow—Tweeting the Future?

On November 21, 2012, President Barack Obama pardoned a turkey, actually a pair of turkeys. A person unfamiliar with American Thanksgiving traditions might think that pardoning a bird is an odd custom. However, the pardoning of the turkeys itself is not that unusual. The saving of the birds from the dinner plate is a regular presidential tradition that has become a popular made-for-media event to celebrate the holiday. For presidents, appearing in the media as both magnanimous and relatable is good, if somewhat simplistic, politics. Modern politics has become very much a visual medium, so pictures of a President and his family with a saved turkey or two is effective politics in the mass media age. This is especially true with the explosion of media outlets such as numerous cable news/entertainment stations and Internet portals looking to fill content on an otherwise slow news day. Obama's own pardoning of the turkeys was not only on multiple television networks, but was also a top political video on the video-sharing website YouTube.

Ironically, the pardoning of turkeys provides a perfect synergy between traditional politics and the increasingly encroaching modern social media sphere that exists today. Turkeys are very much a traditional American symbol and were suggested to be preferable to the bald eagle as the choice as the official bird of the United States by Benjamin Franklin. While the roots of the tradition may stretch back years, the current ceremony is a very much a product of the mass media age. This type of overlap is evidenced by the White House claims that the tradition goes back to Tag Lincoln begging his father, President Abraham Lincoln, to save a turkey (Slack 2011). This history and the story are of course displayed and distributed across the nation via social media and the White House Internet website. Whether Tag Lincoln actually caused his father to save a bird is not entirely clear, but, regardless, it is now a part of the virtual universe where a juicy yarn is far easier to distribute than a dry truth. One is certainly likely to get far more retweets from the compelling Lincoln narrative than from the alternative tale that the entire tradition is one based on good marketing from America's turkey farmers, who first gave a bird to Harry Truman in 1947 (Slack 2011). In truth, it was not until 1989 that the media hoopla really started with President George W. Bush being the first to "officially" offer the turkey a pardon at the White House. Truth, fiction, and something in between are all found somewhere across the information superhighway, though they often move at considerably different rates. On social media, spectacle is speed. Regardless of the history, subsequent years have the sitting president passing judgment, in the tradition of Lincoln, fairly leniently, on a turkey or two for the media cameras and Internet viewers.

So while pronouncing clemency for birds seems odd, it is not unusual. What was particularly unusual in 2012 was that the president left the clemency decision up to the American people. However, he did not leave it to just any people. The White House organized a vote through the social media with the decision left to users of the SNS Facebook (Lindsay 2012). The people could vote to save one of two turkeys by going to the White House Facebook page. Using Facebook, people could read up on the birds, examine their pictures, and even learn their favorite songs. Ultimately the SNS user could choose to save one of the turkeys, named Gobbler and Cobbler. For social media purposes, this is fairly clever as it drives traffic to the White House page, and the act of voting supplies a user account that can be later used to create a larger distribution network for the president and his staff. A voter may have been supporting a turkey, but they were in fact joining a larger community inside the social media. Much to the good fortune of both turkeys, President Obama pardoned the pair, thus supporting both competing elements of this nascent ornithological network. Aside from the two less fortunate, and unnamed birds, who were sent to replace the two celebrity turkeys at the dinner table, everyone was a winner.

While the tale of the turkey pardons seems a small matter, it is evidence of the continued adoption and integration of social media into the political sphere. Political actors are just now starting to come to terms with how to use these networks most effectively, and they are trying different strategies, turkey voting included. Effective or not, the integration of social media into politics is happening rapidly. It is not just a question of whether political actors can develop newer and more clever ways to market themselves, though that is part of it. It is a change in who we communicate with and how that communication occurs. It is a change in how the electorate organizes itself, and how that organization limits old forms of political communication and provides new opportunities for others. The Internet is shifting and changing the world around us. Altering the calculus of information exchange is not just an abstraction. It has very real and durable consequences.

In some cases the changes are very obvious, such as the declining physical circulation of newspapers, and the rapid demise of the music store and the bookstore, which rely on large production, storage, and distribution centers along with tangible physical items sold to consumers in face-to-face transactions. The Internet can sell the same content without any such infrastructure. When there are more efficient ways to obtain and exchange information, the less efficient methods become costly in comparison and increasingly obsolete. This is true whether it is in business or politics. The early adopters are advantaged, while the late adopters are often forced to try and catch up with the new methods. The early advantages in technology adoption do tend to dissipate with time, but the implications of the new methods are more lasting after universal adoption and application.

One of the larger drags on this process is human tradition and practice. More directly, the shift to more efficient Internet-dominated politics itself is likely hampered by our own resistance to change. Though we write about technological evolution, both authors are fond of their increasingly obsolete printed newspapers. Our habits can delay technology-driven shifts, but only for a short time. This resistance to change, when observed, can create a false view that the change might not happen, or that the change will be smaller and less significant. However, the broader patterns are harder to deny. This is most clear looking across the generations. Younger people who matured during the adoption of the Internet are far more comfortable with its use for many purposes, including politics (Gainous and Wagner 2011). With the aging of society, change is not just likely, it is inevitable, as the older methodologies of campaigning and communication increasingly find limited or even vanished audiences.

In the preceding chapters, we explored how technology, and specifically the use of SNSs on the Internet, forces a change in how people engage with each other and the political system. By creating an entirely new system to distribute and engage with news and opinion, social media is altering a long-held power relationship over the control of information. It is substantially shifting who controls information, who consumes information, how that information is distributed, and perhaps even more importantly, how that information is understood. While there are many implications of this new digital politics, we focused on two foundational premises. First, by allowing the consumer to pick their own network of communication, social media allows citizens to self-select their content in a way that avoids any disagreeable ideas or interpretations. Second, the networks themselves exist outside the traditional media machine, allowing political actors—including parties and candidates—to shape and often dictate their content.

We have explored these changes using several different approaches and measures. We have used measures of voters, citizens, SNS users, political actors, political groups, and others to begin to describe how Americans have embraced this new technology and its penetration into society. We examined social media and how its use has become pervasive along with an increasing volume of political communication. We measured and illustrated how users prefer information that matches their own predisposition and the implications of such usage. We explored how members of Congress use the social media by applying a traditional theory of congressional behavior to social media, and we created a typology to see how those behaviors translate into SNS websites like Twitter or Facebook. We offered an analysis of the total Twitter activity across party identification, race of candidate, chamber (House or Senate), and incumbency status.

Beyond the numbers, we created a theoretical foundation to understand how people are likely to use social media. In particular, we focused on the concept of cognitive dissonance and how social media allows the creation of networks that provide information that confirms and reassures people along their preexisting dispositions. We proposed that such a network is highly vulnerable to political actors who can drive tailored information through these networks outside the traditional media which would often temper and limit such a manipulative outreach. We specifically explore that process using data gathered from Twitter itself. Finally, we measure the use of the strategies in the 2010 election.

In this concluding chapter, we will sum up the major patterns that have emerged since the wider adoption of social media in the political sphere. We will consider the implications of this type of change for the future of the American system and how these changes go beyond campaigning and into governance. We conclude with thoughts on the broader implications of social media as an increasingly integral part of our society and lives.

Twitter Politics in the 2012 Campaign

Interestingly, while Republicans were earlier adopters of Twitter, and had higher usage trends in our 2010 data, the Democrats, especially President Obama, have made sizable strides in using Twitter. Republican political actors were early users of the technology, but the social media audience trends young, and that is an opportunity for Democrats who have had greater success with younger voters in recent elections. As noted earlier, President Obama has one of the most followed accounts on Twitter, and his victory photo showing him hugging the First Lady was the most tweeted photo in the short history of that particular SNS. It was also the most "liked" photo in the somewhat longer history of Facebook (Oremus 2012). While candidates and campaigns are still experimenting with how to use Facebook and Twitter in both campaigning and governance strategies, the questions are increasingly about how to use them and not about whether to do so.

Winning dollars or votes is about efficiency and reach. Mailing flyers or buying time on television are still important strategies today, but buying time seems remarkably inefficient in light of the Internet and social media. Internet campaign videos, often marketed directly through social media, can far outreach traditional advertising, as was the case with the video supporting Barack Obama's 2008 campaign for the Democratic presidential nomination titled "Yes, We Can!" (Wallsten 2010). A simple music video that had celebrities lip-syncing an Obama speech to music reached nearly four million viewers in just a few weeks (Memmott and Lawrence 2008). This is a striking contrast to Hillary Clinton's competing nationally televised town hall that was purchased at great cost on multiple networks and reached far fewer people (Rich 2008). In 2008, Obama's viral video strategy was an odd quirk of the campaign, but by 2012 this was a standard part of most major campaign strategy.

The political video genre has become active and frequently draws millions of views. Consider that, in the 2012 election, the Obama campaign promoted a short video from actor/comedian Will Ferrell supporting President Obama's reelection. The video drew nearly 5 million views despite being posted just days before the election. The marketing was primarily through social media, blogs, and email. The success of any of the videos is often based on postings on popular blogs and websites, and on interested people sharing or communicating them to friends and acquaintances. Yet interestingly it is not the traditional media or journalists that account for the popularity of a video. It is more often the product of online bloggers and political actors, such as campaign staff, that account for the growth (Wallsten 2010). Videos have become a persuasive element of the content in online social networks, and the content exists largely outside the traditional media channels.

As a consequence of the growth, the video hosting website YouTube created a separate channel on its website dedicated to political videos. Satire videos making light of the candidates are particularly popular. A video titled, "Mitt Romney Style," from *College Humor*, used the music and visuals from a popular music video to poke fun at Mitt Romney's wealth, manner, and even hair. The video drew over 24 million views in less than two months. The distribution costs for any of these videos are negligible in comparison to buying expensive television time. Candidates need not even make the videos, but simply encourage the consumption of supporting videos through the reach of their

social media networks. Traditional media outlets are left to report on a video's popularity, but have no ability to act as a gatekeeper on the political messaging itself.

While posting campaign videos is not in and of itself a new strategy, the ability of
videos to go "viral," is an increasingly important part of the political campaign. The term
"viral" generally refers to something that, often unexpectedly, receives large amounts
of distribution across the Internet (Wallsten 2010; Boynton 2009). The hope of any
producer of Internet content (especially political content) is for their video, photo, or
post to go "viral." While, in some ways, that is an accident of particular preferences at
particular times, it is also strategic. Even now there are new books which attempt to
teach campaign staff and the candidates themselves how to use social media to produce
this "accidental" effect (Agranoff and Tabin 2011). Suggested strategies range from how
to design a tweet to when the best time to tweet would be. Tweeting one's way to power
is becoming less a strategy and more a regular part of the campaign. As social media
become more important in a campaign, more experts will likely arise to help candidates
marshal their Internet efforts.

Refocusing the resources and strategy of a campaign to the Internet is not simple. The
current campaigns are interesting combinations of old and new technologies, ranging
from social media town halls to traditional mailers. It is not easy to mimic the strategies
that make the political use of social media effective, nor is it easy to convince traditional
campaigners of the value of the Internet and social media in particular. Consider trying
to explain to a long-sitting politician that tweeting is better than sending a mailer. Such a
strategy might have been hard to grasp for politicians such as former Alaska Senator Ted
Stevens, who referred to the Internet as "a series of tubes" (Singel and Poulsen 2006).
It is too easy for both political actors and political observers who are mired in the structure of the traditional campaign tools to dismiss page views or distribution network
numbers as inflated or even irrelevant.

Yet 55% of all registered voters went online in the 2012 election season to watch
political videos (Smith and Duggan 2012). These activities include watching speeches,
news reports, advertisements, and parodies. Significantly, the process of discovering political videos comes back to the power of social networks and as a result social media.
Sixty-two percent of Internet-using registered voters have had others recommend
online political videos to them (Smith and Duggan 2012). This is a trend that is accel-
erating as more people go online and enter the social media web portals. Directing and
redirecting people through social networks is not just a useful strategy, it is an essential
one for modern politics.

2012 is a particular noteworthy year for watching the campaigns attempt to grapple
with this new political sphere. We note that SNSs have no gatekeepers, which provides
an opportunity for the political actors to direct content. But simplistic strategies can
be more harmful than useful. Consider the efforts of groups supporting Republican
candidate Mitt Romney to direct the flow of social media through the promotion of
hashtags on Twitter. As we discussed in previous chapters, hashtags can be useful ways
to organize discussions or suggest how people should view and understand information.
However, once released into the Twitter networks, they can become almost anything.
The Republican National Committee ("RNC") tried to use Twitter to suggest that President Obama had failed to improve the life of most Americans and should therefore be
denied a second term. They pushed this strategy using the hashtag #AreYouBetterOff.

EXAMPLE: REPUBLICAN NATIONAL COMMITTEE

Tweet Americans across the country are talking about how #ObamaIsntWorking. Join the conversation: obamaisntworking.com #AreYouBetterOff.

This played off of the famous debate quote from Ronald Reagan who used the question "Are you better off than you were four years ago?" to help sink the campaign of Jimmy Carter in 1980. In some ways this appeared to be a nice synergy between an old campaign talking point and a new campaign strategy.

Republicans were asking Americans to join the conversation, so they did. Unfortunately, a hashtag that asks a question can be answered in any way. While some people responded as the RNC intended, many did not. Large numbers of Twitter users responded in mass to suggest that they were, in fact, better off (Roston 2012). Some went to great lengths to illustrate how much better off they had become. One more witty response looked as follows:

Tweet #AreYouBetterOff ? Sure am. My wife and I are now gainfully employed and can almost afford to vote #republican but we're still voting #Obama.

Obama supporters took the hashtag and used it as a conversation starter for people to tell stories of how their lives had improved and why the country was better off. One of the early lessons on 2012 and Twitter is that asking open-ended questions is probably not a good approach.

Similarly, the group Americans for Prosperity, in seeking to marshal people on Twitter against President Obama, paid to promote the hashtag #failedagenda. A paid, promoted hashtag is a shortcut for users to draw attention to themselves or to a message. It makes a hashtag appear in trending charts on Twitter and therefore brings it to the attention of users outside the traditional ways such as heavy usage of the hashtag or simply seeing it used by people who one is following on Twitter. The purpose of this particular hashtag was to encourage users to discuss how the president had largely failed the country and how his policies had proven to be a failure.

Once again, despite the money spent, this approach was less than ideal. Only about one in five users used the hashtag to speak about Obama, many more co-opted the hashtag and used it against Mitt Romney and his running mate, Congressman Paul Ryan (Green 2012). Controlling the flow of information is not easy, but gets increasingly hard when the attempts are so obtuse and easily co-opted. A second lesson from 2012 is that open-ended hashtags are a poor technique as well.

Social Media in Governance

We noted in the above chapters that Republicans took to Twitter in larger numbers in 2010. Yet the evidence from 2012 shows that both parties were using the SNSs frequently, though with different levels of success. While Republicans may have had an advantage in adoption rates of Twitter in 2010, Democrats were well-established there by 2012. The Obama Campaign was certainly not disadvantaged on Twitter, and as noted above, Obama rapidly outdistanced Mitt Romney in number of followers. Going forward, both political parties, and just about every political interest, are going to be competing online and especially in social media venues.

What is interesting about the use of social media in the campaign is that it can be transferred into a governing strategy. The networks developed over the course of a campaign are not eliminated at the conclusion of the election. The president's team has attempted to transfer the SNS campaign network into a governing strategy by trying to rally supporters for the president's plan to manage the 2012 budget crisis, often referred to as the "fiscal cliff" (Shaer 2012). Using the hashtag "#my2k" (a reference to the $2,000 increase in taxes for some middleclass families that would happen without a continuation of the preexisting tax policy), the White House was trying to pressure Republicans with a public appeal (Jackson 2012). Again, with reference to the above hashtag, the President Obama took questions through Twitter about his plans regarding tax policy. All people had to do was use the hashtag during a short time period beginning at 2 p.m. on December 3, 2012 and there was a chance to get an individual response. The president personally opened the session on twitter.

EXAMPLE: THE WHITE HOUSE, @WHITEHOUSE

Tweet Good to see lots of folks on twitter speaking out on extending middle class tax cuts. I'll answer some Qs on that at 2ET. Ask w/#My2k—bo

As the president's Twitter account is regularly used by staff, the president used "-bo" to indicate that he was the one actually responding. Unlike some other forms of political outreach, Twitter usage and reach is readily calculable. During his online tweet exchange with constituents, the hashtag #My2k appeared on Twitter over 30,000 times (Schulman 2012). That was a sufficient volume for it to become a nationally trending topic on Twitter and the exchange was reposted on the White House's blog (Schulman 2012).

Appealing to the public to affect policy is not a new idea. Presidents have maximized their power through public appeals based on media access and in more recent years the almost universal penetration of television (Kernell 1997). Yet as revolutionary as video has proven to be, social media is a means of distribution and communication unlike television. It is directed, interactive, and focused in a way that broadcast television could never be. A broadcast is widely dispersed for a time, but hard to direct. On the Internet, video from television itself is organized parsed and distributed at all times through multiple channels including, increasingly, social media. A tweet can include any kind of visual information by linking video content. However, social media is far more than relevant video whenever one wants to view it, which alone would be significant. A tweet can be a short comment with a link to more specific content, including analysis and argument. It can even be part of a larger reinforcing conversation online. As an instantaneous conglomeration of almost every style of information from video to written word distributed worldwide with little or no cost, social media is strikingly different than anything before it.

The value of social media in governance is still not clear. President Obama's attempt to marshal the social media audience to pressure Congress is a novel, if fairly efficient, form of public appeal. However, the success of such an approach has not yet been seen, though the president has tried a few times on issues from student loans to the payroll tax (Cox 2012). The strategy is far too new to have enough data points to allow for a valid measure. If public appeal continues to be an effective political strategy for presidents

(Kernell 1997), then social media should improve its reach and distribution. Yet there are some new variables to consider, including whether 140 character messages or even linked short video clips are similar in impact to a traditional mass media appeal. Ronald Reagan's charisma may not have translated as well from the television screen to the computer tablet. In the social media universe, sometimes wit or clever wordsmithing is far more appealing than long oration.

In the formative years of the social media sphere, questions as to larger political impacts are hard to answer. Even television, which has had decades of use, has conflicting assessments. Some have argued that television has so trivialized politics that its impact will be substantively destructive to the political system (Postman 1985; Putnam 2000), while others have argued for greater knowledge and engagement (Gould 1946; Graber 2006). Depending on which line of reasoning one follows, the effect of television is either destructive to social organization (Putnam 2000) or it is a key component of a more informed and engaged society (Gould 1946; Graber 2006). Regardless, few would argue with the assertion that television has changed how candidates are covered and has had a significant impact on the success or failure of a candidate (Prior 2007). In 1992, Reform Party presidential candidate Ross Perot certainly challenged the idea that candidates had to go out and campaign. Perot ran a presidential campaign almost entirely through the use of television appearances and paid advertisements (Jelen 2001). Television visibility has become a staple of modern politics. Congresspersons regularly give speeches to largely empty chambers just for television consumption.

Beyond organizing political support or campaigning, social media could begin to serve other purposes in the political sphere. The way that politicians interact with their constituents can be very different. One good illustration of this process was Mayor Corey Booker's Twitter presence during the hours and days following the destruction caused to Newark, New Jersey, by Hurricane Sandy in November of 2012. Booker constantly tweeted recovery efforts to citizens in the city to keep them updated (Jeltsen 2012). He also encouraged residents to tweet messages to him about power outages, downed trees, and other storm destruction that needed immediate attention. Booker even invited a resident without power over to his house using Twitter (Jeltsen 2012). Booker's invitation was available for anyone to read.

EXAMPLE: CORY BOOKER, MAYOR NEWARK, NEW JERSEY

Tweet There is someone at my house now (Eric). I've got space u can relax in, charge devices & even a working DVD player. Come by.

While one need not presume that Mayor Booker was acting with appearance in mind, the political optics were very good. The response to the mayor's tweet came a little later from the grateful constituent:

Tweet At @CoryBooker house. Charging everything up. Thx.

Booker then ordered lunch for the 12 people who came to his house. A picture of the meal was, of course, tweeted out as well, and the exchange between Mayor Booker and his constituents was covered by the more traditional media (Jeltsen 2012).

Social media is a very direct channel between decision-makers and their constituents. An average citizen with a Twitter account can speak directly to political figures, and even sometimes have them respond. As we noted above, President Obama has used his Twitter account to answer questions directly from Americans (Schulman 2012). More than just a direct campaign tool, social media is a very useful device for constituent service, which is a significant part of any successful political strategy (Fiorina 1989). In the new social media universe, constituent service can happen at a rapid pace. Increasingly, citizens are going to expect their political leaders to be available through social media and to be responsive far more quickly than in past years. Mayor Booker's Twitter presence was exceptional in 2012, and in a few years that type of social media presence will likely be expected of all politicians. It has the advantage of bringing the political leaders much closer to their constituents, but it also places far greater demands on them. A successful politician in the social media age cannot simply send out periodic platitudes, advertisements, and credit claiming messages. More personalized responses will be demanded and likely rewarded.

Tweeting to the Future

Much of the coverage of social media, including the vast majority of this book, has focused on how the Internet, and social media in particular, affects campaigning and governance. Yet there is surely a larger narrative beyond the campaign. The nature of the political world is changing around us. In some sense these changes are just the natural progression of the adoption of technology. Sometimes it is not revolutionary, but it is hard to miss. Whether it is tweeting from the State of the Union address, or answering constituents with instant help, the digital connections between politicians and people are changing the underlying rules of engagement. Though some of these changes are just alterations of the behaviors and customs of old, many provide the baseline for a new type of politics. For better or worse, politics and people are closer now than ever.

Change in our political system is an inevitable result of the rise of the Internet and SNS use in particular. As the penetration of this technology increases, successful political actors will harness it, and the late adopters will fall behind. Politics has always been about understanding the rules of the system best, and using them to one's advantage rather than as a detriment (Riker 1986). The technological changes are new enough that you can still see some of the efforts to resist the new reality. Older and more experienced politicians and political consultants always prefer the modes and methods that have worked in the past. However, losing elections is the most important stimulus for change in the political sphere (Appleton and Ward 1997). Campaigns are always evolving. Looking backwards for an idealized political system for governing or campaigning is not only poor strategy but also foundationally inaccurate. As all things are constantly adapting and changing, politics and governing have become, and continue to be, a process of adjustment and learning where nothing is fixed and nothing is permanent.

SNSs are a vast medium of communication and we could not hope to capture the totality of it in this book. Any approach to social media is likely to exclude some types of interactions which may prove substantial in time. In fact, because of the evolving nature of SNSs, some websites which are prominent now will be discarded as they are surpassed by the next, more intuitive and useful, protocol. Perhaps the most difficult aspect of writing about such changes is that the changes themselves continue around us as we consider them. So no matter how comprehensive our measures, or complete our theory, the environment will shift and evolve as new stimuli and new innovations are adopted and applied. In short, the focus of our study is very much a moving target. Yet even in such an uncertain environment, there are patterns to observe.

We have demonstrated that the increasing use of SNSs changes how people interact with politicians, each other, and state institutions. These changes are significant since they result in shifts in everything from what people know, to who votes, to ultimately how we understand and participate with the political system. We posit that our contribution will survive the inevitable changes that will occur subsequent to the release of this book. We have presented a grounded theoretical approach to understanding the role of innovations, including social media, in politics. Our empirical tests sought to hold our theories and existing theories to a measurable and reliable standard. While the system will change, our approach should evolve with it. Even in our dynamic political system, we provided generalizable results for others to consider and compare as new rules and types of interaction are added to the networks.

While clearly this book is not the end of the attempts to understand and measure the impact of online engagement on politics, it is among the earliest efforts to bring a systematic approach in both theory and measurement to the study of social media. The underlying truth of social media is a fairly complex one. It is not the panacea for democracy that some have claimed (Allison 2002). Yet it is not the mind-numbing wasteland or corporate supermarket that many have feared. Social media does bring a great opportunity for open interaction in our democracy and greater means and impetus to participate. Yet the system presents an opportunity structure for groups to drive and control the political message. There is great potential for learning by using the Internet, as there is a vast amount of information on virtually anything knowable available.

Ideally, one might surmise that lies and deception would be difficult in such an information-rich environment. People with Internet access have at their fingertips the greatest database of knowledge ever invented. In it is no wonder that this reality is seen as the ideal foundation for greater degrees of democratization. The Internet provides the user with both this knowledge and a multitude of voices unrestrained by a gatekeeper (Hindman 2008). However, having the information and the platform and using them are not the same. As we have observed, people often avoid objectivity if the path to reassuring information, which is consistent with their predispositions, is available. The accessibility of more objective sources of information does not mean that people will find them or even understand them to be worth seeking out. The Internet allows people to choose, but the choices are driven by the desire to reinforce our pre-dispositions, not challenge them.

Does this mean that greater social media use inevitably leads to a divided and ill-informed public? We are not prepared to assume that result. In this book we have provided a beginning with projections that both show the potential of social media as well as the likely pitfalls. One clear lesson in the study of the Internet, and the growing social media phenomena, is that conclusions, even when correct, may not remain correct for long. The study of this dynamic environment teaches caution about making too many long-term determinations. The environment is not static, but then neither are people or political actors. Resultantly, Internet politics, and the study of social media in particular, are becoming a vital area for continued research. In our study, the positives and negatives of social media and the Internet are becoming clearer. With a clearer understanding of these effects, we can chart our future course through this new political reality.

Appendix

(Operationalization of all variables not described in the text or footnotes)

- Internet Use: About how often do you use the Internet or email from ... (1) work, (2) home—several times a day, about once a day, 3–5 days a week, 1–2 days a week, every few weeks, less often, or never? These two items were scaled so that higher values reflected more Internet use and then summed to create a two-item index.
- Attentiveness: (1) We're interested in how people used their cell phones during the recent political campaign, in addition to talking to others on your phone. Again thinking about just your cell phone, in the months leading up to the election, did you use your cell phone to keep up with news related to the election or politics, or did you not do this?, (2) and (3) Please tell me if you ever use the Internet to do any of the following things. Do you ever use the Internet to ... (get news online, look online for news or information about politics or the 2010 campaigns)? These three items were summed to create an index ($\alpha = 0.57$).
- Partisanship Strength: In politics TODAY, do you consider yourself a Republican, Democrat, or independent? (those who volunteered no preference, other party, or don't know were imputed). Independents were asked: As of today do you lean more to the Republican Party or more to the Democratic Party? We then coded partisans as a 2, leaners as a 1, and independents as a 0.
- Demographics: Age (self-reported and collapsed into an ordinal scale representing quartiles), income (self-reported and collapsed into an ordinal scale representing quartiles), education (What is the last grade or class you completed in school?– (1) None, or grades 1–8, (2) High school incomplete (grades 9–11), (3) High school graduate (grade 12 or GED certificate), (4) Technical, trade or vocational school AFTER high school, (5) Some college, no 4-year degree (includes associate degree), (6) College graduate (BS, BA, or other 4-year degree), (7) Post-graduate training/professional school after college (toward a Masters/PhD, Law or Medical school). We collapsed the first four categories (= 1), some college, no 4-year degree (= 2), and collapsed the last two categories.
- Propensity to Join Groups:

  (1–14) I'm going to read you different types of groups and organizations in which some people are active. Please tell me if you are currently active in any of these types of groups or organizations, or not. (First/Next,) are you currently active in any ... ?

a. Community groups or neighborhood associations
b. Church groups or other religious or spiritual organizations
c. Sports or recreation leagues, whether for yourself or for your child
d. Hobby groups or clubs
e. Performance or arts groups, such as a choir, dance group, or craft guild
f. Professional or trade associations for people in your occupation
g. Parent groups or organizations, such as the PTA or local parent support group
h. Youth groups, such as the Scouts, YMCA, or 4-H
i. Social or fraternal clubs, sororities or fraternities
j. Veterans groups or organizations such as the American Legion or VFW
k. Literary, discussion or study groups, such as a book club or reading group
l. Charitable or volunteer organizations, such as Habitat for Humanity or the Humane Society
m. Consumer groups, such as AAA [Triple A] or coupon sharing groups
n. Farm organizations

There were two possible responses: (1) Yes, active, and (2) No, not active. All affirmative responses were coded as a 1 and negative responses as a 0.

(15–27) I'm going to read you another list of groups and organizations in which you might or might not be active. Are you currently active in any ... ?

a. Travel clubs
b. Sports fantasy leagues
c. Gaming communities
d. National or local organizations for older adults, such as AARP
e. Political parties or organizations
f. Ethnic or cultural groups
g. Labor unions
h. Support groups for people with a particular illness or personal situation
i. Alumni associations
j. Fan groups for a particular TV show, movie, celebrity, or musical performer
k. Fan groups for a particular sports team or athlete
l. Fan groups for a particular brand, company, or product
m. Environmental groups

These also had two possible responses: yes and no. Again, these were coded as 0 for the negative and 1 for the affirmative. All 27 items were then summed to create a single index ($\alpha = 0.79$).

• Online Political Participation: There are many different activities related to the campaign and the elections that a person might do on the Internet. I'm going to read a list of things you may or may not have done online in the months leading up to the November elections. Just tell me if you happened to do each one, or not. (First,) did you ... ? (Next,) did you ... in the months leading up to the election?

a. Contribute money online to a candidate running for public office
b. Look for information online about candidates' voting records or positions on the issues
c. Use the Internet to participate in VOLUNTEER activities related to the campaign—like getting lists of voters to call, or getting people to the polls
d. Share photos, videos, or audio files online that relate to the campaign or the elections
e. Send e-mail related to the campaign or the elections to friends, family members, or others
f. Use the Internet to organize or get information about in-person meetings to discuss political issues in the campaign
g. Take part in an online discussion, listserv, or other online group forum like a blog, related to political issues or the campaign

Respondents were given a yes/no option. We coded yes as 1 and no as 0 and then summed these items to construct an index ($\alpha = 0.67$).

- Vote: A lot of people have been telling us they didn't get a chance to vote in the elections this year on November 2. How about you . . . did things come up that kept you from voting, or did you happen to vote? (Yes, voted = 1, No, did not vote = 2).

Notes

Chapter 1

1. Social Media is both singular and plural in common usage. For consistency, we are choosing to leave it singular throughout the book.

Chapter 2

1. The margin of error is plus or minus two percentage points. Many of the results are based on subsamples. As certain questions were only relevant to those who answered affirmatively to other questions, the respondents had to be filtered (e.g., SNS use questions were only asked of those who claim to use the Internet). Also, we apply the weight provided by Pew for all descriptive analyses to assure that the marginal distributions are generalizable. The results presented throughout the book using these data are also based on a multiply imputed dataset. While the total number of missing values across each vector was not large in absolute terms, using listwise deletion in the multivariate models throughout the book would likely bias the estimates because existing information would be lost. We are assuming that the data are missing at random (MAR). Using the multiple imputation procedure, five replicate datasets were generated based on the data, where the missing data in each replication are substituted with draws from the posterior distribution of the missing value conditional on observed values (Little and Rubin 1987; see also Horton and Lipsitz 2001). The observed values used here are standard demographics (age, education race, income) and party identification, and the posterior distributions for each variable in the dataset are based on the prediction model estimates appropriate for each variable (logit for binary outcomes, multinomial logit for categorical nominal outcomes, etc.). The analyses that follow are based on pooled results of the five replicate imputed datasets correcting for underestimation of the standard error in the multivariate models.

2. The survey indicator reads: Overall, how have you been getting most of your news about this year's campaigns and elections . . . from television, from newspapers, from radio, from magazines, or from the Internet?

3. The survey indicator reads: Please tell me if you ever use the Internet to do any of the following things. Do you ever use the Internet to use a social networking site like MySpace, Facebook or LinkedIn?

4. The survey indicator reads: Please tell me if you ever use the Internet to do any of the following things. Do you ever use the Internet to use Twitter?

5. We constructed an additive index of attentiveness indicators that we will refer to as "Attentiveness" in the models throughout the book ($\alpha = 0.57$). The three survey indicators used read: Please tell me if you ever use the Internet to do any of the following things. Do you ever use the Internet to (1) get news online? (2) look online for news or information about politics or the 2010 campaigns?, and (3) We're interested in how people used their cell phones during the recent political campaign, in addition to talking to others on your phone. Again

thinking about just your cell phone, in the months leading up to the election, did you use your cell phone to keep up with news related to the election or politics, or did you not do this?

6. We constructed an additive index of several items measuring online political participation. This will be used as a dependent variable in later chapters ($\alpha = 0.67$). The survey indicators read: There are many different activities related to the campaign and the elections that a person might do on the Internet. I'm going to read a list of things you may or may not have done online in the months leading up to the November elections. Just tell me if you happened to do each one, or not. (First,) did you . . . (Insert item; randomized)? Next, did you . . . (Insert item): in the months leading up to the election? (1) Contribute money online to a candidate running for public office, (2) Look for information online about candidates' voting records or positions on the issues, (3) Use the Internet to participate in VOLUNTEER activities related to the campaign—like getting lists of voters to call, or getting people to the polls, (4) Share photos, videos or audio files online that relate to the campaign or the elections, (5) Send email related to the campaign or the elections to friends, family members or others, (6) Use the Internet to organize or get information about in-person meetings to discuss political issues in the campaign, and (7) Take part in an online discussion, listserv, or other online group forum like a blog, related to political issues or the campaign?

7. An additive index of the six items was constructed for use in models and tests later in the book ($\alpha = 0.65$) and will be referred to as "Political SNS Use." The survey indicators used here and in the index read: Thinking about what you may have done on social networking sites like Facebook and MySpace related to the November elections, did you happen to . . . (Insert Item; Randomize) ? Next, did you . . . (Insert Item), or not?: (1) Get any campaign or candidate information on social networking sites, (2) Discover on a social networking site which candidates your friends voted for this year, (3) Sign up on a social networking site as a "friend" of a candidate, or a group involved in the campaign such as a political party or interest group, (4) Post content related to politics or the campaign on a social networking site, (5) JOIN a political group, or group supporting a cause on a social networking site, (6) START a political group, or group supporting a political cause on a social networking site?

8. An additive index of four items was constructed for use in models and tests later in the book ($\alpha = 0.62$) and will be referred to as "Political Twitter Use." The survey indicators used here and in the index read: Thinking about what you may have done on Twitter related to the November elections, did you happen to . . . (Insert Item; Randomize) ? Next, did you . . . (Insert Item), or not?: (1) Get any campaign or candidate information on Twitter, (2) Follow a candidate, or a group involved in the campaign such as a political party or interest group on Twitter, (3) Include links to political content in your tweets, and (4) Use Twitter to follow the election results as they were happening?

9. The survey indicators in this Table read: People follow candidates or other political organizations on Twitter or social networking sites such as MySpace or Facebook for a number of reasons. Please tell me if each of the following is a MAJOR reason why you follow political candidates or organizations on Twitter or social networking sites, a MINOR reason, or not a reason at all for you. First/Next . . . (Insert; Randomize) : (1) It helps me find out about political news before other people do, (2) I feel more personally connected to the political candidates or groups that I follow, and (3) The information I get on these sites is more reliable than the information I get from traditional news organizations. Is this a MAJOR reason why you follow political candidates or organizations on Twitter or social networking sites, a MINOR reason, or not a reason at all for you?

10. The survey indicator reads: Thinking about the information that is posted to Twitter or social networking sites such as MySpace or Facebook by the political candidates or groups you follow, would you say that most of it is interesting and relevant to you, or is most of it irrelevant and uninteresting? We have some reservations about how this question is worded but, nonetheless, think it provides valuable information. The question is clearly double-barreled. Respondents could believe that is interesting but irrelevant or vice versa but they are forced into accepting both premises based on the wording. Nonetheless, we think showing that they

overwhelmingly selected interesting and relevant suggests that clearly a majority believes at least one of those premises to be true.

11. The survey indicator reads: Thinking about the information posted on Twitter and social networking sites by the political candidates or groups you follow, would you say you pay attention to most of it, some of it, only a little of it, or none of it?

12. The News Feed is the center column of one's Facebook home page where there is a constantly updating list of postings coming from the people and Pages that one follows on Facebook.

13. The survey indicator reads: Would you say the Internet makes it easier to connect with others who share your political views, or that the Internet has no impact on how you connect with others who share your political views? (If the answer is "makes it easier" they were asked the following question): Would you say the Internet makes it A LOT easier, or only a little easier?

14. The survey indicator reads: When you get political or campaign news or information online, would you say most of it comes from sources that SHARE your point of view, DON'T HAVE a particular point of view, or DIFFER FROM your own point of view? A dummy variable is constructed for use in the model displayed in Table 2.5 (1 = share your point of view, 0 = other two response options).

Chapter 3

1. We constructed an additive index of the two indicators of general SNS use and Twitter use that were described in Chapter 2. These two items were statistically significantly related ($p < 0.001$).

Chapter 4

1. Much of the initial work was done by Kevin Fahey, a graduate student at the University of Louisville at the time of the election and presently a doctoral student in political science at Florida State University. He created the account and gathered the data under our guidance. He also contributed significantly to the development of the keywords described below.

2. We also counted the number of tweets with links to external sites, tweets with references to other Twitter accounts using the @ symbol with a Twitter name, and tweets with hashtags. Twitter allows people to use the hashtag symbol # before a relevant keyword or phrase in their tweet to categorize those tweets and cause them show up when someone does a Twitter search. When someone clicks on a hashtagged word in any message, they will be taken to all other tweets marked with that keyword. All of these types of tweets, those with links, other Twitter names, and those with hashtags, are discussed more thoroughly in Chapters 7 and 9 when we further develop the theory that candidates can use Twitter to try to control the flow of information.

Chapter 5

1. We chose not to offer examples for whites and senatorial candidates because the differences here are not central to our argument. They are offered, instead, just to provide some additional context.

2. District competitiveness was measured by taking the absolute value of the difference between the winner's vote total in the previous election and the loser's vote total in the previous elections and then we divided this value by 500 thousand to make the interpretation of estimate clearer. Campaign spending differential was measured by taking the absolute value of the difference between the loser's spending and the winner's spending in the previous election and then dividing that by 10 million. This makes the measure range from a decimal less than one to above four.

3. All models estimated here use negative binomial regression because the Twitter activity measures are count variables. They are also over-dispersed count variables as evidenced in the

high standard deviations presented in Chapter 4. The respective conditional variances exceed the conditional means (we selected chamber as the condition). This makes negative binomial the best distribution assumption as opposed to other count distributions.

4. Our operationalization of political experience is described in a later chapter.

Chapter 6

1. Like the post-election survey, the margin of error is plus or minus 2% for these data containing 2,303 cases. The respondents had to be filtered here also (e.g., SNS use questions were only asked of those who claim to use the Internet) so this sample is smaller for the model estimated in this chapter. Again, we apply the weight provided by Pew for all descriptive analysis to assure that the marginal distributions are generalizable. While the total number of missing values across each vector was not large in absolute terms, we again multiply imputed these data to avoid the biases that may have resulted from using listwise deletion. We replicated the process described in Chapter 2. Thus, five replicate datasets were generated based on the data, where the missing data in each replication were substituted with draws from the posterior distribution of the missing value conditional on standard demographics (age, education, race, income) and party identification (see Little and Rubin 1987; see also Horton and Lipsitz 2001). The observed values used here, and the posterior distributions for each variable in the dataset, are based on the prediction model estimates appropriate for each variable (logit for binary outcomes, multinomial logit for categorical nominal outcomes, etc.). The analyses that follow are based on pooled results of the five replicate imputed datasets correcting for underestimation of the standard error in the multivariate models.

2. The dependent variable is a count variable that is not over-dispersed, making Poisson the best assumed distribution to model this outcome. The means of the propensity to join groups are larger than the variances across SNS use. A description of the control variables is included in the Appendix.

Chapter 7

1. The reason some exceed 1 is because there were instances of tweets with multiple links counted (or @Twitter names or hashtags). We decided, just as we did with the noninformation control tweets that it was optimal, methodologically and theoretically, to count each instance. The idea is that someone who sends out a tweet with multiple links or hashtags has the potential for a larger impact than a tweet with only one. If the tweet were only counted once when one of these appeared, a tweet with four hashtags or links would carry the same weight in the analysis as one that had only a single hashtag.

2. These three models are estimated using negative binomial regression because they are over-dispersed count variables. The respective conditional variances exceed the conditional means (we selected chamber to use as the condition). This makes negative binomial the best distribution assumption as opposed to other count distributions. The district competitiveness and spending differential indicators are the same as those used in Chapter 5.

Chapter 8

1. This argument is consistent with recent media scholarship much of which focuses on the implications of the rise of partisan media and whether this has helped to create an information environment where citizens tend to consume congenial news and screen out opposing viewpoints (Arceneaux and Johnson 2013; Bennett and Manheim 2006; Garrett 2009a, 2009b; Goldman and Mutz 2011; Iyengar and Hahn 2009; Iyengar et al. 2008; Manjoo 2008; Mutz and Martin 2001; Stroud 2008, 2011; Sunstein 2009; Valentino et al. 2009).

2. This status update was taken from the Facebook News Feed of one of the authors of this book with the permission of the person who posted it.

3. For more details on how EdgeRank works see http://edgerank.net.

4. Earlier research by Thomas Patterson (2007) did find that that usage of "aggregators with attitude" or partisan aggregators was rapidly growing. Thus, not all news aggregators present a two-sided information flow.

5. The Elaboration Likelihood Model (ELM) asserts that attitude persuasion can take place through two routes, the central and the peripheral (Petty and Cacioppo 1996; Petty, Priester, and Brinol 2002). Holbert, Garret, and Gleason (2010) make clear that the central route is characterized by cognitive models of persuasion and that the new media environment provides opportunity for this central route. We concur and assert that this cognitive process of attitude persuasion is understood best by looking at this phenomenon through the lens of a combined understanding of the RAS model and the OPM.

6. It is worth noting that not all research concurs that the consumption of opinionated or one-sided news will intensify attitude differences between people with varied predispositions (see Feldman 2011).

7. We rely largely on the description of and arguments about how these two models have shaped the history of the information processing and public opinion literature laid out by Taber (2003) in his descriptive piece in the *Oxford Handbook of Political Psychology* (Sears, Huddy, and Jervis 2003).

8. Although Achen (1975) was able to account for virtually all attitude instability simply as measurement error using Converse's own data, there was nonetheless still not a widely accepted political attitudinal model at the time.

9. This online participation model is estimated using Poisson regression because online political participation is a count variable that is not over-dispersed. The respective conditional variances do not exceed the conditional means (we selected attitude extremity as the condition). This makes Poisson the best distribution assumption. The model of whether people voted is a simple dichotomous variable so we estimated the model using logit.

10. There is also a fair amount of support of the relationship when the index component items are broken out and the bivariate relationships are observed. Those who score on the lower values on the SNS/Twitter scale typically score lower on the folded ideology scale, the awareness of the Tea Party indicator, the folded agreement with the Tea Party indicator, and the anger with the federal government indicator.

11. It is interesting that attentiveness is highly significant in the online participation model but insignificant in the vote model. We can only speculate on reasons why this may be the case. Our best post-hoc speculation is that those who are more attentive are more likely to be educated, and thus, more likely to have the necessary computer/Internet skills needed to effectively participate online. While one would also expect the more educated to vote, this relationship may just not be as strong as is between online skills and education.

Chapter 9

1. Both tweeting indices were divided by 1,000 to make the results that follow easier to interpret.

2. Again, these models are based on data where the missing values were replaced using multiple imputation. The imputation model is described in Chapter 5. The same measures of district competitiveness and spending differential employed in Chapter 5 were used here. Political experience was measured as the number of years the candidate has held elected office and the total number of candidates was simply the count on the number of candidates in the general election for each candidate's respective race.

3. The r^2 is quite large across the models, suggesting that they perform well at explaining the overall variance in vote share.

4. Most in the sample did not have over 1,000 instances of these types of tweets so the units were represented by fractions (decimals). As noted earlier, we divided the variable by 1,000 so that the coefficients would be easier to interpret. We would have had to use scientific notation.

References

Abramowitz, Alan I. 1991. "Incumbency, Campaign Spending, and the Decline of Competition in U.S. House Elections." *Journal of Politics* 53 (1): 34–56.

Achen, Christopher H. 1975. "Mass Political Attitudes and the Survey Response." *American Political Science Review* 69 (4): 1218–1231.

Agranoff, Craig, and Herbert Tabin. 2011. *Socially Elected: How To Win Elections Using Social Media.* New York: Pendant Publishing.

Aldrich, John H. 1995. *Why Parties?* Chicago: University of Chicago Press.

Alexa.com. 2011. http://www.alexa.com. Accessed November 18, 2011.

Allison, Juliann Emmons. 2002. *Technology, Development, and Democracy: International Conflict and Cooperation in the Information Age.* Albany: State University of New York Press.

Almacy, David, Kurt Hauptman, and Marcia Newbert. 2012. "Capitol Tweets: The Yeas and Nays of the Congressional Twitterverse." *Scribd.* http://www.scribd.com/doc/86234716/Capitol-Tweets-New-Edelman-Study-Looks-at-U-S-Congressional-Performance-on-Twitter. Accessed: August 24, 2012.

Alvarez, R. Michael, and John Brehm. 1995. "American Ambivalence towards Abortion Policy: Development of a Heteroskedastic Probit Model of Competing Values." *American Journal of Political Science* 39 (4): 1055–1082.

Ammann, Sky L. 2010. "A Political Campaign Message in 140 Characters or Less: The Use of Twitter by U.S. Senate Candidates in 2010." *Social Science Research Network.* http://ssrn.com/abstract=1725477. Accessed: April 15, 2013.

Ansolabehere, Stephen, and James M. Snyder Jr. 2002. "The Incumbency Advantage in U.S. Elections: An Analysis of State and Federal Offices, 1942–2000." *Election Law Journal: Rules, Politics, and Policy* 1 (3): 315–338.

Appleton, A., and D. Ward. 1997. "Party Response to Environmental Change." *Party Politics* 3 (3): 341–362.

Arceneaux, Kevin, and Martin Johnson. 2013. *Changing Minds or Changing Channels? Partisan News in the Age of Choice.* Chicago: University of Chicago Press.

Arnold, R. Douglas. 1990. *The Logic of Congressional Action.* New Haven: Yale University Press.

Atkinson, J. W. 1964. *An Introduction to Motivation.* Princeton, NJ: Van Nostrand.

Bakker, Tom P., and Claes H. de Vreese. 2011. "Good News for the Future? Young People, Internet Use, and Political Participation." *Communication Research* 38 (4): 451–470.

Barber, Benjamin R. 2001. "The Uncertainty of Digital Politics." *Harvard International Review* 23 (1): 42–47.

Barber, Benjamin R. 2003. *Strong Democracy: Participatory Politics for a New Age.* Berkeley, CA: University of California Press.

Barker, David. 2002. *Rush to Judgment?* New York: Columbia University Press.

Barry, Brian. 1970. *Sociologists, Economists and Democracy.* Chicago: University of Chicago Press.

Bennett, W. Lance. 2004. *News: The Politics of Illusion,* 6th ed. New York: Longman.

Bennett, W. Lance. 2011. *News: The Politics of Illusion,* 9th ed. New York: Longman.

Bennett, W. Lance and Jarol B. Manheim. 2006. "The One-Step Flow of Communication." *The ANNALS of the American Academy of Political and Social Science* 608 (1): 213–232.

Benson, Eric. 2012. "Unskewed Polls Founder Dean Chambers Takes Stock of Obama's Win." *New York Magazine*. http://nymag.com/daily/intel/2012/11/unskewed-polls-founder-dean-chambers-on-polling-bias.html. Accessed: November 9, 2012.

Berelson, Bernard R., Paul F. Lazarsfeld, and William N. McPhee. 1954. *Voting: A Study of Opinion Formation in a Presidential Campaign*. Chicago: University of Chicago Press.

Bergan, Daniel E., Alan S. Gerber, Donald P. Green, and Costas Panagopoulos. 2005. "Grassroots Mobilization and Voter Turnout in 2004." *Public Opinion Quarterly* 69 (5): 760–777.

Bimber, Bruce A. 1999. "The Internet and Citizen Communication With Government: Does the Medium Matter?" *Political Communication* 16 (4): 409–428.

Bimber, Bruce A., and Richard Davis. 2003. *Campaigning Online: The Internet in U.S. Elections*. New York: Oxford University Press.

Bimber, Bruce, and Lauren Copeland. 2013. "Digital Media and Political Participation over Time in the U.S." *Journal of Information Technology & Politics* 10 (2): 125–137.

Bizer, George Y., Zakary L. Tormala, Derek D. Rucker, and Richard E. Petty. 2006. "Memory-Based versus On-Line Processing: Implications for Attitude Strength." *Journal of Experimental Social Psychology* 42 (5): 646–653.

Bode, Leticia. 2012. "Facebooking it to the Polls: A Study in Online Social Networking and Political Behavior." *Journal of Information Technology & Politics* 9 (4): 352–369.

Bode, Leticia, Kajsa Dalrymple and Dhavan Shah. 2011. "Politics in 140 Characters or Less: Campaign Communication, Network Interaction, and Political Participation on Twitter." Paper presented at the 2011 *Annual meeting of the American Political Science Association*.

Bode, Leticia, David Lassen, Benjamin Sayre, Young Mie Kim, Dhavan Vinod Shah, Erika Franklin Fowler, Travis N. Ridout, and Michael Franz. 2011 "Putting New Media in Old Strategies: Candidate Use of Twitter during the 2010 Midterm Elections." Paper presented at the 2011 *Annual Meeting of the American Political Science Association*, Seattle.

Bond, Jon R., Cary Covington, and Richard Fleisher. 1985. "Explaining Challenger Quality in Congressional Elections." *Journal of Politics* 47 (2): 510–529.

Bond, Robert M., Christopher J. Fariss, Jason J. Jones, Adam D. I. Kramer, Cameron Marlow, Jaime E. Settle, and James H. Fowler. 2012. "A 61-Million-Person Experiment in Social Influence and Political Mobilization." *Nature* 489 (7415): 295–298.

Bonfadelli, Heinz. 2002. "The Internet and Knowledge Gaps: A Theoretical and Empirical Investigation." *European Journal of Communication* 17 (1): 65–84.

Boulianne, Shelley. 2009. "Does Internet Use Affect Engagement? A Meta-Analysis of Research." *Political Communication* 26 (2): 193–211.

Boulianne, Shelley. 2011. "Stimulating or Reinforcing Political Interest: Using Panel Data to Examine Reciprocal Effects between News Media Use and Political Interest." Political Communication 28 (2): 147–162.

Bourdieu, Pierre. 1986. "The Forms of Capital." In *Handbook of Theory and Research for the Sociology of Education*, ed. John Richardson. New York: Greenwood Press. 241–258.

Boynton, Robert. 2009. *Going Viral—The Dynamics of Attention*. Paper presented at the *YouTube and the 2008 Election Cycle in the United States Conference*, Amherst, MA.

Breaux, David A., and Anthony Gierzynski. 1991. "'It's Money that Matters': Campaign Expenditures and State Legislative Primaries." *Legislative Studies Quarterly* 16 (3): 429–443.

Brehm, John, and Wendy M. Rahn. 1997. "Individual-Level Evidence for the Causes and Consequences of Social Capital." *American Journal of Political Science* 41 (3): 999–1023.

Browning, Graeme. 2002. *Electronic Democracy: Using the Internet to Transform American Politics*, 2nd ed. Medford, NJ: CyberAge Books.

Burden, Barry C., and David C. Kimball. 2002. *Why Americans Split Their Tickets: Campaigns, Competition and Divided Government*. Ann Arbor: University of Michigan Press.

Campbell, Angus. 1960. "Surge and Decline: A Study of Electoral Change." *Public Opinion Quarterly*. 24 (3): 397–418.

Carmines, Edward G. and James A. Stimson. 1986. "On the Structure and Sequence of Issue Evolution," *American Political Science Review* 80 (3): 901–920.

Carmines, Edward G., and James A. Stimson. 1989. *Issue Evolution: Race and the Transformation of American Politics.* Ithaca: Princeton University Press.

Carpenter, Christopher. 2010. "The Obamamachine: Techno-politics 2.0." *Journal of Information Technology & Politics* 7 (2/3): 216–225.

Cassino, Dan, Charles S. Taber, and Milton Lodge. 2007. "Information Processing and Public Opinion." *Politische Vierteljahresschrift* 48: 205–20.

Chadwick, Andrew. 2006. *Internet Politics: States, Citizens, and New Communication Technologies.* New York: Oxford University Press.

Chen, M. Keith., and Jane L. Risen 2010. "How Choice Affects and Reflects Preferences: Revisiting the Free-Choice Paradigm." *Journal of Personality and Social Psychology* 99 (4): 573–594.

Chi, Feng, and Nathan Yang. 2010. "Twitter in Congress: Outreach vs. Transparency." *Social Science Research Network.* http://papers.ssrn.com/sol3/papers.cfm?abstract_id = 1630943. Accessed: October 17, 2011.

Cho, Jaeho, Dhavan V. Shah, Jack M. McLeod, Douglas M. McLeod, Rosanne M. Scholl, and Melissa R. Gotlieb. 2009. "Campaigns, Reflection, and Deliberation: Advancing an O-S-R-O-R Model of Communication Effects." *Communication Theory* 19 (1): 66–88.

Cohn, Alcia M. 2012. "Obama's 'horses and bayonets' debate comment tops Twitter chatter." *The Hill.* http://thehill.com/blogs/twitter-room/other-news/263431-obamas-horses-and-bayonets-line-tops-social-media-chatter. Accessed: July 15, 2013.

Coleman, James S. 1988. "Social Capital in the Creation of Human Capital." *American Journal of Sociology* 94: S95–S120.

Coleman, James S. 1990. *Foundations of Social Theory.* Cambridge, MA: Harvard University Press.

Conover, Pamela Johnston, and Stanley Feldman. 1984. "How People Organize the Political World: A Schematic Model." *American Journal of Political Science* 28 (1): 95–126.

Conroy, Meredith, Jessica T. Feezell, and Mario Guerrero. 2012. "Facebook and Political Engagement: A Study of Online Political Group Membership and Offline Political Engagement." *Computers in Human Behavior* 28 (5): 1535–1546.

Converse, Philip E. 1962. "Information Flow and the Stability of Partisan Attitudes." *Public Opinion Quarterly* 26 (4): 578–599.

Converse, Philip E. 1964. "The Nature of Belief Systems in Mass Publics." In *Ideology and Discontent,* ed. David Apter. New York: John Wiley. 202–261.

Cornfeld, Michael, Lee Rainie, and John Horrigan. 2003. "Untuned Keyboards: Online Campaigners, Citizens and Portals in the 2002 Elections." In *Pew Internet and American Life Project.* http://pewinternet.org/reports/2003/online-campaigners-citizens-and-portals-in-the-2002-elections.aspx. Accessed: April 15, 2013.

Corrado, Anthony, and Charles M. Firestone, eds. 1996. *Elections in Cyberspace: Towards a New Era in American Politics.* Washington, DC: Aspen Institute.

Cox, Anna Marie. 2012. "How the Obama White House has won the hashtag wars." *The Guardian.* http://www.guardian.co.uk/commentisfree/2012/nov/29/obama-white-house-hashtag-wars#start-of-comments. Accessed: December 5, 2012.

Craig, Stephen C., Jim G. Kane, Michael D. Martinez, and Jason Gainous. 2005. "Core Values, Value Conflict, and Citizens' Ambivalence about Gay Rights." *Political Research Quarterly* 58 (1): 5–17.

Dahl, Robert A. 1961. *Who Governs?* New Haven: Yale University Press.

Dahl, Robert A. 1989. *Democracy and its Critics.* New Haven: Yale University Press.

Dalton, Russell. 1996. "Political Cleavages, Issues, and Electoral Change." In *Comparing Democracies,* eds. Lawrence LeDuc, Richard G. Niemi, and Pippa Norris. Thousand Oaks: Sage. 319–342.

Dalton, Russell J. 2006. *Citizen Politics: Public Opinion and Political Participation in Advanced Industrial Democracies.* New York: Chatham House.

Davis, Richard. 1999. *The Web of Politics: The Internet's Impact on the American Political System.* New York: Oxford University Press.

Davis, Robert. 2009. *Typing Politics: The Role of Blogs in American Politics*. New York: Oxford University Press.

Delli Carpini, Michael X. 2000. "Gen.Com: Youth, Civic Engagement and the New Information Environment." *Political Communication* 17 (4): 341–349.

DiMaggio, Paul, Eszter Hargittai, Coral Celeste, and Steven Shafer. 2004. "Digital Inequality: From Unequal Access to Differentiated Use." In *Social Inequality*, ed. Kathryn Neckerman. New York: Russell Sage Foundation. 355–400.

Dodd, Lawrence C. 1977. "Congress and the Quest for Power." In *Congress Reconsidered*, eds. Lawrence C. Dodd and Bruce I. Oppenheimer. Washington: CQ Press. 269–307.

Dodd, Lawrence C. 1981. "Congress, the Constitution and the Crisis of Legitimation." In *Congress Reconsidered*, eds. Lawrence C. Dodd and Bruce I. Oppenheimer. Washington, DC: CQ Press. 390–420.

Downs, Anthony. 1957. *An Economic Theory of Democracy*. New York: Harper.

Druckman, James N., and Michael Parkin. 2005. "The Impact of Media Bias: How Editorial Slant Affects Voters." *Journal of Politics* 67 (4): 1030–1049.

Dutton, Jane E., and Susan E. Jackson. 1987. "Categorizing Strategic Issues: Links to Organizational Action." *Academy of Management Review* 12 (1): 76–90.

Dyson, Ester. 2011. "Illusions of Democracy." *Daily News Egypt*. http://www.dailynewsegypt. com/2011/05/20/illusions-of-democracy. Accessed: April 2, 2013.

Eagly, Alice H., and Shelly Chaiken. 1993. *The Psychology of Attitudes*. Fort Worth: Harcourt Brace.

Edwards, Ward. 1955. "The Prediction of Decisions among Bets." *Journal of Experimental Psychology* 51 (3): 201–214.

Elliot, Andrew J., and Patricia G. Devine. 1994. "On the Motivational Nature of Cognitive Dissonance: Dissonance as Psychological Discomfort." *Journal of Personality and Social Psychology* 67 (3): 382–394.

Ellison, Nicole B., Charles Steinfield, and Cliff Lampe. 2007. "The Benefits of Facebook "Friends:" Social Capital and College Students' use of Online Social Network Sites." *Journal of Computer-Mediated Communication* 12 (4).

Epstein, David, and Peter Zemsky. 1995. "Money Talks: Deterring Quality Challengers in Congressional Elections." *American Political Science Review*. 89 (2): 295–308.

Erikson, Robert S., and Thomas R. Palfrey. 1998. "Campaign Spending and Incumbency: An Alternative Simultaneous Equations Approach." *Journal of Politics* 60 (2): 355–373.

Farley, Christopher John. 2012. "#horsesandbayonets Gallops across the Internet." *The Wall Street Journal Online*. http://blogs.wsj.com/speakeasy/2012/10/22/horsesandbayonets-gallops-across-the-internet/. Accessed: April 15, 2013.

Feldman, Lauren. 2011. "The Opinion Factor: The Effects of Opinionated News on Information Processing and Attitude Change, Political Communication." *Political Communication* 28 (2): 163–181.

Fenno, Richard F. 1973. *Congressmen in Committees*. Boston: Little & Brown.

Festinger, Leon. 1957. *A Theory of Cognitive Dissonance*. Stanford, CA: Stanford University Press.

Festinger, Leon. 1964. *Conflict, Decision, and Dissonance*. Stanford, CA: Stanford University Press.

Fiorina, Morris P. 1989. *Congress: Keystone of the Washington Establishment*, rev. ed. Princeton, NJ: Yale University Press.

Fiorina, Morris P., and Samuel J. Abrams. 2009. *Disconnect: The Breakdown of Representation in American Politics*. Norman, OK: University of Oklahoma Press.

Fischer, Peter, Eva Jonas, Dieter Frey, and Stefan Schulz-Hardt. 2005. "Selective Exposure to Information: The Impact of Information Limits." *European Journal of Social Psychology* 35 (4): 469–492.

Fischer, Peter, Stefan Schulz-Hardt, and Dieter Frey. 2008. "Selective Exposure and Information Quantity: How Different Information Quantities Moderate Decision Makers' Preference for Consistent and Inconsistent Information." *Journal of Personality and Social Psychology* 94 (2): 231–244.

Freedman, Des. 2006. "Internet Transformations: 'Old' Media Resilience in the 'New Media' Revolution." In *Media and Cultural Theory*, eds. James Curran and David Morley. Abingdon: Routledge. 275–290.

Freeman, Jo. 1986. "The Political Culture of the Democratic and Republican Parties." *Political Science Quarterly* 101 (3): 327–356.

Frey, Dieter. 1986. "Recent Research on Selective Exposure to Information." In *Advances in Experimental Social Psychology*, ed. Leonard Berkowitz. New York: Academic Press. 41–80.

Funk, Carolyn L. 1999. "Bringing the Candidate into Models of Candidate Evaluation." *The Journal of Politics* 61 (3): 700–720.

Gainous, Jason. 2008a. "Who's Ambivalent and Who's Not? Ideology and Ambivalence about Social Welfare." *American Politics Research* 36 (2): 210–235.

Gainous, Jason. 2008b. "Ambivalence about Social Welfare: An Evaluation of Measurement Approaches." *American Review of Politics* 29: 109–134.

Gainous, Jason. 2012. "The New 'New Racism' Thesis: Limited Government Values and Race-Conscious Policy Attitudes." *Journal of Black Studies* 43 (3): 251–273.

Gainous, Jason, Adam David Marlowe, and Kevin M. Wagner. 2013. "Traditional Cleavages or a New World: Does Online Social Networking Bridge the Political Participation Divide?" *International Journal of Politics, Culture, and Society* 26 (2): 145–158.

Gainous, Jason, and Kevin M. Wagner. 2007. "The Electronic Ballot Box: A Rational Voting Model and The Internet." *American Review of Politics* 28 (Spring and Summer): 19–35.

Gainous, Jason, and Kevin M. Wagner. 2011. *Rebooting American Politics: The Internet Revolution.* Lanham, MD: Rowman and Littlefield.

Garrett, R. Kelly. 2009a. "Politically Motivated Reinforcement Seeking: Reframing the Selective Exposure Debate." *Journal of Communication* 59 (4): 676–699.

Garrett, R. Kelly. 2009b. "Echo Chambers Online? Politically Motivated Selective Exposure among Internet News Users." *Journal of Computer-Mediated Communication* 14 (2): 265–285.

Garrett, R. Kelly, Dustin Carnahan, and Emily K. Lynch. 2013. "A Turn Toward Avoidance? Selective Exposure to Online Political Information, 2004–2008." *Political Behavior* 35 (1): 113–134.

Garrison-Sprenger, Nicole. 2008. "Twittery-Do-Dah, Twittering Pays." *Quill* 96 (8): 12–15.

Gibson, Rachel, Wainer Lusoli, and Stephen Ward. 2005. "Online Participation in the UK: Testing a 'Contextualised' Model of Internet Effects." *British Journal of Politics and International Relations* 7 (4): 561–583.

Gibson, Rachel, and Stephen Ward. 1998. "U.K. Political Parties and the Internet: 'Politics as Usual' in the New Media?" *The Harvard International Journal of Press/Politics* 3 (3): 14–38.

Gil de Zúñiga, Homero, Nakwon Jun, and Sebastián Valenzuela. 2012. "Social Media Use for News and Individuals' Social Capital, Civic Engagement and Political Participation." *Journal of Computer Mediated Communication* 17 (3): 319–336.

Giustozzi, Antonio. 2001. *Koran, Kalishnikov, and Laptop: The Neo-Taliban Insurgency in Afghanistan 2002–2007.* New York: Columbia University Press.

Glassman, Matthew, Jacob R. Straus, and Colleen J. Shogun. 2009. "Social Networking and Constituency Communication: Member Use of Twitter during a Two Month Period in the 111th Congress." Washington, DC: Congressional Research Service. http://assets.opencrs.com/rpts/r41066_20100203.pdf. Accessed: April 15, 2013.

Golbeck, Jennifer, Justin M. Grimes, and Anthony Rogers. 2010. "Twitter use by the U.S. Congress." *Journal of the American Society for Information Science and Technology* 61 (8): 1612–1621.

Goldman, Seth K., and Diana C. Mutz. 2011. "The Friendly Media Phenomenon: A Cross-National Analysis of Cross-Cutting Exposure." *Political Communication* 28 (1): 42–66.

Gould, Jack. 1946. "Television: Boon or Bane?" *Public Opinion Quarterly* 10 (3): 314–320.

Graber, Doris A. 2006. *Mass Media and American Politics.* Washington, DC: CQ Press.

Graber, Doris A. 2007. *Media Power in Politics.* Washington, DC: CQ Press.

Graber, Doris A. 2010. *Processing Politics: Learning from Television in the Internet Age.* Chicago: University of Chicago Press.

Gray, Jeffrey A. 1982. *The Neuropsychology of Anxiety: An Enquiry into the Functions of the Septo-Hippocampal System*. New York: Oxford University Press.

Green, Donald P., Alan S. Gerber, and David W. Nickerson. 2003. "Getting out the Vote in Local Elections: Results from Six Door-to-Door Canvassing Experiments." *Journal of Politics* 65 (4): 1083–1096.

Green, Donald P., and Jonathan S. Krasno. 1988. "Salvation for the Spendthrift Incumbent: Reestimating the Effects of Campaign Spending in House Elections." *American Journal of Political Science* 32 (4): 884–907.

Green, Zach. 2012. "Rule 22: Hashtags will be Co-opted." *140Elect*. http://140elect.com/2012-twitter-politics/rule-22-hashtags-will-be-co-opted/. Accessed: November 25, 2012.

Guildford, George. 2011. "Why Improving you EdgeRank Score on Facebook is Now More Important than Ever." *socialmedia today*. http://socialmediatoday.com/george-guildford/383842/why-improving-your-edgerank-score-facebook-now-more-important-ever. Accessed: May 14, 2013.

Hagen, Michael G., and William G. Mayer. 2000. "The Modern Politics of Presidential Selection: How Changing the Rules Really Did Change the Game." In *In Pursuit of the White House 2000: How We Choose Our Presidential Nominees*, ed. William G. Mayer. New York: Chatham House Publishers. 1–55.

Hamilton, James T. 2004. *All the News that is Fit to Sell. How the Market Transforms Information into News*. Princeton, NJ: Princeton University Press.

Hastie, Reid, and Bernadette Park. 1986. "The Relationship between Memory and Judgment Depends on Whether the Judgment Task is Memory-Based or On-Line." *Psychological Review* 93 (3): 258–268.

Hastie, Reid, and Nancy Pennington. 1989. "Notes on the Distinction between Memory-Based versus On-Line Judgments." In *On-Line Cognition in Person Perception*, ed. John N. Bassili. Hillsdale, NJ: Lawrence Erlbaum Associates, Inc. 1–17.

Headcount.com. 2011. http://www.headcount.com. Accessed: November 12, 2011.

Heberlig, Eric, Marc Hetherington, and Bruce Larson. 2006. "The Price of Leadership: Campaign Money and the Polarization of Congressional Parties." *Journal of Politics* 68 (4): 992–1005.

Heider, Fritz. 1958. *The Psychology of Interpersonal Relations*. New York: Wiley.

Hendriks Vettehen, Paul. G., C. P. M. Hagemann, and Leo B. Van Snippenburg. 2004. "Political Knowledge and Media use in the Netherlands." *European Sociological Review* 20 (5): 415–424.

Herman, Edward, and Noam Chomsky. 2002. *Manufacturing Consent: The Political Economy of the Mass Media*. New York: Pantheon.

Higgins, E. Tory. 1997. "Beyond Pleasure and Pain." *American Psychologist* 52 (12): 1280–1300.

Hill, Kevin A., and John E. Hughes. 1998. *Cyberpolitics*. New York: Rowman and Littlefield.

Hillygus, Sunshine, and Simon Jackman. 2003. "Voter Decision Making in Election 2000: Campaign Effects, Partisan Activation, and the Clinton Legacy." *American Journal of Political Science* 47 (4): 583–596.

Hindman, Mathew. 2008. *The Myth of Digital Democracy*. Princeton, NJ: Princeton University Press.

Hoge, Patrick. 2009. "Facebook Dethrones MySpace." *Jacksonville Business Journal*. http://www.bizjournals.com/jacksonville/stories/2009/01/26/daily5.html. Accessed: July 20, 2013.

Holbert, Lance R., Kelly Garrett, and Laurel S. Gleason. 2010. "A New Era of Minimal Effects? A Response to Bennett and Iyengar." *Journal of Communication* 60 (1): 15–34.

Holbrook, Thomas M., and Charles M. Tidmarch. 1993. "The Effects of Leadership Positions on Votes for Incumbents in State Legislative Elections." *Political Research Quarterly* 46 (4): 897–909.

Honeycutt, Courtenay, and Susan Herring. 2009. "Beyond Microblogging: Conversation and Collaboration via Twitter." *Proceedings of the Forty-Second Hawai'i International Conference on System Sciences (HICSS-42)*, CD-ROM, IEEE Computer Society 1–10.

Horton, Nicholas J., and Stuart R. Lipsitz. 2001. "Multiple Imputation in Practice: Comparison of Software Packages for Regression Models with Missing Variables." *The American Statistician* 55 (3): 244–254.

Howard, Philip N. 2011. *The Digital Origins of Dictatorship and Democracy: Information Technology and Political Islam*. New York: Oxford University Press.

Iyengar, Shanto, and Kyu S. Hahn. 2009. "Red Media, Blue Media: Evidence of Ideological Selectivity in Media Use." *Journal of Communication* 59 (1): 19–39.

Iyengar, Shanto, Kyu S. Hahn, Jon A. Krosnick, and John Walker. 2008. "Selective Exposure to Campaign Communication: The Role of Anticipated Agreement and Issue Public Membership." *Journal of Politics* 70 (1):186–200.

Jackson, David. 2012. "Obama Hosts 'Fiscal Cliff' Chat on Twitter." *USA Today*. http://www.usatoday. com/story/theoval/2012/12/03/obama-twitter-fiscal-cliff/1742807/. Accessed: April 11, 2013.

Jacobs, Lawrence R., and Robert Y Shapiro. 1994. "Issues, Candidate Image, and Priming: The Use of Private Polls in Kennedy's 1960 Presidential Campaign. *American Political Science Review* 88 (3): 527–540.

Jacobson, Gary C. 1992. *The Politics of Congressional Elections*, 3rd ed. New York: HarperCollins Publishers.

Jelen, Ted G. 2001. *Ross for Boss: The Perot Phenomena and Beyond*. New York: State University of New York Press.

Jeltsen, Melissa. 2012. "Cory Booker, Newark, New Jersey Mayor, Invites Hurricane Sandy Victims to His House." *The Huffington Post*. http://www.huffingtonpost.com/2012/11/01/cory-booker-neighbors-hurricane-sandy_n_2059971.html. Accessed: December 12, 2012.

Jones, Jeffery M. 2010. "Congress' Job Approval Rating Worst in Gallup History." *Gallup Politics*. http://www.gallup.com/poll/145238/congress-job-approval-rating-worst-gallup-history. aspx. Accessed: December 8, 2012.

Kahn, Kim Fridkin, and Patrick J. Kenney. 2001. "The Importance of Issues in Senate Campaigns: Citizens' Reception of Issue Messages." *Legislative Studies Quarterly* 26 (4): 573–597.

Kahn, Kim Fridkin, and Patrick J. Kenney. 2002. "The Slant of the News." *American Political Science Review* 96 (2): 381–394.

Kahneman, Daniel, and Amos Tversky. 1979. "Prospect Theory: An Analysis of Decision under Risk." *Econometrica* 47 (2): 263–291.

Kallen, Stuart. 2004. *Media Bias*. San Diego: Greenhaven Press.

Kaplan, Andreas M., and Michael Haenlein. 2010. "Users of the World, Unite! The Challenges and Opportunities of Social Media." *Business Horizons* 53 (1): 62–64.

Kaufmann, Karen M. 2002. "Culture Wars, Secular Realignment, and the Gender Gap in Party Identification." *Political Behavior* 24 (3): 283–307.

Kelley, Jr., Stanley. 1983. *Interpreting Elections*. Princeton, NJ: Princeton University Press.

Kenney, Patrick J., and Tom W. Rice. 1988. "Presidential Prenomination Preferences and Candidate Evaluations." *American Political Science Review* 82 (4): 1309–1319.

Kernell, Samuel. 1994. *Going Public: New Strategies of Presidential Leadership*, 4th ed. Washington, DC: CQ Press.

Kernell, Samuel. 1997. "The Theory and Practice of Going Public." In *Do the Media Govern?: Politicians, Voters, and Reporters in America*, eds. Shanto Iyengar and Richard Reeves. Thousand Oaks, CA: Sage Publications. 323–333.

Key, V. O. 1966. *The Responsible Electorate*. Cambridge, MA: Belknap Press.

Kinder, Donald R. 1986. "The Continuing American Dilemma: White Resistance to Racial Change 40 Years after Mydral." *Journal of Social Issues* 42 (2): 151–171.

Kinder, Donald R. 2003. Communication and Politics in the Age of Information. In *Oxford Handbook of Political Psychology*, eds. Leoni Huddy, Robert Jervis, and David O. Sears. New York: Oxford University Press. 357–393.

Kittilson, Miki Caul, and Russell J. Dalton. 2011. "Virtual Civil Society: The New Frontier of Social Capital?" *Political Behavior* 33 (4): 625–644.

Klofstad, Casey A. 2007. "Talk Leads to Recruitment: How Discussions about Politics and Current Events Increase Civic Participation." *Political Research Quarterly* 60 (2): 180–191.

Klofstad, Casey A. 2009. "Civic Talk and Civic Participation: The Moderating Effect of Individual Predispositions." *American Politics Research* 37 (5): 856–878.

Klotz, Robert J. 2004. *The Politics of Internet Communication.* Lanham, MD: Rowman and Littlefield Publishers.

Koetzle, William. 1998. "The Impact of Constituency Diversity upon the Competitiveness of U.S. House Elections, 1962–96." *Legislative Studies Quarterly* 23 (4): 561–573.

Krebs, Timothy B. 1998. "The Determinants of Candidates' Vote Share and the Advantages of Incumbency in City Council Elections." *American Journal of Political Science* 42 (3): 921–935.

Krueger, Brian S. 2002. "Assessing the Potential of Internet Political Participation in the United States." *American Politics Research* 30 (5): 476–498.

Krueger, Brian S. 2006. "A Comparison of Conventional and Internet Political Mobilization." *American Politics Research* 34 (6): 759–776.

Lake, Ronald La Due and Robert Huckfeldt. 1998. "Social Capital, Social Networks, and Political Participation." *Political Psychology* 19 (3): 567–584.

Lashley, Marilyn. 2009. "The Politics of Cognitive Dissonance: Spin, the Media, and Race (and Ethnicity) in the 2008 US Presidential Election." *American Review of Canadian Studies* 39 (4): 364–377.

Lassen, David S., Adam R. Brown and Scott Riding. 2010. "Twitter: The Electoral Connection?" Presented at the 2010 *Annual meeting of the Midwest Political Science Association,* Chicago.

Lau, Richard R., Lee Sigelman, and Ivy Brown Rovner. 2007. "The Effects of Negative Political Campaigns: A Meta-Analytic Reassessment." *Journal of Politics* 69 (4): 1176–1209.

Lavine, Howard. 2002. "On-line vs. Memory-Based Models of Political Evaluation." In *Political Psychology,* ed. Kristen Renwick Monroe, Majwah, NJ: Erlbaum. 225–248.

Leighley, Jan E., and Arnold Vedlitz. 1999. "Race, Ethnicity, and Political Participation: Competing Models and Contrasting Explanations." *Journal of Politics* 61 (4): 1092–1114.

Lenhart, Amanda. 2009. "Adults and Social Network Websites." *Pew Internet and American Life Project.* http://www.pewInternet.org/Reports/2009/Adults-and-Social-Network-Websites.aspx. Accessed: March 18, 2010.

Lijphart, Arend. 1979. "Religious vs. Linguistic vs. Class Voting: The 'Crucial Experiment' of Comparing Belgium, Canada, South Africa, and Switzerland." *American Political Science Review* 73 (2): 442–458.

Lindsay, Erin. 2012. "Thanksgiving Decision 2012: Cobbler or Gobbler?" The White House Blog. http://www.whitehouse.gov/blog/2012/11/20/thanksgiving-decision-2012-cobbler-or-gobbler. Accessed: December 6, 2012.

Little, Roderick J.A. Donald, and B. Rubin. 1987. *Statistical Analysis with Missing Data.* New York: Wiley.

Livene, Avishay, Mathew Simmons, W. Abraham Gong, Eytan Adar, and Lada A. Adamic. 2011. "Networks and Language in 2010 Election." Presented at the *4th Annual Political Networks Conference,* University of Michigan: June 14–18.

Lodge, Milton. 1995. "Toward a Procedural Model of Candidate Evaluation." In *Political Judgment: Structure and Process,* eds. Milton Lodge and Kathleen McGraw. Ann Arbor: University of Michigan Press. 110–140.

Lodge, Milton, Kathleen M. McGraw, and Patrick Stroh. 1989. "An Impression-Driven Model of Candidate Evaluation." *American Political Science Review* 83 (2): 399–420.

Lodge, Milton, Marco R. Steenbergen, and Shawn Brau. 1995. "The Responsive Voter: Campaign Information and the Dynamics of Candidate Evaluation," *American Political Science Review* (89): 309–326.

Lodge, Milton, and Charles S. Taber. 2000. "Three Steps toward a Theory of Motivated Political Reasoning." In *Elements of Reason: Cognition, Choice, and the Bounds of Rationality,* eds. Arthur Lupia, Matthew D. McCubbins, and Samuel L. Popkin. Cambridge: Cambridge University Press. 183–213.

Lowi, Theodore. 1963. "Toward Functionalism in Political Science. The Case of Innovation in Party Systems." *American Political Science Review* 57 (3): 570–583.

Lupia, Arthur, and Gisela Sin. 2003. "Which Public Goods Are Endangered? How Evolving Technologies Affect the Logic of Collective Action." *Public Choice* (117): 315–331.

Manjoo, Farhad. 2008. *True Enough: Learning to Live in a Post-fact Society*. New York: Wiley.

Mann, Kevin. 2012. "Leading birther Donald Trump offers Barack Obama £5m charity donation for school records." *TNT*. http://www.tntmagazine.com/news/world/video-donald-trump-offers-barack-obama-charity-donation-for-school-records. Accessed: April 15, 2013.

Margolis, Michael, and David Resnick. 2000. *Politics as Usual: The Cyberspace Revolution*. London: Sage.

Markus, Gregory B. 1982. "Political Attitudes during an Election Year: A Report on the 1980 NES Panel Study." *American Political Science Review* 76 (3): 538–560.

Markus, Gregory B., and Philip E. Converse. 1979. "A Dynamic Simultaneous Equation Model of Electoral Choice." *American Political Science Review* 73 (2): 1055–1077.

Martin, Leonard L., and Abraham Tesser, eds. 1992. *The Construction of Social Judgments*. Hillsdale, NJ: Erlbaum.

Mayhew, David. 1974. *Congress: The Electoral Connection*. Newhaven, CT: Yale University Press.

Mayhew, David. 2004. *Congress: The Electoral Connection*, 2nd ed. Newhaven, CT: Yale University Press.

McClurg, Scott D. 2003. "Social Networks and Political Participation: The Role of Social Interaction in Explaining Political Participation." *Political Research Quarterly* 56 (4): 449–464.

McGraw, Kathleen M., Milton Lodge, and Patrick Stroh. 1990. "On-line Processing in Candidate Evaluation: The Effects of Issue Order, Issue Importance, and Sophistication." *Political Behavior* 12 (1): 41–58.

McKenna, Laura, and Atoinette Pole. 2008. "What do Bloggers do: An Average Day on an Average Political Blog." *Public Choice* 134 (1): 97–108.

McNally, Terrence. 2004. "Moveon as an Instrument of the People." *AlterNet*. http://www.alternet.org/story/19043/moveon_as_an_instrument_of_the_people. Accessed: April 15, 2013.

Memmott, M., and J. Lawrence. 2008. "Yes We Can has Topped 3.7M Views." *USA Today*. February 6.

Miller, Arthur H., and Warren E. Miller. 1976. "Ideology in the 1972 Election: Myth or Reality—a Rejoinder." *American Political Science Review* 70 (3): 832–8349.

Miller, Warren E., and J. Merrill Shanks. 1996. *The New American Voter*. Cambridge: Harvard University.

Morales, Lymari. 2012. "U.S. Distrust in Media Hits New High." *Gallup Poll*. http://www.gallup.com/poll/157589/distrust-media-hits-new-high.aspx. Accessed: September 24, 2012.

Morris, Dick. 2012. "Prediction: Romney 325, Obama 213." *The Hill*. http://thehill.com/opinion/columnists/dick-morris/266027-prediction-romney-325-obama-213-. Accessed: November 5, 2012.

Mossberger, Karen, Caroline J. Tolbert, and Mary Stansbury. 2003. *Virtual Inequality: Beyond the Digital Divide*. Washington, D.C: Georgetown University Press.

Mossberger, Karen, Caroline J. Tolbert, and Ramona S. McNeal. 2008. *Digital Citizenship: The Internet, Society and Participation*. Cambridge: MIT Press.

Mowrer, O. Hobart. 1960. *Learning Theory and Behavior*. New York: Wiley.

Mutz, Diana C. and Jeffery J. Mondak. 1997. "Dimensions of Sociotropic Behavior: Group-Based Judgements of Fairness and Well-Being." *American Journal of Political Science* 41 (1): 284–308.

Mutz, Diana C., and Paul M. Martin. 2001. "Facilitating Communication across Lines of Political Difference: The Role of Mass Media." *American Political Science Review* 95 (1): 97–114.

Nie, Norman, Sidney Verba, and John R. Petrocik. 1976. *The Changing American Voter*. Cambridge, MA: Harvard University Press.

Nie, Norman H., Jane Junn, and Kenneth Stehlik-Barry. 1996. *Education and Democratic Citizenship in America*. Chicago: University of Chicago Press.

Nielsen. 2010. "Led by Facebook, Twitter, Global Time Spend on Social Media Sites up 82% Year over Year." Nielsenwire.com. http://blog.nielsen.com/nielsenwire/global/led-by-facebook-twitter-global-time-spent-on-social-media-sites-up-82-year-over-year/. Accessed: March 15, 2010.

Norris, Pippa. 2001. *Digital Divide, Civic Engagement, Information Poverty, and the Internet Worldwide*. New York: Cambridge University Press.

Norris, Pippa. 2002. *Democratic Phoenix: Reinventing Political Activism*. New York: Cambridge University Press.

Oremus, Will. 2012. "Here's Facebook's Most-Liked Photo of All Time." *Slate.com*. http://www.slate.com/blogs/future_tense/2012/11/07/facebook_photo_of_barack_obama_hugging_michelle_is_most_liked_most_retweeted.html. Accessed: December 3, 2012.

Ostermeier, Eric. 2009. "How Do Politicians Use Twitter? A Case Study of Rep. Laura Brod." *Smart Politics*. http://blog.lib.umn.edu/cspg/smartpolitics/2009/07/how_do_politicians_use_twitter.php. Accessed: October 17, 2012.

Page, Benjamin I., and Calvin Jones. 1979. "Reciprocal Effects of Policy Preferences, Party Loyalties, and the Vote." *American Political Science Review* 73 (3): 1071–1089.

Page, Benjamin I., and Robert Y. Shapiro. 1992. *The Rational Public: Fifty Years of Trends in Americans' Policy Preferences*. Chicago: University of Chicago Press.

Pasek, Josh, Eian More, and Daniel Romer. 2009. "Realizing the Social Internet? Online Social Networking Meets Offline Civic Engagement." *Journal of Information Technology & Politics* 6 (3/4): 197–215.

Patterson, Thomas E. 2007. "Creative Destruction: An Exploratory Look at News on the Internet." A report from the Joan Shorenstein Center on the Press, Politics and Public Policy, John F. Kennedy School of Government. Boston: Harvard University.

Patterson, Troy. 2007. "Who's the Fairest of Them All? A Comparison of all of the Women's Television Networks." *Slate.com*. http://www.slate.com/articles/arts/television/2007/12/whos_the_fairest_of_them_all.html. Accessed: April 15, 2013.

Peterson, Rolfe Daus. 2012. "To Tweet or not to Tweet: Exploring the Determinants of Early Adoption of Twitter by House Members in the 111th Congress." *Social Science Journal* 49 (4): 430–438.

Peterson, Rolfe Daus, and Lena Surzhko-Harned. 2011. "To Tweet or not to Tweet: Comparative Analysis of Twitter Adoption in the United States Congress and the European Parliament." Paper presented at the 2011 *Annual Meeting of the American Political Science Association*, Seattle.

Petty, Richard E., and John T. Cacioppo. 1996. *Attitudes and Persuasion: Classic and Contemporary Approaches*. Boulder, CO: Westview Press.

Petty, Richard E., Joseph R. Priester, and Pablo Brinol. 2002. "Mass Media Attitude Change: Implications of the Elaboration Likelihood Model of Persuasion. In *Media Effects: Advances in Theory and Research*, 2nd ed., eds. Jennings Bryant and Dolf Zillmann, Mahwah, NJ: Erlbaum. 155–198.

Pew Internet and American Life Project. 2010. "Internet Update." http://www.pewinternet.org/reports. Accessed: November 17, 2011.

Pew Internet and American Life Project. 2011a. "Twitter Update 2011." http://www.pewinternet.org/reports. Accessed: October 22, 2011.

Pew Internet and American Life Project. 2011b. "8% of Online Americans Use Twitter." http://www.pewinternet.org/reports. Accessed: October 22, 2011.

Pew Internet and American Life Project. 2012a. "The Rise of the Connected Viewer." http://www.pewinternet.org/reports. Accessed: August 24, 2012.

Pew Internet and American Life Project. 2012b. "Cell Internet Use 2012." http://www.pewinternet.org/reports. Accessed: August 24, 2012.

Pew Internet and American Life Project. 2012c. "Twitter Update 2012." http://www.pewinternet.org/reports. Accessed: August 24, 2012.

Polat, Rabia Karakaya. 2005. "The Internet and Political Participation: Exploring the Explanatory Links." *European Journal of Communication* 20 (4): 435–459.

Popkin, Samuel L. 1994. *The Reasoning Voter: Communication and Persuasion in Presidential Campaigns*. Chicago: University of Chicago Press.

Postman, Neil. 1985. *Amusing Ourselves to Death: Public Discourse in the Age of Show Business*. New York: Penguin Books.

Prior, Markus. 2005. "News vs. Entertainment: How Increasing Media Choice Widens Gaps in Political Knowledge and Turnout." *American Journal of Political Science* 49 (3): 577–592.

Prior, Markus. 2007. *Post-Broadcast Democracy: How Media Choice Increases Inequality in Political Involvement and Polarizes the Elections*. New York: Cambridge University Press.

Putnam, Robert D. 1995a. "Tuning in, Tuning Out: The Strange Disappearance of Social Capital in America." *PS: Political Science and Politics* 28 (4): 664–683.

Putnam, Robert D. 1995b. "Bowling Alone: America's Declining Social Capital." *Journal of Democracy* 6 (1): 65–78.

Putnam, Robert D. 2000. *Bowling Alone: The Collapse and Revival of American Community*. New York: Simon and Schuster.

Putnam, Robert D., Lewis M. Feldstein, and Don Cohen. 2003. *Better Together: Restoring the American Community*. New York: Simon and Schuster.

Quantcast.com. 2010. http://www.quantcast.com. Accessed: November 11, 2011.

Rahn, Wendy M., John H. Aldrich, Eugene Borgida, and John L. Sullivan. 1990. "A Social-Cognitive Model of Candidate Appraisal." In *Information and Democratic Processes*, eds. John A. Ferejohn and James H. Kuklinski. Urbana: University of Illinois Press. 136–159.

Rainie, Lee, and Peter Bell. 2004. "The numbers that count." *New Media & Society* 6 (1): 44–54.

Ramirez, Ricardo 2005. "Giving Voice to Latino Voters: A Field Experiment on the Effectiveness of a National Nonpartisan Mobilization Effort." *The ANNALS of the American Academy of Political and Social Science* 601 (1): 66–84.

Rash, Wayne. 1997. *Politics on the Net: Wiring the Political Process*. New York: Freeman.

Rich, Frank. 2008. "Next up for the Democrats: Civil War." *New York Times*. http://www.nytimes.com/2008/02/10/opinion/10rich.html. Accessed: April 11, 2013.

Riker, William H. 1986. *The Art of Political Manipulation*. New Haven: Yale University Press.

Riker, William H., and Peter C. Ordeshook. 1968. "A Theory of the Calculus of Voting." *American Political Science Review* 62 (1): 25–42.

Risen, Jane, and M. Keith Chen. 2010. "How to Study Choice-Induced Attitude Change: Strategies for Fixing the Free-Choice Paradigm." *Social and Personality Psychology Compass* (4): 1151–1164.

Romero, Daniel, Wojciech Galuba, Sitraram Asur, and Bernardo Huberman. 2010. "Influence and Passivity in Social Media." *Machine Learning and Knowledge Discovery in Databases* 6913: 18–33.

Romero, Daniel, Brendan Meeder, and Jon Kleinberg. 2011. "Differences in the Mechanics of Information Diffusion Across Topics: Idioms, Political Hashtags, and Complex Contagion on Twitter." Presented at the *20th International Conference on the World Wide Web*. March 28, 2011.

Ronayne, Kathleen. 2011. "OpenSecrets.org Unveils 2010 'Big Picture' Analysis." http://www.opensecrets.org/news/2011/07/2010-election-big-picture.html. Accessed: September 18, 2012.

Roston, Michael. 2012. "Republicans Ask 'Are You Better Off' and Many Reply 'Yes'." *New York Times*. http://thecaucus.blogs.nytimes.com/2012/09/04/republicans-ask-are-you-better-off-and-many-reply-yes/. Accessed: November 25, 2012.

Rosenstone, Steven J., and John Mark Hansen. 1993. *Mobilization, Participation, and Democracy in America*. New York: Macmillan.

Say Media. 2012. "*Voters Going Off The Grid: 2012* [White Paper]." http://saymedia.typepad.com/_pdf/VotersOTG2012-whitepaper-FINAL.pdf. Accessed: April 15, 2012.

Scheufele, Dietram A., and Dhavan V. Shah. 2000. "Personality Strength and Social Capital- The Role of Dispositional and Informational Variables in the Production of Civic Participation." *Communication Research* 27 (2): 107–131.

Schuller, Tom. 2000. "Social and Human Capital: The Search for Appropriate Technomethodology." *Policy Studies* 21 (1): 25–35.

Schulman, Kori. 2012. "Watch: President Obama's Twitter Q&A on #My2k." *The White House Blog*. http://www.whitehouse.gov/blog/2012/12/04/watch-president-obama-tweets-middle-class-tax-cuts. Accessed: December 5, 2012.

Sears, David O., and Jonathan L. Freedman. 1967. "Selective Exposure to Information: A Critical Review." *Public Opinion Quarterly* 31 (2):194–213.

Sears, David O., Leonie Huddy, and Robert Jervis, eds. 2003. *Oxford Handbook of Political Psychology*. London: Oxford University Press.

Semiocast. 2012. "Twitter reaches half a billion accounts: More than 140 millions in the U.S." http://semiocast.com/publications/2012_07_30_Twitter_reaches_half_a_billion_accounts_140m_in_the_US. Accessed: December 8, 2012.

Senak, Mark. 2010. "Twongress: The Power of Twitter in Congress." *Eye on the FDA*. www.eyeonfda.com. Accessed: October 17, 2011.

Shaer, Mathew. 2012. "#My2K: Can Facebook and Twitter sway 'fiscal cliff' debate?" *Christian Science Monitor*. http://www.csmonitor.com/Innovation/Horizons/2012/1128/My2K-Can-Facebook-and-Twitter-sway-fiscal-cliff-debate. Accessed: April 15, 2013.

Shah, Dhavan V. 1998. "Civic Engagement, Interpersonal Trust, and Television Use: An Individual-Level Assessment of Social Capital." *Political Psychology* 19 (3): 469–496.

Shah, Dhavan V., Jaeho Cho, William P. Eveland, Jr., and Nojin Kwak. 2005. "Information and Expression in a Digital Age: Modeling Internet Effects on Civic Participation." *Communication Research* 32 (5): 531–565.

Shah, Dhavan V., Jaeho Cho, Seungahn Nah, Melissa R. Gotlieb, Hyunseo Hwang, Nam-Jin Lee, and Douglas M. McLeod. 2007. "Campaign Ads, Online Messaging, and Participation: Extending the Communication Mediation Model." *Journal of Communication* 57 (4): 676–703.

Shah, Dhavan V., Nojin Kwak, and R. Lance Holbert. 2001. "'Connecting' and 'Disconnecting' with Civic Life: Patterns of Internet Use and the Production of Social Capital." *Political Communication* 18 (2): 141–162.

Shaw, Daron R. 1999. "A Study of Presidential Campaign Event Effects from 1952 to 1992." *Journal of Politics* 61 (2): 387–422.

Sheppard, Si. 2008. *The Partisan Press: A History of Media Bias in the United States*. Jefferson, NC: McFarland.

Sherpenzeel, Annette C., and Willem E. Saris. 1997. "The Validity and Reliability of Survey Questions: A Meta-Analysis of MTMM Studies." *Sociological Methods Research* 25 (3): 341–383.

Shogan, Coleen. 2010. "Blackberries, Tweets, and YouTube: Technology and the Future of Communication with Congress." *PS: Political Science and Politics* 43: 231–233.

Sifry, Micah. 2009. "The Politics of Twitter." *Tech President*. http://techpresident.com/blog-entry/politics-twitter. Accessed: October 17, 2011.

Singel, Ryan, and Kevin Poulsen. 2006. "Your Own Personal Internet." *Threat Level Blog, Wired Magazine*. http://www.wired.com/threatlevel/2006/06/your_own_person/. Accessed: April 2, 2013.

Slack, Megan. 2011. "The Definitive History of the Presidential Turkey Pardon." *The White House Blog*. http://www.whitehouse.gov/blog/2011/11/23/definitive-history-presidential-turkey-pardon. Accessed: December 5, 2012.

Smith, A. 2011. "22% of Online American Used Social Networking or Twitter for Politics in 2010 Campaign." *Pew Internet Research Center*. http://www.pewinternet.org/~/media/Files/Reports/2011/PIP-Social-Media-and-2010-Election.pdf. Accessed: October 22, 2011.

Smith, A., and M. Duggan. 2012. "Online Political Videos and Campaign 2012." *Pew Internet Research Center*. http://pewinternet.org/Reports/2012/Election-2012-Video.aspx. Accessed: April 2, 2013.

Smith, Stephen A. 1994. *Bill Clinton on Stump, State, and Stage: The Rhetorical Road to the White House*. Fayetteville: University of Arkansas Press.

Sommers, Paul M. 2002. "Is Presidential Greatness Related to Height?" *The College Mathematics Journal* 33 (1): 14–16.

Sparks, Colin. 2000. "Media Theory after the Fall of European Communism: Why the Old Models from East and West Won't Do Anymore." In *De-Westernizing Media Systems*, eds. James Curran and Myung-Jin Parks. London: Routledge. 35–49.

Squire, Peverill. 1989. "Challengers in U.S. Senate Elections." *Legislative Studies Quarterly* 14 (4): 531–537.

Stanyer, James. 2008. "Web 2.0 and the Transformation of News and Journalism." In *The Handbook of Internet Politics*, eds. A. Chadwick and P. N. Howard. London: Routledge.

Stimson, James A. 1999. *Public Opinion in America: Moods, Cycles, and Swings*. Boulder, CO: Westview Press.

Stimson, James A. 2004. *Tides of Consent: How Public Opinion Shapes American Politics*. New York: Cambridge University Press.

Stroud, Natalie J. 2008. "Media Use and Political Predispositions: Revisiting the Concept of Selective Exposure." *Political Behavior* 30 (3): 341–366.

Stroud, Natalie J. 2011. *Niche News: The Politics of News Choice*. New York: Oxford University Press.

Sunstein, Cass. 2002. *Republic.com*. Princeton: Princeton University Press.

Sunstein, Cass. 2009. *Going to Extremes: How Like Minds Unite and Divide*. New York: Oxford University Press.

Taber, Charles S. 2003. "Information Processing and Public Opinion." In *Handbook of Political Psychology*, eds. David O. Sears, Leonie Huddy, and Robert L. Jervis. London: Oxford University Press. 433–476.

Taber, Charles S. and Milton Lodge. 2006. "Motivated Skepticism in the Evaluation of Political Beliefs." *American Journal of Political Science* 50 (3): 755–769.

Teachout, Zephyr, and Thomas Streeter. 2007. *Mousepads, Shoe Leather, and Hope*. Boulder, CO: Paradigm Publishers.

Tewksbury, David H. 2003. "What do Americans Really Want to Know? Tracking the Behavior of News Readers on the Internet." *Journal of Communication* 53 (4): 694–710.

Tewksbury, David H. 2005. "The Seeds of Audience Fragmentation: Specialization in the use of Online News Sites." *Journal of Broadcasting and Electronic Media* 49 (3): 332–348.

Tewksbury, David H., and Jason Rittenberg. 2008. "News on the Internet: Audience Selection, Consumption, and Retention of Public Affairs News." In *The Handbook of Internet Politics*, eds. Andrew Chadwick and Philip N. Howard, London: Routledge. 186–200.

Thorndike, E. L. 1935. *The Psychology of Wants, Interests, and Attitudes*. New York: Appleton-Century-Crofts.

Tolbert, Caroline J., and Ramona S. McNeal. 2003. "Unraveling the Effects of the Internet on Political Participation? *Political Research Quarterly* 56 (2): 175–85.

Tourangeau, Roger, Lance J. Rips, and Kenneth Rasinski. 2000. *The Psychology of Survey Response*. Cambridge: Cambridge University Press.

Trippi, Joe. 2005. *The Revolution Will Not Be Televised: Democracy, the Internet and the Overthrow of Everything*. New York: HarperCollins.

Tullock, Gordon. 1967. *Toward a Mathematics of Politics*. Ann Arbor: University of Michigan Press.

Turner, Joel. 2007. "The Messenger Overwhelming the Message: Ideological Cues and Perceptions of Bias in Television News." *Political Behavior* 29 (4): 441–464.

TweetCongress.com. 2012. http://www.tweetcongress.com. Accessed: July 15, 2012.

Tweney, Dylan. 2011. "Why Do Republicans Tweet more Than Democrats?" *Venture Beat*. http://venturebeat.com/2011/06/11/republican-democrat-tweets/. Accessed: April 15, 2013.

Twitter Blog. 2012. http://blog.twitter.com/2012/09/dnc2012-night-3-obamas-speech-sets.html. Accessed: September 7, 2012.

Valentino, Nicholas A., Antoine J. Banks, Vincent L. Hutchings, and Anne K. Davis. 2009. "Selective Exposure in the Internet Age: The Interaction between Anxiety and Information Utility." *Political Psychology* 30 (4): 591–613.

Valenzuela, Sebastián, Namsu Park, and Kerk F. Kee. 2009. "Is There Social Capital in a Social Network Site?: Facebook Use and College Students' Life Satisfaction, Trust, and Participation." *Journal of Computer-Mediated Communication* 14 (4): 875–901.

Van Alstyne, Marshall, and Erik Brynjolfsson. 2005. "Global Village or Cyberbalkans: Modeling and Measuring the Integration of Electronic Communities." *Management Science* 51 (6): 851–868.

Verba, Sidney, and Norman H. Nie. 1972. *Participation in America: Political Democracy and Social Equality*. Chicago: University of Chicago Press.

Verba, Sidney, Kay Lehman Schlozman, Henry Brady, and Norman H. Nie. 1993. "Race, Ethnicity and Political Resources: Participation in the United States." *British Journal of Political Science* 23 (4): 453–97.

Verba, Sidney, Kay Lehman Schlozman, and Henry E. Brady. 1995. *Voice and Equality: Civic Voluntarism in American Politics*. Cambridge, MA: Harvard University Press.

Wagner, Kevin M. 2010. "Rewriting the Guarantee Clause: Justifying Direct Democracy in the Constitution." *Willamette Law Review* 47: 66–79.

Wagner, Kevin and Jason Gainous. 2013. "Digital Uprising: The Internet Revolution in the Middle East." *Journal of Information, Technology and Politics.* DOI: 10.1080/19331681.2013.778802.

Wagner, Kevin, and Jason Gainous. 2009. "Electronic Grassroots: Does Online Campaigning Work?" *Journal of Legislative Studies* 15 (4): 502–520.

Wallsten, Kevin. 2008. "Political Blogs: Transmission Belts, Soapboxes, Mobilizers, or Conversation Starters?" *Journal of Information Technology & Politics.* 4 (3):19–40.

Wallsten, Kevin. 2010. "Yes We Can: How Online Viewership, Blog Discussion, Campaign Statements, and Mainstream Media Coverage Produced a Viral Video Phenomenon." *Journal of Information Technology & Politics.* 7 (2/3): 163–181.

Wallsten, Kevin. 2011. "Microblogging and the News: Political Elites and the Ultimate Retweet." Presented at the 2011 *Annual Meeting of the American Political Science Association.*

Ward, Stephen, and Rachel Gibson. 2003. "On-Line and on Message? Candidate Websites in the 2001 General Election." *British Journal of Politics and International Relations* 5 (2): 188–205.

Ward, Stephen, Rachel Gibson, and Wainer Lusoli. 2003. "Online Participation and Mobilization in Britain: Hype, Hope and Reality." *Parliamentary Affairs* 56 (4): 652–688.

Weber, Lori M., Alysha Loumakis, and James Bergman. 2003. "Who Participates and Why? An Analysis of Citizens on the Internet and the Mass Public." *Social Science Computer Review* 21 (1): 26–42.

Welch, Susan, and John R. Hibbing. 1997. "The Effects of Charges of Corruption on Voting Behavior in Congressional Elections, 1982–1990." *Journal of Politics* 59 (1): 226–239.

West, Darrell. 2005. *Digital Government: Technology and Public Sector Performance.* Princeton, NJ: Princeton University Press.

Wilcox, Clyde, and Barbara Norrander. 2002. "Of Moods and Morals: The Dynamics of Opinion on Abortion and Gay Rights." In *Understanding Public Opinion*, 2nd ed., eds. Barbara Norrander and Clyde Wilcox, Washington, DC: Congressional Quarterly Press. 121–148.

Wilhelm, Anthony G. 2000. *Democracy in the Digital Age: Challenges to Political Life in Cyberspace.* New York: Routledge.

Williams, Christine B., and Girish J. Gulati. 2008. "The Political Impact of Facebook: Evidence from the 2006 Midterm Elections and 2008 Nomination Contest." *Politics and Technology Review* (March): 11–21.

Williams, Christine B., and Girish J. Gulati. 2010. "Communicating with Constituents in 140 Characters or Less: Twitter and the Diffusion of Technology Innovation in the United States Congress." Presented at the 2010 *Annual Meeting of the Midwest Political Science Association,* Chicago.

Williams, Christine B., and Girish J. Gulati. 2011. "Social Media in the 2010 Congressional Election." Presented at the 2011 *Annual Meeting of the Midwest Political Science Association,* Chicago.

Wojcieszak, Magdalena. 2006. "Does Online Selectivity Create a Threat to Deliberative Democracy: Cyber Skepticism Reconsidered." *International Journal of Technology, Knowledge and Society* 1 (5): 165–174.

Wojcieszak, Magdalena, and Diana C. Mutz. 2009. "Online Groups and Political Discourse: Do Online Discussion Spaces Facilitate Exposure to Political Disagreement?" *Journal of Communication* 59 (1): 40–56.

Xenos, Michael, and Patricia Moy. 2007. "Direct and Differential Effects of the Internet on Political and Civic Engagement." *Journal of Communication* 57 (4): 704–718.

Yang, Jiang and Scott Counts. 2010. "Predicting the Speed, Scale, and Range of Information Diffusion in Twitter." *Proceeding of the International AAAI Conference on Weblogs and Social Media.* New York: AAAI.

YouTube.com. 2011. http://www.YouTube.com. Accessed: November 12, 2011.

Zaller, John. 1992. *The Nature and Origins of Mass Opinion*. New York: Cambridge University Press.

Zaller, John. 2004. "Floating Voters in U.S. Presidential Elections 1948–2000." In *Studies in Public Opinion*, eds. William E. Saris and Paul Sniderman. Princeton, NJ: Princeton University Press. 166–212.

Zaller, John, and Stanley Feldman. 1992. "A Simple Theory of the Survey Response: Answering Questions versus Revealing Preferences." *American Journal of Political Science* 36 (3): 579–616.

Zinni, Jr., Frank P., Laurie A. Rhodebeck, and Franco Mattei. 1997. "The Structure and Dynamics of Group Politics: 1964–1992." *Political Behavior* 19: 247–282.

Index